Am I a Person of the Beatitudes?

HOLYPEARL

Original Korean edition published in Korea by HolyPearl Publications.
First published in Korea under the title of 산상수훈(상) 나는 팔복의 사람인가?

Copyright © 2022 by Seung-woo Byun
Published by HolyPearl Publications
27-22, Wiryeseong-daero 22-gil, Songpa-gu Seoul, Republic of Korea

All rights reserved. No part of this publication may be reproduced, stored in a retrieval system, or transmitted in any form by any means, electronic, mechanical, photocopy, recording, or otherwise, without the prior permission of the publisher.

All Scripture quotations, unless otherwise indicated, are taken from the ESV® Bible (The Holy Bible, English Standard Version®), copyright © 2001 by Crossway Bibles, a publishing ministry of Good News Publishers. Used by permission. All rights reserved.

Scripture quotations marked NLT are from the Holy Bible, New Living Translation.
© 1996, 2004, 2007, 2013 by Tyndale House Foundation.
Used by Permission of Tyndale House Publishers, Inc., Carol Stream, Illinois 60188.
All rights reserved.

Scripture quotations marked NRSV are taken from the New Revised Standard Version Bible, copyright © 1989 the Division of Christian Education of the National Council of the Churches of Christ in the United States of America. Used by permission. All rights reserved.

Translated by Faith Huh
Cover design by Jinhee Kim

Website
www.belovedc.com
www.belovedc.com/en
www.cafe.daum.net/Bigchurch

Youtube
www.youtube.com/user/gfctvmedia

E-mail
holypearlpubl@gmail.com

RESTARTING WITH THE SERMON ON THE MOUNT

Volume I

Am I a Person of the Beatitudes?

Seung-woo Byun

HOLYPEARL

CONTENTS

I. An Introduction to the Sermon on the Mount
(Matt. 5:1-16)

1. Am I a Beatitude Person? 53

    1) The Context of Matthew 63

    2) The Concept of Blessing 79

    3) The Structure of the Beatitudes 86

    4) The Matching Interpretations of the Scholars 88

(1) Am I Poor in Spirit? 94

    1) What Exactly Does It Mean to Be Poor in Spirit? 97

    2) Being Poor in Spirit and a Humble Heart 121

    3) The Important Meaning
       That is Incorporated in Being Poor in Spirit! 124

    4) The Heaven Promised to Those Who Are Poor in Spirit 125

    5) The Key to Becoming Poor in Spirit! 128

       ① Romans 1-3
       ② The 10 Commandments
       ③ The Sermon on the Mount
       ④ The Verses That Show One's Inner Depravity!

(2) Am I One Who Mourns? 156

    1) The Exact Meaning of Mourning 157

       ① The Characteristics of Poverty in the Beatitudes
       ② The Order of the Beatitudes
       ③ The Parallelism with Isaiah 66:2

2) Another Meaning of Mourning … 164
3) God Does Not Desire Cheap Tears. … 167
4) The Heavenly Comfort
   That Will Be Given to Those Who Mourn! … 172
   ① A Level of Comfort "Already" Given
   ② A Level of Comfort "Not Yet" Given

(3) Am I Meek? … 190

1) "Blessed Are the Meek" … 190

① Meekness Towards Other People
  (a) A Christian is a beatitude person who has been saved
      by repentance and faith.
  (b) A Christian has righteousness that exceeds that of the scribes
      and Pharisees.
  (c) A Christian is one who bears the fruits of the Spirit.

② Meekness Towards God
  (a) It matches the order of Isaiah 66.
  (b) It is the meaning of meekness in the Bible.
  (c) The beatitudes before and after the meek are about God.
  (d) It is the context of Matthew's statements.
  (e) This interpretation is highly probable.

2) "For They Shall Inherit the Earth!" … 207

① The Meaning of the Earth We Have 'Already' Received.
② The Meaning of the Earth We Have "Not Yet" Received.

(4) Am I One Who Hungers and Thirsts for Righteousness?   234

    1) What is the Righteousness Jesus Spoke of?   235

    2) What Exactly Does It Mean to Hunger and Thirst?   242

    3) Why Must We Become One Who Hungers and Thirsts for Righteousness?   252

       ① If We Do Not Hunger and Thirst for Righteousness, We Cannot Truly Be Happy.

       ② If We Do Not Hunger and Thirst for Righteousness, We Will Never Find Happiness.

    4) If You Are Hungry and Thirsty for Righteousness, Can You Enter Heaven Without Being Satisfied?   259

(5) Am I Merciful?   271

    1) What Is Mercy?   274

    2) Mercy Is Not a Choice but a Mandatory Obligation!   278

       ① A Philippine Pastor's Testimony

       ② Angelica Zambrano's Testimony

       ③ Victoria Nehale's Testimony

       ④ Carmelo Brenes' Testimony

    3) Anyone Can Be Merciful and Forgive Others!   293

(6) Am I Pure in Heart?   298

    1) What Does Being Pure in Heart Mean?   300

       ① Jesus Believed It Was Possible to Be Pure in Heart.

       ② There Are People in the Bible Who Are Actually Pure in Heart.

       ③ The Bible Says the Hearts of All Christians Are Pure.

       ④ If Your Heart Is Not Pure, You Cannot Enter the Kingdom of Heaven.

2) What Does the Promise "to See God" Mean? — 318
- ① Those Who Are Pure in Heart Can See God on This Earth.
- ② Those Who Are Pure in Heart Will See God's Face in Heaven.

3) What Must We Do to Become Pure in Heart? — 329
- ① We Must Repent!
- ② We Must Believe!
- ③ Must Listen to the Word!
- ④ We Must Strive to Live by the Word!
- ⑤ We Must Seek the Face of God!

(7) Am I a Peacemaker? — 360

1) The Duty of a Peacemaker! — 361
- ① The Duty to be at Peace with One Another
- ② The Duty to Make Peace between Other People
- ③ The Duty to Make Peace Between God and Other People

2) The Blessing That the Peacemakers Will Receive! — 375
- ① Those Who Are Peacemakers Are Those Who Are True Sons of God, Namely the Truly Saved.
- ② Those Who Are Peacemakers Will Receive the Ultimate Salvation and Enter Heaven.

(8) Am I One Who Is Persecuted For Righteousness? — 389

1) The Cowardly Cannot Enter the Kingdom of Heaven! — 392
2) Not All Who Receive Persecution Will Be Blessed! — 398
3) Torture and Murder Are Not the Only Forms of Persecution! — 403
4) The Tragedy of Spiritual Fratricide Is Still Happening Today! — 411

5) Blessed Are Those Who Are Persecuted,
   but Woe to Those Who Persecute Others!   422

   ① Do Not Be Doctrine-Orientated
      If You Do Not Want to Be a Persecutor!

   ② Do Not Be Religious If You Do Not Want to Be a Persecutor!

6) You Who Are Persecuted for Righteousness' Sake,
   Rejoice and Be Glad!   434

   ① The Reason We Can Rejoice While Being Persecuted Is
      Because Ours Is the Kingdom of Heaven.

   ② The Reason We Can Rejoice While Being Persecuted Is
      Because Our Reward Is Great in Heaven.

   ③ The Reason We Can Rejoice While Being Persecuted Is
      Because They Did So to the Prophets Before Us.

2. Am I the Salt of the Earth and Light of the World?   457

(1) Am I the Salt of the Earth?   464

1) The Meaning of Being the Salt of the Earth!   466
2) Why Must We Be the Salt of the Earth?   471
3) What Must We Do to Excel at Being the Salt of the Earth?   475

   ① We Must Live a Life Completely Distinct From the World.

   ② We Must Live a Distinct Life from the World
      While Living Inside the World.

4) A Severe Warning — Do Not Lose Your Taste!   480

   ① If You Lose Your Taste, You Will Become Useless!

   ② If You Lose Your Taste, You Will Be Thrown Away!

   ③ If You Lose Your Taste, You Will Be Trampled On!

5) The Heart-Breaking Reality of Modern Day Churches!   494

(2) Am I the Light of the World?   499
   1) Light of the World   500
   2) A City on a Hill   504
   3) A Lamp on a Stand   511
   4) Good Works   516

It was when I was ministering in Ulsan that I first preached on the Sermon on the Mount, and this is now my second time approaching this topic. It has taken me over 24 years to revisit this sermon series.

Back then, I was greatly blessed by John Wesley's sermons on The Sermon[1] in *Forty-Four Sermons*, and I could tell how important and precious they were. I also read Lloyd Jones' *Studies in the Sermon on the Mount*, and it further deepened the importance of this message for me. And so, I started my first exposition on the Sermon on the Mount. This time around, Dr. Yong-eui Yang's *How Will You Read the Book of Matthew?* greatly moved me. I had spent the past few years studying the Bible and reading exceptional commentaries and expository writings, and Dr. Yang's book was one such resource that I read for research. While reading, however, I discovered that Wesley

---

[1] From this point on the Sermon on the Mount will also be referred to as "The Sermon."

and Lloyd-Jones' view on soteriology in The Sermon is not just one out of many possible interpretations; it is thoroughly biblical and exactly what the Bible is trying to say. Thus, because of how impressive and important this is, the desire to preach again on The Sermon started fervently burning inside of me.

The following is what Jesus commanded to his disciples and preachers of all ages.

> **"[Teach] them to observe all that I have commanded you."** (Matthew 28:20a)

Now the Sermon on the Mount is the most representative and exemplary teaching of Jesus. Thus as a preacher, I felt incredible guilt over my ignorance. It even led me to think that as a preacher, it would be a dereliction of duty to not teach on The Sermon. This is why I began to prepare for this series in repentance.

First and foremost, I will explain the most fundamental aspects of The Sermon.

We call Matthew 5-7 the Sermon on the Mount. This title was first used by Augustine of Hippo (354-430), a theologian from North Africa. The phrase was derived from the fact that Jesus preached this exceedingly precious sermon on top of a mountain (5:1). Although we do not know the exact location of this mountain, most views agree that it was on the site of Tabgha, near Capernaum.

Throughout the book of Matthew, there are a total of 5 collections of Jesus' sermons. (This is reminiscent of the Pentateuch!) The Sermon on the Mount is the first and longest of these. David Turner pointed to The Sermon "as the representative ethical teaching of Jesus."[2] Although correct, it is an unduly inadequate expression, for The Sermon is more than just a representative sermon. It shows the collective truth that Jesus taught and spread. Scot McKnight explains this as follows.

> "When the gospel of Matthew was written, no chapter divisions were used. To indicate transitions authors in the ancient world used a quarry of devices, one of which was summary statements. Matthew's summary statement in 4:23-25 is nearly repeated verbatim in 9:35 and 10:1.
>
> 4:23-25 'Jesus went throughout Galilee, **teaching in their synagogues, proclaiming the good news of the kingdom, and healing every disease and sickness among the people**. News about him spread all over Syria, and people brought to him all who were ill with various diseases, those suffering severe pain, the demon-possessed, those having seizures, and the

---

[2] David L. Turner, *Matthew*, BECNT (Grand Rapids, MI: Baker Academic, 2008) 142.

paralyzed; and he healed them. Large crowds from Galilee, the Decapolis, Jerusalem, Judea and the region across the Jordan followed him.'

9:35 'Jesus went through all the towns and villages, **teaching in their synagogues, proclaiming the good news of the kingdom and healing every disease and sickness**.'

10:1 'Jesus called his twelve disciples to him and gave them authority to drive out impure spirits and **to heal every disease and sickness**.'

The italicized connections are obvious, but they are even more obvious in Greek. The only three places where these Greek words are used together in Matthew are in these three sets of verses, which leads me to this observation: Matthew 4:23-25 outlines what Matthew will tell us about Jesus' ministry (teachings, preaching, healing) in Matthew 5-9, Matthew 9:35 tells us that Matthew has completed his sketch of Jesus' ministry of teaching, preaching, and healing, and then Matthew 10:1 shows that Jesus empowered his twelve apostles to extend that sketched ministry of Jesus to others.

Put together, here's what we get: Matthew 4:23-9:35 is a sketch of the mission and ministry of Jesus: he teaches and preaches in Matthew 5-7 and he heals in Matthew 8-9. The Sermon on the Mount, then, is a comprehensive sketch of the

teaching and preaching message of Jesus."[3]

Dr. Yong-eui Yang reiterates the same point.

"The Sermon on the Mount is the first discourse of Matthew's five teaching discourses (5-7; 10; 13; 18; 24-25). As the first, **it effectively presents the core of Jesus' teachings.** The locational importance of the placement of The Sermon is further highlighted in light of its relationship with the narrative paragraph (ch. 8) that follows it. **As many scholars have taken notice, chapters 5-7, which is the Sermon on the Mount, along with chapters 8-9, introduce to us respectively the ministry of Jesus as the Messiah shown through his 'teachings' and 'teachings' and 'practices'. The interrelated nature of chapters 5–9 are firmly revealed by the near identical 'inclusio' structure of the start of this paragraph in 4:23 and the end in 9:35. The starting and final verses both simplify Jesus' ministry of declaring the Kingdom of Heaven as consisting of 'teaching' and 'working of miracles'** …

These two parallel verses seem to be Matthew's own interpretation, which shows us that this 'inclusio' passage was an intentional act by Matthew. In this manner, Matthew was

---

[3] Scot McKnight, *Sermon on the Mount*, SGBC, Vol. 21 (Grand Rapids, MI: Zondervan, 2013) 18-9.

revealing through the 'inclusio' passage that The Sermon correlates to the teaching portion of the Messiah's ministry of declaring the Kingdom of God."[4]

In order to prepare for this Sermon on the Mount series, I spent roughly a month solely focusing on research and reading many books. Through this process, I was able to find out that many scholars agree with the aforementioned viewpoint. Thus, The Sermon is not merely the most exemplary sermon. It is infinitely valuable and important, for it shows the whole kingdom gospel and the core truth that Jesus taught.

From this point on, I will be discussing The Sermon with a heart of trepidation and excited anticipation, for it is the most outstanding and important sermon in the history of mankind. I plan to focus on the following three points.

1. I will mainly focus on the original meaning of the Sermon on the Mount.

The Sermon is one of the best known messages that is familiar to believers. Yet, it is not a message that is best understood. In fact, it is a message that people know only superficially.

---

[4] Yong-eui Yang, *How Will You Read the Book of Matthew? (in Korean)* (Seoul, Korea: Scripture Union, 2011) 87-8.

This is why John Stott said the following.

> "The Sermon on the Mount is probably the best-known part of the teaching of Jesus, **though arguably it is the least understood, and certainly it is the least obeyed.**"[5]

The Sermon is the most representative sermon of Jesus, and it comprehensively shows his teachings. Therefore, it should have rightfully become the foundation of the teachings of the church. However, the church has failed to do so. This is why the church has become as perverted and weakened as it is today. The modern-day church would not have gotten to this point had we simply understood The Sermon correctly.

Because of this, rather than treating this topic as a simple word of blessing, I want to focus in this book on finding the exact meaning of each verse in The Sermon. I will concentrate on finding this accurate meaning over everything else.

Currently, there are too many different interpretations concerning The Sermon, starting from the beatitudes all the way to the parable of the house built on the rock. It was thus difficult to find what was right and wrong while researching. In each moment of confusion, I read carefully and paid special

---

[5] John R. W. Stott, *The Message of the Sermon on the Mount*, (Downers Grove, IL: InterVarsity Press, 2020) 1.

attention to the context while looking at the main passage for proper discernment. Through the context, I was able to discern which viewpoint was biblical. In my experience, most of these verses were discernible with this method. However, this was not always the case. At times, I meticulously pored over the original languages, the grammar, different translations, and cross-referenced verses in order to discern the views of these different scholars. Thus, there were also many moments I had to discern with difficulty.

The reason I poured my heart and soul like so to find the original meaning of The Sermon was because the Word of God is perfect in and of itself.

> "This **God—his way is perfect;** the word of the LORD proves true; he is a shield for all those who take refuge in him." (2 Samuel 22:31)

> "This **God—his way is perfect;** the word of the LORD proves true; he is a shield for all those who take refuge in him." (Psalm 18:30)

> "**The law of the LORD is perfect, reviving the soul;** the testimony of the LORD is sure, making wise the simple; the precepts of the LORD are right, rejoicing the heart; the command-

ment of the LORD is pure, enlightening the eyes;" (Psalm 19:7-8)

The Bible is fully perfect, and this includes the law. Then how much more perfect would The Sermon be, when it was Jesus himself that preached it? The Word of God is perfect. No matter who is preaching, the word of man cannot be more perfect than the Bible. This is why it is so important to uncover the original meaning found in Scripture just the way it is. There is no need to forcefully extract a message from The Sermon. We only need to reveal the meaning that is already there. And that will become the greatest sermon for one's soul.

The Word of God itself is the light, the bread, the fire and hammer, the two-edged sword. Thus, if we properly reveal the meaning of The Sermon, it will be the shining light. It will become the best bread and the strongest fire and hammer. It will be a two-edged sword that is sharper than any other sword. Therefore, I put all my effort in finding the original meaning of The Sermon over everything else. Thus, I dare hope that the content of this book will be as precious for you as if you were listening to Jesus' sermon in person. I hope through this book that you will hear and understand the Lord's voice as Mary did when she sat at the feet of her Lord to listen to His words. I pray that it will break and transform you. I believe that with this book series, many will truly come to experience such things.

Before we move on, I want to briefly talk about sermons in general. Preaching topical sermons is inadvisable, except when God strongly pours out revelations (Eph. 6:19). In the past, I used to preach on the revelatory things that God revealed to me. But rather than stay devoted to the main passage, I utilized many parallel verses on the grounds of having read the Bible many times. I gave a type of topical sermon, using all the related verses from Genesis to Revelations for they came to mind one after another. I preached in this manner, by integrating in many relatable interpretations, resonating content, and also the brilliant, fresh, and grace-filled points from various books I read. However, the above is an incomplete style of preaching.

In order to properly preach, one must primarily be faithful to the main passage and identify the exact meaning of the main passage itself. You also need the help of professional scholars to do so. It is not enough to just receive revelations. It is also not enough to read many books. It is only by looking at the original language and grammar, countless readings, and through extensive scholarly research that you can figure out the exact meaning of each verse. Thus, one must actively utilize the works of scholars to figure out the true meaning of the main passage. And one should make it the foundational structure for all sermons. On top of this, we must add the various materials we gain through other readings and practical teachings that fit the situations of the generation or the situations of the believers. That is how you can preach a sermon that is not only biblical but also the most beneficial and nutritional for your members.

After realizing this, my reading and sermon patterns changed. In the past, I tended to preach topical sermons. Now, I mostly pay attention to figuring out what each verse in the main passage means and what exactly Jesus or Paul meant when saying certain words. Although I still look at similar verses in the Bible in relation to the main passage, it is of a lesser interest. For in many cases, these Bible verses are simply similar in nature and not saying the exact same thing. I now focus instead on grasping what Jesus and the biblical authors were truly trying to say and exactly what it is, for each context has a different flow of thought on what is actually being said. I have learned through experience that when you grasp this fact and preach on this foundation, you are able to preach the most biblical and sound sermon that is not mixed in with the thoughts of man. You are thus able to give the most beneficial and necessary sermon to your church members.

To reiterate, topical sermons are not good sermons unless the Holy Spirit strongly pours it out to you in particular. Additionally, expository sermons are likewise not the best way to preach. For when we look at expository sermons, many of them seem to perform acts with shallow intellectual one-liners instead of dutifully following the intentions of the author. Then, what kind of sermons should we be preaching? We must preach on the content that God reveals to us on the basis of exegesis. Obviously, there is no need for us to plaster the wall with difficult jargon or extensive grammar of the original language like professional scholars do. However, we must preach a sermon that is first based on thorough exegesis and then use examples or testimonies, grace-filled explanations, or practical applications with it. I believe that this type of sermon is the best sermon for souls.

Preachers, heed my words. From today on, when you prepare your sermons, focus on figuring out the accurate meaning of each verse. Otherwise, there will be no progress even after all these years. However, if you prepare your sermons like I aforementioned, even if you were of similar competence as other pastors, you will be on a different level in the future. Differing from topical or expository sermons, a sermon that accurately grasps the meaning of the sermon passage and respective verses with the aid of professional scholars, will astoundingly improve the preacher. The former simply gains miscellaneous Bible knowledge but cannot go deeper into the Word. The latter however, as more time goes by, will be able to see the Bible more in depth and more accurately and will be able to interpret it. We might not see a difference right now, but in 5 years' time, 10 years', and as the years continue to pass, they will be pastors on a completely different level. Therefore, preachers heed my words and put them into action at all costs.

On the other hand, what I have just written is not only for ministers. This is also extremely important for all believers. As most of you know, choosing your church is as important as, if not more, than choosing your spouse. Even though this is the case, the majority of Christians choose their church without giving much thought to it. In order to go to a good school or workplace no one hesitates to move across the country. Yet, when choosing a church, so many people pick the one closest to home and register there with the hopes to attend comfortably. The worst result of such a decision could very well be that you will end up crying sadly in hell, gnashing your teeth with regrets.

Beloved, what do you look for when choosing a church? Generally, people choose based on the sermons. I think that this in itself is good. The problem rather arises in the criteria for judging a sermon. We do not listen to sermons to enjoy ourselves. We listen to hear the Word of life that determines where we will spend our eternity. Furthermore, we listen to realize the biblical truth and to enter the narrow gate and walk the narrow path and have a proper faith life. Therefore, when choosing a church by listening to sermons, our standard should not be on whether the sermon is short, easy, fun, touching, academic, informative, etc. Rather, we must ask: are they correctly discerning the truth and thus proclaiming the scripture as is instead of proclaiming doctrine? Are they shouting the truth without a hint of compromise or worry about what others will say? And are they receiving not only the teachings of the Spirit but also doing extensive research to understand an accurate interpretation of the Bible message when preaching? We should not be attracted to sermons that simply have witty remarks or amusing anecdotes, but instead desire and receive grace from the kind of sermons I mentioned, even if they are harder to listen to. This is how we can stop being fooled by the false prophets. And this is how we can become true believers that God is delighted in and not nominal Christians or hypocrites. Therefore, we must take this to heart and remember it.

2. I will focus on the soteriology that is revealed in the Sermon on the Mount.

After reading Dr. Yong-eui Yang's book *How Will You Read*

the Book of Matthew? I felt the need to write on The Sermon, at least once in my lifetime. For I felt it was necessary to properly explain soteriology.

The Sermon is not just a wonderful lesson. The Sermon is soteriology! Yet, so many have preached on it in a moral way. Therefore, we need to re-preach it from the viewpoint of salvation. And this is the reason why I am trying to talk about it from this viewpoint.

Please do not misunderstand my words. I am not saying that you can preach the Sermon on the Mount in a variety of ways and that I will be doing so through the viewpoint of soteriology. The Sermon has always been soteriology. For Jesus, from the very start of it all, preached from the viewpoint of salvation. And the evidence for this is in the aforementioned inclusio seen in Matthew 4:23 and 9:35. Herman Ridderbos accurately caught the meaning implied in the structure and wrote the following.

> "In 4:12-25 the Evangelist has given a broad sketch of the Lord's ministry in word and deed after He made His public appearance in Galilee. Here he proceeds to fill out his general description by giving detailed illustrations both of Jesus' teaching activity and of His miracles. The former is found in the Sermon on the Mount (5:3-7:27), and the latter in the series of

miracles that follow it (8:1-9:34).

The Sermon on the Mount thus can generally be regarded as an example of the Lord's teaching activity during His first period, which is described very briefly in 4:12-25 (particularly vv. 17 and 23). This means that it has the character of an announcement of the kingdom of heaven. For in verses 17 and 23, the content of Jesus' initial teaching is characterized as (1) an announcement that the kingdom of heaven is near (v. 17), which in verse 23 is called 'good news,' and (2) a call to repentance in view of the approach of this kingdom. Both of these things are worked out in detail in the Sermon on the Mount; the good news of the kingdom is present in the Beatitudes and the call to repentance in the commandments and admonitions, which are pressed on the listeners with reference to the kingdom's nearness."[6]

Scot McKnight also caught on to this fact. He said the following.

"The Sermon is not theory: the Sermon itself gospels the gospel. The Sermon casts forth the image of Jesus and of his vision for how kingdom people are to live, and then Jesus looks

---

[6] Herman N. Ridderbos, *Matthew*, (Grand Rapids, MI: Regency Reference Library, 1987) 81.

his listeners in the eyes and summons them to choose to follow him."[7]

Hallelujah! We praise the Lord. In this manner, the Sermon on the Mount is altogether soteriology. However, because soteriology has been seriously perverted in the church and has fallen apart, most scholars and preachers have not noticed this truth. This is why so many preachers have committed the mistake of preaching The Sermon from an ethical or moral standpoint rather than a soteriological one. As a result, many believers continue to walk in darkness. They delude themselves into thinking that they are walking on the narrow path to life even though they are on the wide path to destruction. How tragic and unfortunate a situation is this?

In spite of this, there are many who will still misunderstand me when I say I will write on The Sermon from the perspective of soteriology.

'Why does he say that we need to live by the Sermon on the Mount when salvation is earned through grace and by faith?'

Such a question might arise inside of you. Yet, rest assured.

---

[7] McKnight, *Sermon on the Mount*, (2013) 260.

To say that I will be writing on The Sermon from the perspective of soteriology is not in contradiction with being saved by faith or grace. I can explain this in the following manner.

I believe too many pastors and Christians have a narrow interpretation of salvation. They are stuck in the doctrinal frame of 'faith alone' and 'once saved, always saved.' Thus, they narrow salvation to be just about justification or regeneration for they believe that they are saved by faith alone and that this salvation is eternal. However, according to the Bible, salvation has a much broader meaning. In other words, the spectrum of soteriology is far wider than they thought it to be.

> "For by grace **you have been saved** through faith. And this is not your own doing; it is the gift of God," (Ephesians 2:8)

> "Therefore, my beloved, as you have always obeyed, so now, not only as in my presence but much more in my absence, **work out your own salvation** with fear and trembling," (Philippians 2:12)

> "The Lord **will** rescue me from every evil attack and **save me** for his heavenly kingdom. To him be the glory forever and ever. Amen." (2 Timothy 4:18, NRSV)

Like so, the Bible shows us that salvation can be in the past, present, and future tense. These then respectively point to justification, sanctification, and glorification, which are 'the order of salvation'. Soteriology does not only consist of justification or regeneration. Soteriology is also sanctification and glorification. And The Sermon deals with all of them. Thus, The Sermon shows us who is saved (justification), how a saved person can work out their salvation and who will receive ultimate salvation and enter heaven (glorification).

First, the introduction of the Sermon on the Mount, the 'beatitudes', correlates with justification or regeneration.

If you look in Matthew 3:2, John the Baptist cried out "Repent, for the kingdom of heaven is at hand." Jesus, in 4:17, also shouted "Repent, for the kingdom of heaven is at hand."

'Heaven' here is not talking about the heaven you go to when you die, but the heaven that is present in us. It is this heaven that came closer through Jesus coming to this earth and we are able to gain it when we repent. That is why Jesus said "From the days of John the Baptist until now the kingdom of heaven has suffered violence, and the violent take it by force" (Matt. 11:12).

Also, to say that the violent take heaven by force shows that heaven dwells in me and thus Jesus is my Lord and I have become His subject. Like so, it is the beatitudes that show the characteristics of His people in heaven. The metaphor of the salt and light shows this as well. Therefore, Matthew 5:3-16 correlates with justification or regeneration.

Next, the body of the Sermon on the Mount, the explanations and teachings of the law, correlates with sanctification.

Jesus came not to abolish the law but to fulfill it. Because of this, He warned His disciples that unless their righteousness exceeds that of the scribes and Pharisees, they will never enter the kingdom of heaven (5:20). After this, He showed us what the will of God that the law demands is, including a perfect interpretation of the commandments. This section shows how the disciples who have repented and are saved should live out their lives. Thus, Matthew 5:17-7:12 correlates with sanctification.

Lastly, the conclusion of the Sermon on the Mount, the message on judgment, correlates with glorification.

When we look inside this message, we are told to enter by the narrow gate and walk the narrow path. We are advised to beware the false prophets who will lead us to the wide gate and wide path along with a message on differing eternal fates. The well known Matthew 7:21-23 is also present in this passage as well as the parable of building the house on the rock or sand. Thus, Matthew 7:13-27 correlates with glorification, which is the completion of one's salvation.

In this manner, the entirety of The Sermon is truly soteriology. Therefore, we should not regard it as simply ethics or morals. We must realize that it is about salvation and clearly reveal the soteriology that Jesus wished to reveal. We need to vividly bring the meaning of The Sermon to life in order to wake up all souls and lead them to the narrow path to life. If we preach this so, Jesus' original intention for the absolute importance, gravity, severity, and impact of each verse will be revived. It will strike your spirit without any weakening or diluting. As a result, you will not be able to help but tremble and mourn for repentance. Thus, I hope you will prepare your hearts as you continue to read.

Before we move on, there is one more thing that I would like to tell you all. I have read many books in order to write on The Sermon and at times I was in shock over what I read. For there were many more scholars than I had imagined who also caught on to the fact that The Sermon is soteriology. This truth will give many of you who are reading a greater confidence and sense of stability. Thus, I would like to introduce to you several of these sources.

First, John Wesley, a wonderful man of God, spoke thus.

"And what is it which he is teaching? The Son of God, who came from heaven, is here showing us the way to heaven, to the place which he hath prepared for us, the glory he had before the world began. He is teaching us the true way to life everlasting, the royal way which leads to the kingdom. And the only true way; for there is none besides—all other paths lead to destruction."[8]

Herman Ridderbos said the following.

"In keeping with the glad character of Jesus' preaching of the kingdom (4:23), the Sermon on the Mount begins with blessings or Beatitudes. This opening determines the character of the whole Sermon, and the true meaning of Jesus' commandments in 5:13-7:27 can only be understood in its light… The first eight Beatitudes also form a unity in another sense: the blessings named in their second halves are a further description of what verses 3 and 10 call 'the kingdom of heaven.' The coming of this kingdom is the basis for the promises that

---

[8] John Wesley, *The Sermons of John Wesley: A Collection for the Christian Journey*, ed. Kenneth J. Collins and Jason E. Vickers (Nashville, TN: Abingdon Press, 2013) 475.

Jesus gives in the Beatitudes. **The Beatitudes thus contain, in the most profound sense of the word, the gospel of the kingdom. Speaking generally one could say that Jesus here is describing the kind of people the kingdom of heaven has been prepared for."**[9]

Scot McKnight said the following.

"The Sermon on the Mount, when read from special contextual clues Matthew provides at 4:23-25 and 9:35, which in Matthew's narrative is a sketch of Jesus' teaching, preaching, and healing ministries, is just that: it is a compelling presentation of Jesus and his moral vision. Pushed to the next level, **what this means is that reading or teaching or preaching the Sermon on the Mount is evangelism."**[10]

Michael J Wilkins also said the following.

"Since Jesus' teaching in the SM is designed primarily for disciples, it can be designated as training in discipleship. **It is the first basic instruction for those who have made a commitment to Jesus and his proclamation of the gospel of the

---

[9] Ridderbos, *Matthew*, (1987) 86-7.
[10] McKnight, *Sermon on the Mount*, (2013) 25.

kingdom. In addition, the SM also contains at certain points an invitation to the crowd to enter the kingdom of heaven (e.g., 5:20; 7:28-29)."[11]

Additionally, in the World Biblical Commentary's *Matthew*, Donald Hagner said,

> "An adequate understanding of the sermon is thus hardly possible apart from the context of the Gospel and the proclamation of the good news of the now dawning kingdom of God."[12]

Lastly, on November 7th, 2011, Dr. Seyoon Kim, a world-renowned theologian born in South Korea, spoke at a fall biblical convention at Chungeoram in Myeongdong, Seoul. "The Korean Church and the Sermon on the Mount" was written on the banner as the theme for the event. A newspaper published an article on it, and surprisingly, this is what was written.

> "Dr. Seyoon Kim explained that for the reformation of the Korean church, one must properly understand Paul's justification. Dr. Kim said, 'justification is when sinners receive the forgiveness

---

[11] Michael J. Wilkins, *Matthew: from Biblical Text to Contemporary Life* (Grand Rapids, MI: Zondervan, 2004) 193.
[12] Donald A. Hagner, *Matthew 1-13*, vol. 33A (Nashville, TN: Thomas Nelson, 1993) 83.

of sins through faith and become new citizens in the kingdom of God. This is in accordance with the gospel of the kingdom of God that Jesus preached.'

It does not end here. **The 'justification' that Paul speaks of is to live by keeping the law of the kingdom of God as subjects of the kingdom of God until the end-times. This is what it means to put the Sermon on the Mount (Matt. 5-7) into practice. Dr. Kim further said that 'the original meaning of justification that Paul spoke of is to follow the teaching of the Sermon on the Mount and that this is the way to reform the Korean Church.'**

Dr. Seyoon Kim also told us that the **'beatitudes' in The Sermon, are the disposition of the people of the kingdom of God and that the 'salt of the earth and light of the world' are their identity.** He stated, 'In order to have the disposition of a person of the kingdom of God and sustain this identity, we need to keep the double commandment of love: to love God and love our neighbors. **The main message of The Sermon is on how to keep this double commandment.'**"[13]

Isn't this amazing? As such, you can see that there are a surprising number of scholars who are cognizant of the fact that

---

[13] Tae-wan Kim, "Church Reformation, Starts from Straightening Out Crooked Justification (in Korean)," Newsnjoy, November 9, 2011, https://www.newsnjoy.or.kr/news/articleView.html?idxno=36202.

the Sermon on the Mount is soteriology! I too was astonished by how many scholars there were. But what is more astonishing is the fact that regardless of this, a distorted soteriology like the Salvation Sect[14] has spread in the Korean Church and in Christianity across the entire world and is endangering souls. Furthermore, I could not help but lament over how the denominations could have labeled my book *Christians Going to Hell* as a doctrine of works based salvation and slander our church. At the same time, I also lamented over souls as there are so many pastors in the church who are leading the blind as the blind. Thus, I cannot stop myself from warning them.

"And if the blind lead the blind, both will fall into a pit."
(Matthew 15:14b)

Pastors, pull yourselves together! Please wake up! At least stop yourselves from becoming the blind leaders who lead their entrusted members to hell. And to you believers, I plead that you will not blindly believe in these pastors because they are from orthodox denominations. Instead, I pray you will discern carefully when choosing a church. Thus, I hope that you

---

[14] The Salvation Sect is a cult that proclaims the heresy that once one receives salvation, one is eternally saved. They thus believe that they are exempt from hell, regardless of how they live their lives on earth.

will not become the blind fool who followed the blind into the pits of fire.

3. I will focus on the genuine transformation of you and me.

Scot McKnight as a theologian, is one of the leading authorities in the world on the research of historical Jesus. He has taught on the Book of Matthew and on The Sermon at seminaries for over 30 years. Yet, he said the following in a Sermon on the Mount commentary.

> "The Sermon on the Mount is the moral portrait of Jesus' own people. Because this portrait doesn't square with the church, this Sermon turns from instruction to indictment.
>
> To those ends—both instruction and indictment—this commentary has been written with the simple goal that God will use this book to lead us to become in real life the portrait Jesus sketched in the Sermon."[15]

He also said the following in the same book.

"The apostle Paul, when describing the ultimate aim of the

---

[15] McKnight, *Sermon on the Mount*, (2013) 1.

Scriptures, says they are revealed to transform us:

'All Scripture is God-breathed and is useful for teaching, rebuking, correcting, and training in righteousness, so that the servant of God may be thoroughly equipped for every good work.' (2 Tim 3:16-17)

To be sure, the apostle was not thinking particularly of the Sermon but instead the Scriptures of Israel. Yet what he says applies all the more to the New Testament: **the *aim of the Scriptures is to transform us into people who are ready to do every good work.*** I can think of no more appropriate words for the aim of this Sermon."[16]

Jesus, who is our King, does not simply want us to understand the Sermon on the Mount. He wants us to obey it. So, in accordance with Jesus' will, I will write This Sermon series with the goal to transform myself, my family and relatives, and all our ministers and members. Therefore, I hope you will all read this with the heart to accept nothing less than full transformation in your lives.

The Bible further helps us to change. For it says the Word of God is an example and even compares it to a mirror.

---

[16] Ibid., 276.

"For I do not want you to be unaware, brothers, that our fathers were all under the cloud, and all passed through the sea, and all were baptized into Moses in the cloud and in the sea, and all ate the same spiritual food, and all drank the same spiritual drink. For they drank from the spiritual Rock that followed them, and the Rock was Christ. Nevertheless, with most of them God was not pleased, for they were overthrown in the wilderness. Now these things **took place as examples** for us, that we might not desire evil as they did. Do not be idolaters as some of them were; as it is written, 'The people sat down to eat and drink and rose up to play.' We must not indulge in sexual immorality as some of them did, and twenty-three thousand fell in a single day. We must not put Christ to the test, as some of them did and were destroyed by serpents, nor grumble, as some of them did and were destroyed by the Destroyer. Now these things happened to them **as an example**, but they were written down for our instruction, on whom the end of the ages has come." (1 Corinthians 10:1-11)

"Just as Sodom and Gomorrah and the surrounding cities, which likewise indulged in sexual immorality and pursued unnatural desire, serve **as an example** by undergoing a punishment of eternal fire." (Jude 1:7)

"But be doers of the word, and not hearers only, deceiving yourselves. For if anyone is a hearer of the word and not a doer, he is like a man who looks intently at his natural face in a **mirror**. For he looks at himself and goes away and at once forgets what he was like. But the one who looks into the perfect law, the law of liberty, and perseveres, being no hearer who forgets but a doer who acts, he will be blessed in his doing." (James 1:22-25)

The Bible is an example and a spiritual mirror that shows my true self. And amongst mirrors, the Sermon on the Mount is the mirror of mirrors. It is a full-length mirror. The Sermon makes me reflect upon all things like my character, my words and actions, prayer, alms-giving, fasting, worship, ministry, etc. Above all else, it accurately shows whether I will go into heaven or not.

There are several places in the Bible that show us what judgment we will receive at the Last Judgment. Some prime examples are the parable of the ten virgins, the parable of the talents, and the parable of the sheep and goats. These parables clearly show us who will receive eternal life and who will receive eternal punishment at the Second Coming.

Furthermore, the following Bible verses clearly reveal who amongst us will go to heaven or to hell.

"Or do you not know that the unrighteous will not inherit the kingdom of God? Do not be deceived: neither the sexually immoral, nor idolaters, nor adulterers, nor men who practice homosexuality, nor thieves, nor the greedy, nor drunkards, nor revilers, nor swindlers will inherit the kingdom of God." (1 Corinthians 6:9-10)

"Now the works of the flesh are evident: sexual immorality, impurity, sensuality, idolatry, sorcery, enmity, strife, jealousy, fits of anger, rivalries, dissensions, divisions, envy, drunkenness, orgies, and things like these. I warn you, as I warned you before, that those who do such things will not inherit the kingdom of God." (Galatians 5:19-21)

"But as for the cowardly, the faithless, the detestable, as for murderers, the sexually immoral, sorcerers, idolaters, and all liars, their portion will be in the lake that burns with fire and sulfur, which is the second death." (Revelation 21:8)

However, there is one other message that gives even more airtight evidence on who will go to heaven or hell than all of these verses combined! It is the message of the Sermon on the

Mount. Most of the content from start to finish is on who will go to heaven and who will go to hell. This is the reason why we must stand in front of The Sermon before we are to stand in front of the judgment seat.

For all these reasons, I wanted to write on The Sermon, as soon as possible. In fact, because I was itching to do so, I grew impatient and my heart burned with desire. For I knew that if I properly wrote on the meaning of The Sermon that many would see their true selves and would deeply repent. It would be impossible to vaguely reflect on oneself and live in delusions. You would not be able to help but become someone who trembles in fear in front of the Word. You would be able to know in detail what you have been doing wrong, what you need to repent, and what you need to be careful of.

Is this not what we need the most? This is why, even though I have many other books I need to write, I wanted to hurry up and write on The Sermon. I know that you too have been awaiting this. But we must be careful. We must not read simply to learn. We must read The Sermon in order to stay alive. If not, we will not be able to avoid judgment and will instead receive an even harsher judgment.

That being said, there is no need to be afraid or to cower. We are only at the introduction, yet, The Sermon has already changed me and is also changing all of you. I have been able to verify this by looking at all of your thousands of comments online.[17] So, I believe that this book series will change every moment of your lives. I hope you will also firmly believe in this. And I hope that those who truly want to be transformed will adhere to the following advice when reading these books.

First, open up your Bible to the Sermon on the Mount and read it again.

Take the Word as a mirror and look at your own reflection through it. Open your eyes to your current state. And make up your mind to fix the things that need to be fixed.

There is not a single person who will not be pricked by their conscience when reading The Sermon. Nominal Christians will be shocked at being exposed as frauds and will repent. True believers will be stricken by how different they are from their heavenly Father, who is perfect, and will repent. In this way, non-believers and nominal believers will become true believers. The Sermon makes the young become mature and even the most mature believers redouble their efforts, like how a horse runs better when given the stick. Therefore, this is an incredibly precious message!

---

[17] This is in reference to the sermon series on YouTube by Pastor Seung-woo Byun that this book is based on.

Second, when reading the Sermon on the Mount series, do not skip over even one chapter.

This book series will make a groundbreaking change in you and it has the power to elevate the level and dimensions of the entire church. So, make this promise with me, to be determined to not skim over even one chapter. I hope that with each chapter you all will be able to see your true state under the light of the Word, be deeply pierced by the double-edged sword of the Word, and be completely broken and crushed by the hammer of the Word.

Additionally, I hope you take plenty of time in repenting and weeping after you read this message, for I do not want you to let the words you read disappear in vain.

Third, whenever you pray, use the Sermon on the Mount as a full-length mirror.

The Sermon is a spiritual mirror. We look at mirrors on a daily basis. In the same way, we need to stand in front of The Sermon daily.

So, starting from today, whenever you pray, think of The Sermon. Stand naked in front of all the teachings. Repent, and make the decision to live by The Sermon, and ask for the grace to actually live it out. Do this every time you pray.

It is not enough to only pray right after reading a chapter.

Every day as you pray, pray with The Sermon as your prayer request and repent accordingly. Then all of you can be transformed. Therefore, I hope you will all do this.

Let us now look at the actual content of this most treasured Sermon on the Mount.

"Seeing the crowds, he went up on the mountain, and when he sat down, his disciples came to him. And he opened his mouth and taught them, saying:

"Blessed are the poor in spirit,

for theirs is the kingdom of heaven.

"Blessed are those who mourn, for they shall be comforted.

"Blessed are the meek, for they shall inherit the earth.

"Blessed are those who hunger and thirst for righteousness,

for they shall be satisfied.

"Blessed are the merciful, for they shall receive mercy.

"Blessed are the pure in heart, for they shall see God.

"Blessed are the peacemakers,

for they shall be called sons of God.

"Blessed are those who are persecuted for righteousness' sake,

for theirs is the kingdom of heaven.

"Blessed are you when others revile you and persecute you

and utter all kinds of evil against you falsely on my account.

Rejoice and be glad, for your reward is great in heaven,

for so they persecuted the prophets who were before you.

"You are the salt of the earth,

but if salt has lost its taste, how shall its saltiness be restored?

It is no longer good for anything except to be thrown out

and trampled under people's feet.

"You are the light of the world.

A city set on a hill cannot be hidden.

Nor do people light a lamp and put it under a basket,

but on a stand,

and it gives light to all in the house.

In the same way, let your light shine before others,

so that they may see your good works

and give glory to your Father who is in heaven."

Matthew 5:1-16

I

Sermon on the Mount's Introduction

(Matt. 5:1-16)

The introduction to the Sermon on the Mount is Matthew 5:1-16. It is the section that shows the characteristics and role of the disciple.

The body of The Sermon is Matthew 5:17-7:12.

"Do not think that I have come to abolish the Law or the Prophets; I have not come to abolish them but to fulfill them." (Matthew 5:17)

"So whatever you wish that others would do to you, do also to them, for this is the Law and the Prophets." (Matthew 7:12)

As you can see, this section creates an inclusio with the expression "the Law and the Prophets."

In the Old Testament, God used the Law and the Prophets

to show us His will. In this section, we see Jesus likewise interpret the commandments. And by giving us the necessary instructions like the prophets did, He shows us God's will.

The conclusion of The Sermon is Matthew 7:13-27. It is the section that urges those who listened to The Sermon to enter by the narrow gate and walk the narrow path to gain life, to beware false prophets, and to live by God's will. This is the structure of the Sermon on the Mount.

1

Am I a Beatitude Person?

Many years ago, Juan Carlos Ortiz wrote a book called *Disciple* and it took the world by storm. It was a book that showed the true disciple, that is, the true Christian's identity. However there is something even better than this book that shows what kind of person a true disciple is: the beatitudes!

Around 24 years ago, when I first preached on The Sermon, I realized for the first time that the beatitudes portray the disciples, namely, the believers who are saved. At the time, several people's writings were of great help to me.

First, were the writings of John Wesley. He wrote on the beatitudes that, "**our Lord, first, lays down the sum of all true religion in eight particulars.**"[18]

Next is John Stott's. He said, "**the Beatitudes emphasize eight principal marks of Christian character and conduct, especially** … the divine blessing which rests on those whose lives show

---

[18] Wesley, *The Sermons of John Wesley,* (2013) 478.

these qualities."[19]

Then there is Martin Lloyd-Jones' writings. He wrote the most in relation to this point. He described the beatitudes as "the **character of the Christian** described in and of itself"[20] and that the beatitudes are a "delineation of the Christian man in his essential features and characteristics."[21] He further wrote, "as we have seen, **all these Beatitudes when taken together are meant to be a delineation of the Christian man.** They present a composite picture, so that each one of them should show a part of the Christian character."[22] He also made an important point that the beatitudes are not just portraying the characteristics of a portion of Christians.

> "*All Christians are to be like this* ... **It is not merely the description of some exceptional Christians.** Our Lord does not say here that He is going to paint a picture of what certain outstanding characters are going to be and can be in this world. **It is His description of every single Christian.**"[23]

---

[19] Stott, *The Message of the Sermon on the Mount*, (2020) 10.
[20] Martin Lloyd-Jones, *Studies in the Sermon on the Mount*, Vol. 1 (Grand Rapids, MI: William B. Eerdmans, 1959) 24.
[21] Ibid., 32.
[22] Ibid., 138.
[23] Ibid., 33.

John Stott also made the same claim.

"Furthermore, the group exhibiting these marks [the marks of the beatitudes] is not the elite, a small spiritual aristocracy remote from ordinary Christians. On the contrary, the Beatitudes are Christ's own specification of what every Christian ought to be. All these qualities are to characterize all his followers."[24]

Additionally, Lloyd-Jones claimed that the entire beatitudes appear in all true Christians.

"*All Christians are meant to manifest all of these characteristics.* Not only are they meant for all Christians, but are a necessity, therefore, all Christians are meant to manifest all of them. In other words it is not that some are to manifest one characteristic and others to manifest another. It is not right to say some are meant to be 'poor in spirit', and some are meant to 'mourn', and some are meant to be 'meek', and some are meant to be 'peacemakers', and so on. **No; every Christian is meant to be all of them, and to manifest all of them, at the same time.** Now I think it is true and right to say that in some Christians some will be more manifest than others; but that is not because it

---

[24] Stott, *The Message of the Sermon on the Mount*, (2020) 15.

is meant to be so. It is just due to the imperfections that still remain in us. When Christians are finally perfect, they will all manifest all these characteristics fully … **The point I am emphasizing is that we are every one of us meant to manifest all of them together and at the same time … The Beatitudes are a complete whole and you cannot divide them.**"[25]

John Stott also agreed with this.

"The Beatitudes set out the balanced and diverse character of Christian people. **These are not eight separate and distinct groups of disciples**, some of whom are meek, while others are merciful and yet others are called upon to endure persecution. **They are rather eight qualities of the same group who at one and the same time are meek and merciful, poor in spirit and pure in heart, mourning and hungry, peacemakers and persecuted.**"[26]

In addition, Dr. Yun-sun Park in his Matthew commentary, wrote that Christians are **"those who participate in the beatitudes (those who are saved)."**[27]

---

[25] Lloyd-Jones, *Studies in the Sermon on the Mount,* (1959) 34.
[26] Stott, *The Message of the Sermon on the Mount*, (2020) 15.
[27] Yun-sun Park, *A Commentary on the Synoptic Gospels*, Vol. 1 *(in Korean)* (Seoul:

Like so, I learned long ago through their writings that the beatitudes are portraying the Christian. There is a reason why I have introduced this fact so elaborately. It is to assure you that this amazing interpretation of the beatitudes is not something I conceived on my own. It is not a personal self-righteous or strange assertion. This is a trustworthy interpretation that you can accept with confidence.

Meanwhile, many people are shocked by the fact that this is what the beatitudes mean, for false soteriology has spread far and wide in the church. Many believers have made a profession of faith on the basis of Romans 10:9-10, and feel assured of their salvation. They read 1 Corinthians 12:3 where it says, "… no one can say 'Jesus is Lord' except in the Holy Spirit," and are comforted. It now makes sense why these people are shocked when I explain to them that the beatitudes are the depiction of the one who is saved. It is likely the same type of shock one might receive when first listening to my sermon, **"The Kingdom of Overcomers!"** For in regards to one's salvation, the fact that the beatitudes portray the saved inevitably raises the question **"are you a beatitude person?"** just like it raised the question **"are you an overcomer?"**

Lloyd-Jones accurately caught on to this fact and he realized

---

Yungeumsa,1992) 171.

how incredibly important it is. So, while lecturing on The Sermon, he wrote the following in three different passages.

> "These descriptions [about the beatitudes], I suggest, indicate clearly (perhaps more clearly than anything else in the entire realm of Scripture) the essential, utter difference between the Christian and the non-Christian. This is the thing that should really concern us; and that is why I say it is most important to consider this Sermon on the Mount. This is not just a description of what a man does; the real point is this difference between the Christian and the non-Christian. The New Testament regards that as something absolutely basic and fundamental; and, as I see things at the present time, the first need in the Church is a clear understanding of this essential difference. It has become blurred; the world has come into the Church and the Church has become worldly. The line is not as distinct as it was."[28]

> "There, then is the general account of the Christian which is given in the Beatitudes. Do you see how essentially different he is from the non-Christian? The vital questions which we therefore ask ourselves are these.

---

[28] Lloyd-Jones, *Studies in the Sermon on the Mount*, (1959) 36-7.

Do we belong to this kingdom? Are we ruled by Christ? Is He our King and our Lord? Are we manifesting these qualities in our daily lives? Is it our ambition to do so? Do we see that this is what we are meant to be? Are we truly blessed? Are we happy? Have we been filled? Have we got peace? I ask, as we have looked together at the general description, **what do we find ourselves to be?** ...

It is a simple question. My immediate reaction to these Beatitudes proclaims exactly what I am."[29]

"But, to put it positively, what we look for in anybody who claims to be Christian is the evidence of the Beatitudes."[30]

Scot McKnight likewise asked the same question.

"Those who first heard this list of the truly blessed by God immediately began to wonder about themselves by asking, 'Am I in or out?'

The Beatitudes are a radical manifesto of a kingdom way of life **because Jesus reveals who is in and who is not.**"[31]

---

[29] Lloyd-Jones, *Studies in the Sermon on the Mount*, (1959) 41
[30] Martin Lloyd-Jones, *Studies in the Sermon on the Mount*, Vol. 2 (Grand Rapids, MI: William B. Eerdmans, 1960) 258.
[31] McKnight, *Sermon on the Mount*, (2013) 30.

You now know how vitally important it is to realize the beatitudes are not simply an ethical teaching but rather depicting the characteristics of a Christian!

Beloved, the beatitudes inevitably raise the following questions in us.

Am I indeed a beatitude person? Are the beatitudes a characteristic in my heart and life? Am I poor in spirit? Do I mourn for my sins? Is my heart meek? Do I hunger and thirst for righteousness? Am I merciful? Am I pure in heart? Am I a peacemaker? Am I persecuted for righteousness' sake?

These are all vitally important questions. They are also the most important questions. Therefore, we must ask ourselves these questions right now. I hope that through them, you are able to accurately recognize whether you are one of the true believers or not.

24 years ago, I personally realized that the beatitudes are the portrait of a Christian. From that point on, I continued to emphasize this fact. Yet, to be honest, I believed this to be one of many possible interpretations. And since the interpretation was beneficial, I thought it was acceptable to emphasize. I did not realize then that the beatitudes Jesus spoke of had exactly such a meaning. Time passed by, and it wasn't until I read Dr.

Yong-eui Yang's *How Will You Read the Book of Matthew?* and other world-renowned scholars' books on The Sermon that I realized this was not just a possible interpretation but the very meaning of the beatitudes themselves.

It is incredibly important for us to grasp this, for it creates a tremendous difference. It is the difference between choice and necessity. This realization makes your loosely developed thoughts of trying to become a beatitude person turn, instead, into one that is fueled with desperation. It raises the value and importance of the beatitudes to now be absolute.

Besides, with just receiving grace or being challenged, it is hard for that fervor to last longer than a week or at most, more than a month. Yet, if we learn that the beatitudes are thus the portrait of a Christian and are confident of this through thorough verification, that Word will forever take hold inside of us. The Word will take hold of us for life and we will live with a heart that desires to become a beatitude person. Thus, our chances of being true Christians will exponentially increase. You can see how very important this is!

Therefore, I want you to be sure of this and exhaustively prove to you that the beatitudes really are depicting Christians. Thankfully, there is much evidence for this and most are even decisive.

1) The Context of Matthew

The Sermon on the Mount starts with the beatitudes and the first one is to be poor in spirit. Yet, in order to accurately understand the beatitudes, we cannot start here. In other words, research for The Sermon does not start with the beatitudes. This is because The Sermon is not something independent but rather one portion of the book of Matthew.

Thus, research for The Sermon should start not with Matthew 5:3, but with Matthew 4:17.

> "From that time Jesus began to preach, saying, **"Repent, for the kingdom of heaven is at hand.""**

This verse is key to understanding The Sermon and especially for understanding the beatitudes. Scot McKnight said this verse has "words that butt up against the Sermon on the Mount and propel the words of Jesus throughout."[32] I agree with this statement.

Jesus started to proclaim "Repent, for the kingdom of heaven is at hand," only after John the Baptist was locked in prison. Many people disregarded His words. Yet, out of the poor and

---

[32] McKnight, *Sermon on the Mount*, (2013) 11.

oppressed, some repented and received the kingdom gospel. These people were the "disciples" that we see in Matthew 5:1.

> "Seeing the crowds, he went up on the mountain, and when he sat down, his **disciples** came to him."

They received the heaven that Jesus promised (Matt. 4:17). This is why Jesus proclaims the following about them in the first and last beatitude.

> "Blessed are the poor in spirit, for **theirs is the kingdom of heaven.**" (Matthew 5:3)

> "Blessed are those who are persecuted for righteousness' sake, for **theirs is the kingdom of heaven.**" (Matthew 5:10)

There is something that we need to rightly establish here before moving on. I am not saying you are saved by keeping the beatitudes. Rather, those who truly repent are the ones who become beatitude people. In any case, the people who repent and are saved then become beatitude people. Therefore, is it right or wrong to say that the beatitudes depict people who are saved? I would say it is right, wouldn't you?

On the other hand, this also explains why there are so few

beatitude people in the church. Why are there so many people who think they believe in Jesus and are saved, but are not beatitude people? To be more straightforward, why are so many of them fake? It is because preachers are not talking about repentance. That is why the crowds say they believe but do not repent.

Look at the Bible carefully. John the Baptist preached first on repentance.

> **"Repent, for the kingdom of heaven is at hand."** (Matthew 3:2)

Jesus also preached on repentance first.

> "From that time Jesus began to preach, saying, **'Repent, for the kingdom of heaven is at hand.'"** (Matthew 4:17)

Additionally, Peter and the 12 apostles also preached on repentance.

> "And he called the twelve and began to send them out two by two … **So they went out and proclaimed that people should repent."** (Mark 6:7,12)

"Now when they heard this they were cut to the heart, and said to Peter and the rest of the apostles, **'Brothers, what shall we do?'** And Peter said to them, '**Repent** and be baptized every one of you in the name of Jesus Christ for the forgiveness of your sins, and you will receive the gift of the Holy Spirit.'" (Acts 2:37-38)

"**Repent therefore, and turn back, that your sins may be blotted out**, that times of refreshing may come from the presence of the Lord." (Acts 3:19-20a)

Moreover, Apostle Paul also cried for repentance.

"The times of ignorance God overlooked, but **now he commands all people everywhere to repent**, because he has fixed a day on which he will judge the world in righteousness by a man whom he has appointed; and of this he has given assurance to all by raising him from the dead." (Acts 17:30-31)

"Therefore, O King Agrippa, I was not disobedient to the heavenly vision, but declared first to those in Damascus, then in Jerusalem and throughout all the region of Judea, and also to the Gentiles, **that they should repent and turn to God, performing deeds in keeping with their repentance**." (Acts 26:19-20)

However, how many pastors today preach strongly on repentance? They are nearly non-existent. It is why the church has been filled with fake Christians.

Many pastors are instead like parrots and repeat "faith alone". They only emphasize faith, which is completely wrong. For Jesus did not do so. Jesus emphasized repentance and faith.

> "And saying, 'The time is fulfilled, and the kingdom of God is at hand; **repent and believe in the gospel.**'" (Mark 1:15)

Likewise, Apostle Paul did not focus on just one. He emphasized repentance and faith.

> **"Testifying both to Jews and to Greeks of repentance toward God and of faith in our Lord Jesus Christ."** (Acts 20:21)

Moreover, no person in the Bible only preached on faith. All of them emphasized repentance with faith. How do I know this? The evidence for this is in the following verse.

> "Therefore let us leave the **elementary doctrine of Christ** and go on to maturity, not laying again a foundation of **repentance from dead works and of faith toward God**, and of instruc-

tion about washings, the laying on of hands, the resurrection of the dead, and eternal judgment." (Hebrews 6:1-2)

Like the phrase "the elementary doctrine of Christ" shows us, repentance and faith were the most elementary teachings of the church. Therefore, in other translations, this sentence is translated as follows.

> NASB "Therefore leaving the **elementary teaching about the Christ**, let us press on to maturity."

> NIV "Therefore let us move beyond the **elementary teachings about Christ** and be taken forward to maturity."

The verse is clear evidence that all the preachers of the early church cried out for repentance and faith. Thus, the pastor who only preaches on "faith alone" (the slogan of the religious reformation), and does not preach on repentance is not a true orthodox, although he pretends to be. And even if he is of great character, he is not a true servant. This pastor becomes the blind leading the blind.

So, think about it. What is the first thing you need to know when learning about The Sermon? It does not start with being poor in spirit from the beatitudes. It is the absolute necessity for repentance! In other words, it is realizing the need to repent and actually repenting. You cannot automatically become a beatitude person just because you believe in Jesus. You must repent to become a beatitude person. Without repentance, you cannot become one. Therefore, you must examine yourself with the beatitudes. For anyone who is not a beatitude person is a person who has not truly repented. We must repent.

Additionally, we need to believe and accept the gospel. For in accordance with Mark 1:15, a beatitude person is not just one who repents, but one who also believes in the gospel.

> "and saying, **'The time is fulfilled, and the kingdom of God is at hand; repent and believe in the gospel.'"**

The "gospel" that comes out in this verse is the "kingdom gospel" that Jesus proclaimed.

> "And he went throughout all Galilee, teaching in their synagogues and proclaiming the **gospel of the kingdom** and healing every disease and every affliction among the people." (Matthew 4:23)

> "And Jesus went throughout all the cities and villages, teaching in their synagogues and proclaiming the **gospel of the king-**

dom and healing every disease and every affliction." (Matthew 9:35)

"The gospel of the kingdom" is a gospel that strongly urges for repentance (Matt. 4:17). It is also a gospel that urges us to receive Jesus as our Lord and live according to His will (Matt. 7:21). Therefore, we must all decide to not only repent but also receive Jesus as our Lord and live a life of obedience.

Nevertheless, these days, so many pastors and believers misunderstand the kingdom gospel. It is as if the gospel is transitional for them. They have obscure delusions with no evidence and think that after the cross, resurrection, and after Paul wrote Romans, the gospel of justification replaced the kingdom gospel. And the expression "justification by faith" further aggravates this delusion, for it has no mention of repentance in it.

This is a delusion. This is not true at all! The kingdom gospel has not been abolished nor can it ever be abolished. Think about it. According to Matthew 5:17-20, even the law has not been abolished. If that is the case, then how can the kingdom gospel that Jesus preached be abolished?

The author of Hebrews also believed the words of Jesus to be the most final (Heb. 1:1-2).

The author further believed that the gospel and truth that

Jesus proclaimed held more authority than the laws of the Old Testament (Heb. 2:1-4).

Jesus also believed that until the day the gospel has been proclaimed to all nations, all of His teachings, including the kingdom gospel, would still be valid (Matt. 28:18-20).

Jesus went as far as to even directly say the following.

> "And this **gospel of the kingdom** will be proclaimed throughout **the whole world** as a testimony to all nations, and **then the end will come.**" (Matthew 24:14)

Thus, just as Jesus said, until the end comes, the gospel of the kingdom will not be abolished. For the gospel Paul proclaimed is not a different one and rather just a more specific version of the kingdom gospel. That is to say, the start of the gospel of justification is the gospel of the kingdom, and the conclusion of the kingdom gospel is the gospel of justification. The two are thus one. It is why Jesus said the kingdom gospel, not the gospel of justification, will be proclaimed to all nations till the end of time.

Beloved, the gospel Jesus proclaimed and the gospel Paul proclaimed are not in contradiction with one another. They are in accord and in harmony with one another. Because of this, Dr. Seyoon Kim, in his excellent book, *Justification and Sancti-*

fication, wrote the following.

> "What we want to do is examine the **Pauline gospel of justification** beyond the simple level that Rudolf Bultmann and Eberhard Jüngel thought it to be. We want to go to a deeper level and see that this gospel corresponds to **Jesus' gospel of the kingdom of God**. To put it more accurately, **the Pauline gospel of justification is the 'soteriological expression of Jesus' gospel of the kingdom of God.' This is the proposition that we are going to prove. In other words, the Pauline justification needs to be understood in the framework of Jesus' gospel of the kingdom of God to be rightly understood without distortion.**
>
> So far, in the protestant tradition, the Pauline gospel of justification has been interpreted apart from Jesus' gospel of the kingdom of God. Because of this, the meaning of justification has been understood in a biased or distorted manner. As a result, the doctrine of justification has become a doctrine that produces people who claim to be righteous even though they do not live a righteous life. It has even degenerated into a doctrine that hinders the life of the righteous. Thus, most protestant believers understand faith separately from ethics. They believe they will be saved from the wrath of God at the final judgment with just faith and no ethical requirements. This is the most fundamental cause of the tragedy of the Korean

Church today. To overcome this, it is important to correctly understand the Pauline gospel of justification as the soteriological expression of Jesus' gospel of the kingdom of God."[33]

This is such an important point. Yet, right now, I have no intention to explain this any further. If you desire to know more, please read his book, pages 93-194.

I will instead give you a short and easy explanation of this topic that the Holy Spirit revealed to me.

When Jesus proclaimed the kingdom gospel, it was before the events of the cross and resurrection. Thus, while preaching the kingdom gospel, he did not discuss it all in detail. The following verse is evidence.

> **"I still have many things to say to you, but you cannot bear them now."** (John 16:12)

The reason Jesus did not reveal everything was not because he did not know. It was because the 12 apostles would not have been able to bear them. Then, what was the truth that the apostles could not bear? It was the death of the cross and the resurrection.

---

[33] Seyoon Kim, *Justification and Sanctification, (in Korean)* (Seoul, Korea: Duranno, 2014) 94.

"From that time Jesus began to show his disciples that he must go to Jerusalem and suffer many things from the elders and chief priests and scribes, and be killed, and on the third day be raised. **And Peter took him aside and began to rebuke him, saying, 'Far be it from you, Lord! This shall never happen to you.'**" (Matthew 16:21-22)

"They went on from there and passed through Galilee. And he did not want anyone to know, for he was teaching his disciples, saying to them, 'The Son of Man is going to be delivered into the hands of men, and they will kill him. And when he is killed, after three days he will rise.' **But they did not understand the saying, and were afraid to ask him.**" (Mark 9:30-32)

"And taking the twelve, he said to them, 'See, we are going up to Jerusalem, and everything that is written about the Son of Man by the prophets will be accomplished. For he will be delivered over to the Gentiles and will be mocked and shamefully treated and spit upon. And after flogging him, they will kill him, and on the third day he will rise.' **But they understood none of these things. This saying was hidden from them, and they did not grasp what was said.**" (Luke 18:31-34)

In this way, whenever Jesus talked of the death on the cross, the disciples trembled and were afraid. They could not understand.

Then, what is the gospel of justification that Paul preached?

"Now I would remind you, brothers, of **the gospel I preached to you,** which you received, in which you stand, and by which you are being saved, if you hold fast to the word I preached to you—unless you believed in vain. **For I delivered to you as of first importance what I also received: that Christ died for our sins in accordance with the Scriptures, that he was buried, that he was raised on the third day in accordance with the Scriptures**, and that he appeared to Cephas, then to the twelve. Then he appeared to more than five hundred brothers at one time, most of whom are still alive, though some have fallen asleep. Then he appeared to James, then to all the apostles. Last of all, as to one untimely born, he appeared also to me." (1 Corinthians 15:1-8)

As shown, it is the doctrine of the cross and resurrection. For justification comes from the cross and resurrection. However, the disciples did not understand the death on the cross. And the resurrection was an even harder concept to believe in. How then could Jesus have explained the gospel of justification that comes from this cross and resurrection?

You can now understand why Jesus said that His disciples could not bear them and why He did not explain the gospel of justification.

At the time, it was impossible for Jesus to explain being called righteous through the cross and resurrection. That is why He inevitably only preached on the kingdom gospel that talked of repentance and emphasized the Lord's reign. Still, Jesus thankfully also said the following.

> **"When the Spirit of truth comes, he will guide you into all the truth, for he will not speak on his own authority, but whatever he hears he will speak, and he will declare to you the things that are to come. He will glorify me, for he will take what is mine and declare it to you."** (John 16:13-14)

This was spoken to the 12 apostles, but it also naturally applied to Paul. Thus, this message that Jesus could not preach, because it was too much to bear for the disciples, was revealed after Pentecost. The Holy Spirit taught and revealed it in detail to the 12 disciples and especially to Paul. A message that is centered on the cross and resurrection: where we die on the cross with the Lord, and we rise again with the Lord. Where we die to sin, and are called to righteousness by living to God through the Spirit. It is how this message was finalized to become the gospel of justification. Therefore, the kingdom gospel and the gospel of justification are not two separate things. It is the same gospel. The two cannot be in contradiction with one another, for the kingdom gospel has not been degraded at all. Furthermore, it is the gospel of justification that works inside the boundaries of the kingdom gospel to actualize and replenish it. Hallelujah!

The gospel of the kingdom that Jesus proclaimed and the gospel of justification that Paul proclaimed are thus one (Matt. 24:14). Therefore, when we proclaim the gospel of justification, we must do it in the manner Jesus preached the kingdom gospel and should not emphasize faith alone. We should instead preach to repent and believe in the gospel. We also need to emphasize the reign of God as we need to receive Jesus as our Lord and obey. It is the same for the cost a disciple must pay. For the gospel of justification is not something being taken away from the kingdom gospel but is rather something being added to it. The gospel of justification thus elaborates the gospel and replenishes it inside the boundaries of the kingdom gospel!

It is incredibly unfortunate, however, that the church has lost sight of this important fact. It is why a severely distorted salvation sect-like false gospel has permeated throughout many churches. Therefore, I cannot help but strictly and sincerely warn you. Wake up, quickly, from your delusions and turn away from the salvation sect-like false gospel! A gospel that does not emphasize the absolute need for repentance is not the gospel that Jesus and Paul preached. It is a different gospel! It is also not the gospel that Jesus and Paul preached if you believe that you can be saved just by believing and professing and do not need to receive Jesus as your Lord nor live a life of obedience. It is a different gospel! Apostle Paul warns us in the following verses.

> "I am astonished that you are so quickly deserting him who called you in the grace of Christ and are turning to a different gospel—not that there is another one, but there are some who trouble you and want to distort the gospel of Christ. But even if we or an angel from heaven should preach to you a gospel contrary to the one we preached to you, let him be accursed. As we have said before, so now I say again: If anyone is preaching to you a gospel contrary to the one you received, let him be accursed." (Galatians 1:6-9)

Therefore with a trembling heart, pastors need to repent preaching a different gospel to countless souls and leading them to the wide path of destruction. And through this sermon, believers need to come to their senses. You should, for the sake of your own soul and your partner's, childrens', parents', and siblings' souls, never follow the blind leaders who preach a false gospel.

2) The Concept of Blessing

The beatitudes deal with eight different blessings. In the beatitudes, Jesus stated that "the poor in spirit, those who mourn, the meek, those who hunger and thirst for righteousness, the merciful, the pure in heart, the peacemakers, and those who are persecuted for righteousness' sake" are blessed.

But what does it mean to be "blessed?" Dr. Yong-eui Yang understood blessing to mean happiness.

> "The key word that is repeated in the Beatitudes, **makarios (blessed)** seems to be based on its usage in the Septuagint. The Septuagint mostly uses this word when translating the Hebrew word **ashrē**. The basic definition of this Hebrew word is to be 'very happy' or **'extremely fortunate.'** It generally means that **one's current condition is exceedingly content**. In that case, this word in the beatitudes depicts a state of happiness that cannot be expressed with words. And this happiness is enjoyed by those who Jesus declared to be in the kingdom of heaven. **The happiness described here is naturally not a worldly hap-**

piness. It is actually vastly different from worldly happiness and is even often the direct opposite. **It is the true happiness that only those who enjoy the reign of God (kingdom of heaven) can experience. For it is a profound inner joy experienced by those who enjoy the fulfillment of the salvation God promised."** [34]

Lloyd-Jones also understood blessing to be happiness and said the following.

"Happiness is the great question confronting mankind. The whole world is longing for happiness and it is tragic to observe the ways in which people are seeking it. The vast majority, alas, are doing so in a way that is bound to produce misery. Anything which, by evading the difficulties, merely makes people happy for the time being, is ultimately going to add to their misery and problems. That is where the utter deceitfulness of sin comes in; it is always offering happiness, and it always leads to unhappiness and to final misery and wretchedness. The Sermon on the Mount says, however, that if you really want to be happy, here is the way." [35]

---

[34] Yang, *How Will You Read the Book of Matthew?*, (2011) 91.
[35] Lloyd-Jones, *Studies in the Sermon on the Mount*, (1959) 32.

Certainly, there is some truth in this. For as Sundar Singh said, those who have heaven in their hearts are the ones who actually go into heaven.[36] However, this interpretation is not perfect. It is why John Stott raised this objection.

> "All Christians can testify from experience that there is a close connection between holiness and happiness. Nevertheless, it is seriously misleading to render makarios as simply 'happy'. For happiness is a subjective state, whereas Jesus is making an objective judgment about these people.
>
> He is declaring not what they may feel like ('happy'), but what God thinks of them and what on that account they are: they are 'blessed'."[37]

This is a very accurate point! Michael J. Wilkins raised the same objection.

> "Some recent versions translate makarios as 'happy' or 'fortunate', which can be good renderings, but the modern usage of those terms tends to trivialize the meaning by simply suggesting a temporary emotional or circumstantial state ... Ma-

---

[36] Sadhu Sundar Singh, *At The Master's Feet*, (London, England: Fleming H Revell Company, 1922), 30.
[37] Stott, *The Message of the Sermon on the Mount*, (2020) 18.

> karios is a state of existence in relationship to God in which a person is 'blessed' from God's perspective even when he or she doesn't feel happy or isn't presently experiencing good fortune."[38]

This is correct. Therefore, the "blessed" Jesus talks of are beyond a feeling of happiness. Then what exactly does being the "blessed" that Jesus mentions entail? I looked for hints and the answer in many different scholarly books. Then I discovered several meaningful explanations.

First, let me introduce to you Douglas Hare's very interesting interpretation.

> "It is even suggested that the original force of the word would be better captured in English by rendering it as 'congratulations'– 'Congratulations to the pure in heart, because they are going to see God!'"[39]

This shines a light on what "blessed" could mean.

Next, Scot McKnight made a basic remark on the word "blessed" that Jesus used.

---

[38] Wilkins, *Matthew*, (2004) 204.
[39] Douglas R. A. Hare, *Matthew: Interpretation: A Bible Commentary for Teaching and Preaching*, (Louisville, KY: John Knox Press, 1993) 35.

> "First, the one who is 'blessed' is blessed by the God of Israel … Second, there is a clear eschatological focus in the word 'blessed.'"[40]

This also provides an important foundation for understanding the word "blessed".

Next, Sinclair Ferguson gave the following more important explanation about the word "blessed".

> "The beatitude is clearly familiar language to the reader of the Old Testament. But what does it mean? Who is the 'blessed' man?
>
> *Blessing* and its biblical opposite, curse, are words intimately related to God's covenant with his people. According to the Lord's promise and commitment, those who were faithful to him would experience his blessing on their lives. Those who turned from him would experience his curse and judgement."[41]

Above all, Herman Ridderbos spoke boldly and specifically that "the word 'blessed,' [is] a reference to salvation."[42] Is this not

---

[40] McKnight, *Sermon on the Mount*, (2013) 32-3.
[41] Sinclair B. Ferguson, *Sermon on the Mount*, (Carlisle, PA: Banner of Truth, 1987) 12.
[42] Herman N. Ridderbos, *Matthew*, (Grand Rapids, MI: Regency Reference Library, 1987) 87.

a breath of fresh air?

When we compile all of this together, I believe David Turner's claim to be most attractive and correct.

> "A beatitude, or macarism (from μακάριος, makarios, blessed), consists of a pronouncement concerning who are blessed, often followed by a promise as to why they are blessed (here introduced by ὅτι, hoti, for, since, because). To be blessed is to be the happy recipient of divine favor or approval. The focus, however, is not on the subjective feelings of the blessed person but on the objective reality of the inauguration of the rule of God in Jesus. The opposite of 'blessed' is not 'unhappy' but 'cursed'[43] …
>
> The word 'beatitude' is related to the Latin beatus, which means 'blessed.' To be blessed (μακάριος, makarios) is to receive God's approval, favor, endorsement, congratulations. To be 'blessed' is to be so much more than 'happy' since the word 'happiness' conveys only a subjective, shallow notion of serendipity, not the conviction of being a recipient of God's grace."[44]

Therefore, the word "blessed" that is used in the beatitudes does not simply mean those who are happy. It is God's ac-

---

[43] Turner, *Matthew*, (2008) 146.
[44] Ibid., 149.

knowledgement that they will not receive curses or damnation and instead will receive the present salvation as well as the ultimate salvation. This is the true meaning of the blessed in the beatitudes.

As I have formerly discussed, I tracked this meaning of blessed from the books of scholars. However, this is not just the view of these scholars. When Jesus preached on the beatitudes, this view was the actual meaning He intended. The evidence for this is as follows.

First, as I have already explained, the beatitudes are for the "disciples" (Matt. 5:1) who heard the message to "repent, for the kingdom of heaven is at hand" (Matt. 4:17). They heard the kingdom gospel that Jesus spoke of and received salvation. The beatitudes are to congratulate and show them how blessed they are. Thus, the "blessed" obviously must be about those who are saved.

Additionally, we can confirm this through the reasons why Jesus called them blessed. Jesus promised to those he called blessed, the immediate heaven as well as a future ultimate heaven. That is why they are blessed. Therefore, the "blessed" that Jesus truly spoke of, points to the "saved". Then, it is right to say that the beatitudes depict the characteristics of those who are saved.

On the other hand, there is something else that is also incredibly important. It is the fact that through the beatitudes we see Jesus' heart. In other words, we see where the focus of his attention is. When people are interested in the blessings, Jesus is completely interested in the salvation of souls. That is why he called those who keep the beatitudes the blessed (saved). Thus, we need to focus and be interested in not the worldly blessings, but in the blessing of blessings that is salvation. We should, in turn, not only work out our own salvation but also pray for the salvation of others and strive to save them.

3) The Structure of the Beatitudes

The first and eighth beatitudes are an inclusio structure.

"Blessed are the poor in spirit, **for theirs is the kingdom of heaven.**" (Matthew 5:3)

"Blessed are those who are persecuted **for righteousness' sake, for theirs is the kingdom of heaven.**" (Matthew 5:10)

The characteristic of such a structure clearly shows that the second to the seventh beatitudes all promise this heaven as well. Most scholars agree on this point. I will introduce just a few of these views. Michael Wilkins wrote the following.

"The first and the eighth beatitudes (5:3, 10) form a sort of bookends, another example of the common Hebrew literary device called an inclusio, because the causal clause of the first beatitude is repeated in the last beatitude – 'for theirs is the kingdom of heaven' (cf. 5:3, 10).

The repetition of the present tense clause signals the main theme of the Beatitudes, that the blessedness of the kingdom of heaven is a present possession and operation among those who respond to Jesus' ministry."[45]

Sinclair Ferguson wrote the following about this.

"Jesus himself makes this plain by beginning and ending the Beatitudes with the same promised blessing: 'Theirs is the kingdom of heaven (v. 3 and 10). In verses 4–9, this chief blessing is further explained and illustrated in a series of six specific blessings: comfort (v. 4), inheriting the earth (v. 5), being filled (v. 6) receiving mercy (v. 7), seeing God (v. 8), and being called sons of God (v. 9)."[46]

Dr. Yong-eui Yang also wrote as follows.

---

[45] Wilkins, *Matthew*, (2004) 205.
[46] Ferguson, *Sermon on the Mount*, (1987) 45.

> "The last apodosis ('for theirs is the kingdom of heaven') exactly repeats the first apodosis (v. 3). This creates an inclusio structure, surrounding the entire beatitudes with the same phrase. Such a structure implies that all of the eight beatitudes express the same fact that 'theirs is the kingdom of heaven' from various aspects."[47]

Hence, the beatitudes are a depiction of the people who have heaven inside of them and will go into heaven in the future. Therefore, it is a very biblically accurate interpretation to say that the beatitudes portray the disciple–the Christian.

4) The Matching Interpretations of the Scholars

Long ago, when I was preaching in Ulsan on The Sermon, I learned through reading books that the beatitudes are the depiction of the true disciple, the depiction of Christians. This time around as well, as I prepared this message on The Sermon, I read the books of many scholars. And in this process I discovered that many more scholars than I had originally thought actually viewed the beatitudes as the characteristics of a Christian. I can't explain how happy I was to realize this! It

---

[47] Yang, *How Will You Read the Book of Matthew?*, (2011) 97.

also gave me more confidence about the truth that I have been proclaiming. And so, in order to ease your mind in following me and also as further confirmation, I want to introduce a few of these resources.

First, Sinclair Ferguson said the following.

"Christians vary greatly in every conceivable way, including personality, interests, social background and intellectual abilities. How different from one another we are! And yet, according to the New Testament, we all belong to the same family and have the same basic family likenesses. They are listed in the Beatitudes …[48] [Jesus] is not, after all, telling us what we should be. Rather, he is describing what the power of God's kingdom makes us. Jesus assumes that his people will show these hallmarks."[49]

Arthur Pink also said the following.

"In these Beatitudes the Lord Jesus delineates the distinguishing characteristics and privileges of those who are 'His disciples indeed,' or the birthmarks by which the true subjects of

---

[48] Ferguson, *Sermon on the Mount*, (1987) 14.
[49] Ibid., 44.

His kingdom may be identified."[50]

And Dr. Seyoon Kim said the following.

"Those people [beatitude people] are the people of God, and this is saying that they will be comforted in the kingdom of God that is to soon come. Through these 8 points, it is telling us in detail what kind of people make up the community of God's people. Therefore, this message of the beatitudes is in reality also talking about the identity of God's people."[51]

This is more than enough evidence and there is no need to cite anymore! The beatitudes list eight characteristics of Christ. Therefore, if you are a Christian, you must have all eight of these characteristics. Whoever does not, is not a Christian but a fake.

We have now firmly established that the beatitudes depict the Christian. And we have also learned that a Christian must be a beatitude person.

Still, some scholars say that the beatitudes are grammati-

---

[50] Arthur W. Pink, *An Exposition of the Sermon on the Mount*, (Mansfield Centre, CT: Martino Publishing, 2011) 29.

[51] Seyoon Kim, *The Lord's Prayer Expounded, (in Korean)* (Seoul, Korea: Duranno Academy, 2014) 26.

cally not in the imperative to require our obedience but are in the indicative to show us the result of the grace of God. They emphasize this fact and try to relax or dilute this message. They say that the beatitudes are the characteristics of a saved person, but that they are not commanded as qualifications for entering heaven. For example, Professor David Turner said the following.

> "There are two contrasting views of the meaning of the Beatitudes. One sees them as indicative pronouncements of gracious kingdom blessings. The other sees them as ethical exhortations about entrance requirements. If the latter view is correct, human effort must produce the characteristics mentioned here so that one might earn God's approval. If the former view is correct, one can only thankfully acknowledge these characteristics as evidence of God's gracious working in one's life and cultivate them as one lives as a disciple of Christ. Certainly the view that regards them as blessings rather than requirements is correct. Those who repent at the message of the kingdom (3:2; 4:17) acknowledge their own spiritual bankruptcy and rejoice in God's blessings of salvation.
>
> The Beatitudes reveal key character traits that God approves in his people. These character traits are gracious gifts indicating God's approval, not requirements for works that merit

God's approval. Those who repent receive these character traits in principle but must cultivate them in the process of discipleship."[52]

He is not wrong. It makes sense. However, does anything change by arguing this? Yes, the beatitudes are the grace-filled gifts that those who repent and are saved receive by principle. But in the end, is it not true that only the people who have the characteristics of the beatitudes will enter heaven? There is no difference when you look at the end result.

Moreover, there are so many people in the church today who believe that they are saved but none of the characteristics of the beatitudes are visible in their lives. Because of this, I believe Douglas Hare's viewpoint is more advisable.

> "The question whether the beatitudes are best described as *eschatological warnings or entrance requirements* for those who wish to participate in the kingdom is still vigorously debated. Are they indicatives, testifying to God's grace, or imperatives, demanding obedient action? If scholars have difficulty reaching a consensus, it is probably because truth lies on both sides of the issue. We should understand Matthew's

---

[52] Turner, *Matthew*, (2008) 146-7.

beatitudes both as expressions of eschatological grace and as implicit commands."[53]

Therefore, do not think that you will be able to get away with it like a slippery snake. If you are a beatitude person already, give thanks to God. But if you are not a beatitude person, repent with a contrite spirit and seek God's grace so that you may undoubtedly become a beatitude person.

So now, with this in mind, let us actually study the beatitudes.

---

[53] Hare, *Matthew,* (1993) 35.

1. AM I POOR IN SPIRIT?

The beatitudes, after the Lord's Prayer, are the most well known verses in the Sermon on the Mount. And the first of these beatitudes is to be poor in spirit.

> **"Blessed are the poor in spirit, for theirs is the kingdom of heaven."** (Matthew 5:3)

Here, they are the "poor in spirit". However, in Luke, which was written before Matthew, they are simply the "poor."

> "And he lifted up his eyes on his disciples, and said: **'Blessed are you who are poor**, for yours is the kingdom of God.'" (Luke 6:20)

Thus, Matthew changed the "poor" to become the "poor in spirit". Although this may seem like Matthew voluntarily altered the words of Jesus, that is actually not the case.

Why then did Matthew do this? Douglas Hare gives the following reason.

> "The opening beatitude in Luke's series must have sounded particularly paradoxical to Greek ears: 'How happy are the poor' (Luke 6:20)...
>
> In Matthew's version, the first beatitude is turned in a very different direction by the additional phrase 'in spirit.' **Perhaps life experience convinced the Evangelist that the dichotomy of pious poor and wicked rich was a gross oversimplification.** Despite the powerful tradition in Israel contrasting the piety of the poor and the godless arrogance of the wealthy, the wise did not forget that poverty too can breed injustice (Prov. 28:3) and disobedience to the commandments (Prov. 30:8-9)."[54]

In short, Hare is saying that Matthew added the word "in spirit" because he felt a burden against oversimplifying the division as simply between the pious poor who have the kingdom of heaven vs. the wicked rich who cannot get into heaven. But if this is true, it would make Jesus' words imperfect. Therefore, this is not a correct interpretation.

David Turner most accurately explained the reason why the

---

[54] Hare, *Matthew*, (1993) 36.

poor became the poor in spirit.

> "Matthew's phrase is 'poor in spirit'... but Luke's version of this beatitude has only 'blessed are you who are poor' (Luke 6:20). **Although some scholars believe that Matthew has spiritualized Luke's more accurate version of a saying originally about material poverty... it is much more likely that Matthew has only clarified the original intent of Jesus by focusing on the inner disposition of those in poverty (Hagner 1993: 91)."**[55]

Dr. Yong-eui Yang said something similar.

> **"In the first beatitude, 'the poor in spirit', seem to refer to those who have the characteristic state of mind of the materially poor."**[56]

Just think about it. One does not receive heaven just because they are poor. If that were the case, then what "Emperor Julian wrote mockingly in a letter (No. 43), that he only confiscated the property of Christians so as to make them poor enough to enter the kingdom of heaven",[57] would be correct. All of the

---

[55] Turner, *Matthew*, (2008) 150.
[56] Yang, *How Will You Read the Book of Matthew?*, (2011) 92.
[57] Dietrich Bonhoeffer, *The Cost of Discipleship*, (New York, NY: Touchstone, 1959) 110.

poor will not enter heaven, but only those who through their poverty become poor in spirit. The rich are also not an exception. Thus, Matthew did not alter Jesus' words by changing "the poor" to "the poor in spirit". If anything, Matthew rather revealed its correct meaning. Therefore, it is not a correct perspective to focus on "the poor" from Luke, like many scholars have done, and to interpret the rest of the meaning of the beatitudes through such a lens.

With this in mind, let us look closer at this vitally important topic of being poor in spirit.

1) What Exactly Does It Mean to Be Poor in Spirit?

The good news is primarily preached to the poor (Matt. 11:5). And the poor primarily receive salvation (1 Cor. 1:26-28). This however, does not mean the rich are excluded. Even if you are rich, if you are poor in spirit, you can receive salvation. What is ultimately important is not whether you are rich or poor but rather that you are poor in spirit. For being poor in spirit is of absolute importance.

Then what exactly does this important phrase 'poor in spirit' mean?

In order to accurately figure out the meaning, I read many different books about The Sermon. However, all of them discuss only the concept behind being poor in spirit. I could not find any that talk of why it means what it means nor any with biblical explanations that would help us understand it further. Still, I was able to salvage one explanation from Professor Yong-eui Yang.

> "In the Old Testament, the Hebrew words 'Ani and 'Anav, which refer to 'the poor', indicate those who are weak and dependent and as a result, are easily open to exploitation by those in power. Those who are poor have no one to appeal to except God. That is why 'the poor' are pictured as being wholly dependent on God (Ps. 14:6, 25:16, 68:29. Isa. 61:1, etc.). There is no doubt that 'the poor' in the beatitudes have this Old Testament background."[58]

This was all I could find. This explanation helps us grasp, to a certain extent, what being poor in spirit is. However, it is not a sufficient explanation.

I desired to know, in more detail, why the poor in spirit means what it does. Yet, in the Bible, there are only two places that refer to those who are poor in spirit (Isa. 66:2, Matt. 5:3). Both of these verses do not have further explanations about

---

[58] Yang, *How Will You Read the Book of Matthew?*, (2011) 92.

what it means. Thus, I quickly gave up thinking there was no way to understand this topic.

But as I woke up on the morning of June 18th, 2020, our good God suddenly explained itl to me. I want to share this explanation with you all.

Being poor in spirit, in short, is opening one's eyes to one's true self.

> "Delivering you from your people and from the Gentiles— to whom I am sending you **to open their eyes**, so that they may turn from darkness to light and from the power of Satan to God, that they may receive forgiveness of sins and a place among those who are sanctified by faith in me." (Acts 26:17-18)

Thus, it signifies a state of deeply realizing one's own sin and inner depravity. The conclusive evidence that this is the meaning of being poor in spirit is shown in Isaiah 66:2-4.

> "All these things my hand has made, and so all these things came to be, declares the LORD. **But this is the one to whom I will look: he who is humble and contrite in spirit and trembles at my word.** "He who slaughters an ox is like one who kills a man; he who sacrifices a lamb, like one who breaks a dog's neck; he who presents a grain offering, like one who of-

fers pig's blood; he who makes a memorial offering of frankincense, like one who blesses an idol. **These have chosen their own ways, and their soul delights in their abominations;** I also will choose harsh treatment for them and bring their fears upon them, because when I called, no one answered, when I spoke, they did not listen; **but they did what was evil in my eyes and chose that in which I did not delight."**

Through this, I was able to reconfirm the fact that the answer is always in the Bible. For I had thought there was no answer, but the answer was right here. Let me explain for those who still cannot see it.

First, the people who appear after verse 3 were diligent in their various religious duties. Yet, they lived life choosing their own ways, and their souls delighted in their abomination. They did what was evil in God's eyes, and God did not delight in their actions. Somehow, they still believed they were faithful. And that is why they did not become poor nor contrite in spirit, nor did they tremble in front of God's Word. The fact that such people are differentiated from those in verse 2 is further evidence. Therefore this is the state of those who are rich in spirit.

Being poor in spirit is the exact opposite of such a state. The poor in spirit do not think that they are right just because they are earnest in their religious duties. They search their hearts and are deeply aware of their sins and inner depravity. Moreover, they do not take their sin lightly. They realize how spiritually wretched, pitiful, poor, blind, and naked they are. They are extremely ashamed, and troubled. They lament and cry out in spirit to God. This is what it means to be poor in spirit!

Sadly, there are so many who are not poor in spirit inside the church and outside. The non-believer largely says the following to oneself.

"I'm a kind person. I have a good conscience. I live a lawful life even without the law. I have morals, and am polite. I'm a good person. So, when I die, I know I'll be going to the good place!"

When these people hear that 'all people are sinners, and that is why Jesus took up the cross, and we must therefore repent and receive Jesus as our Lord,' they are offended and do not accept such a message.

There are also people like this in the church, and not just in the outside world. They diligently keep religious duties like the Lord's Day, tithing, reading the Bible, praying, volunteering, evangelizing, etc. However, they live in sin and do not live by God's Word. Yet, strangely, they still believe themselves to be faithful and believe they will go to heaven. Even when listening to sermons, they do not become poor nor contrite in spirit, nor do they tremble in front of God's Word.

We see people like this in the Bible as well. They are the Pharisees that Jesus severely rebuked as snakes and a brood of vipers. These Pharisees were not truly righteous. Certainly, like those in the verses after Isaiah 66:3, they were diligent in their religious duties. They were righteous on the outside, but were like whitewashed tombs on the inside.

> **"Woe to you, scribes and Pharisees, hypocrites! For you clean the outside of the cup and the plate, but inside they are full of greed and self-indulgence. You blind Pharisee! First clean the inside of the cup and the plate, that the outside also may be clean. Woe to you, scribes and Pharisees, hypocrites! For you are like whitewashed tombs, which outwardly appear beautiful, but within are full of dead people's bones and all uncleanness. So you also outwardly appear righteous to others, but within you are full of hypocrisy and lawlessness."** (Matthew 23:25-28)

Surprisingly, they were unaware of their horrifying reality. On the contrary, they believed themselves to be righteous. That is why Jesus used the following parable to rebuke them.

"He also told this parable **to some who trusted in themselves that they were righteous, and treated others with contempt:** Two men went up into the temple to pray, one **a Pharisee** and the other a tax collector. **The Pharisee, standing by himself, prayed thus: 'God, I thank you that I am not like other men, extortioners, unjust, adulterers, or even like this tax collector. I fast twice a week; I give tithes of all that I get.'"** (Luke 18:9-12)

The Pharisees are the prime example of those who are not poor in spirit. Repentance was impossible for them because they did not know themselves. They did everything but repent. Thus, they did not receive salvation and were thrown into the fires of hell.

However, there are still many people like this inside the church. They are the modern-day Pharisees. I know that most people who attend church today believe themselves to be different from the Pharisees in the Bible. Yet, in reality, many are just like them. As evidence of this, Jesus said this in a letter, not to the Pharisees, but to the members of the Church of Laodicea.

"**'I know your works**: you are neither cold nor hot. Would that you were either cold or hot... **For you say, I am rich, I** have prospered, and I need nothing, not realizing that you are wretched, pitiable, poor, blind, and naked." (Revelation 3:15, 17)

These people were Christians who attended church. However, they were completely blind to their spiritual state, just like the Pharisees. Thus, they were the Pharisees of the church.

If you think about it, in a way these people were even worse than the Pharisees. The Pharisees could not see themselves and believed that they were righteous because of their diligence in religious duties and their ethical way of life. Yet, the members of the church of Laodicea think that there is nothing wrong with their faith because of their material wealth. How foolish were they!

I see such a delusion prevalent inside the church. In society, money determines whether one is rich or poor. For our spirit, our status is determined by righteousness. What is important is not money but rather righteousness. Whoever does not have righteousness will be spiritually poor. Yet, being spiritually poor does not always equate to being poor in spirit. It is when you deeply recognize your spiritual poverty that you can become one who is poor in spirit. However, there are so many people in the church who are not like this.

For example, think about how in the church, among those

who have a good job, are socially successful, and rich, many believe themselves to be righteous. Yet, they are just like the Pharisees, performing religious duties and living with outward righteousness. Even amongst pastors, many feel pride when their church grows bigger, more people attend, and they receive more offerings. There are too many blind leaders to count, who mistakenly believe that they are ministering the right way.

I hope that this chapter will be like a salve for their eyes. And not only them, but I hope that all those in the church who do not know themselves will be able to open their eyes. Please, do a reality check on yourselves. For I desperately wish for everybody to become poor in spirit and truly be saved.

Being poor in spirit now makes sense and it is clearly understandable. However, I do not want you all to just know this in your mind but I want you to really become poor in spirit. Thus, I want to introduce to you several excellent explanations from all the books that I have read on being poor in spirit. For I felt like my heart was melting when I read them in preparation for this book. I hope that all of you will have an equivalent experience.

First, Kathryn Kuhlman explained being poor in spirit as the following.

"One must become poor—poor in a deep sense of nothingness before God—to truly be rich in the things of God. I will admit that is a most difficult hurdle and one of the hardest achievements for any man. We are part of a generation whose doctrine is self-sufficiency ... man's rules for living are, in a sense, a code of self-sufficiency; and that is why it is very difficult for man to get to the place where he can come into the presence of Almighty God and actually have a feeling of complete nothingness, where he can be absolutely resigned before the giving hand of his Lord.

The foundation of all spiritual happiness is a consciousness before God of one's emptiness and one's need.

Jesus tells us in this first beatitude—poverty of spirit—that we must be aware of our lack of God. When we get to that place (and it is not easy, believe me), we have laid the foundation for genuine wealth. **You and I will never inherit the Kingdom of Heaven until we get to the place where we acknowledge our absolute nothingness...**

If you want to be truly rich, you must come to the place where you have a deep sense of nothingness before God; and that, my friend, is what Jesus meant when He said, 'Blessed are the poor in Spirit.'"[59]

---

[59] Kathryn Kuhlman, *In Search of Blessings: Sermons on the Beatitudes*, (Gainesville, Fl: Bridge-Logos Publishers, 1989) 2-3.

Lloyd-Jones also explained being poor in spirit in the following manner.

> "Being 'poor in spirit' … means a complete absence of pride, a complete absence of self- assurance and of self-reliance. It means a consciousness that we are nothing in the presence of God. It is nothing, then, that we can produce; it is nothing that we can do in ourselves. **It is just this tremendous awareness of our utter nothingness as we come face to face with God. That is to be 'poor in spirit'**…
>
> I say again, **it is to feel that we are nothing, and that we have nothing, and that we look to God in utter submission to Him and in utter dependence upon Him and His grace and mercy.**"[60]

Additionally, John Stott said this about being poor in spirit.

> "To be poor in spirit is therefore to acknowledge our spiritual poverty, indeed our spiritual bankruptcy, before God. For we are sinners, under the holy wrath of God, and deserving nothing but the judgment of God. We have nothing to offer, nothing to plead, nothing with which to buy the favour of heaven…
>
> We do not belong anywhere except alongside the tax col-

---

60 Lloyd-Jones, *Studies in the Sermon on the Mount*, (1959) 50-1.

lector in Jesus' parable, crying out with downcast eyes, 'God, have mercy on me, a sinner!'...

In our Lord's own day it was not the Pharisees who entered the kingdom, who thought they were rich, so rich in merit that they thanked God for their accomplishments; nor the Zealots who dreamed of establishing the kingdom by blood and sword; but tax collectors and prostitutes, the rejects of human society, who knew they were so poor they could offer nothing and achieve nothing. All they could do was to cry to God for mercy; and he heard their cry...

Still today the indispensable condition of receiving the kingdom of God is to acknowledge our spiritual poverty. God still sends the rich away empty."[61]

Charles Hodge also talked about the poor in spirit in detail.

"The poor in spirit are those who are conscious of their spiritual poverty. They stand opposed to those who falsely assume and assert that they are rich and know not that they are wretched and miserable, and poor and blind and naked. Poorness in spirit includes therefore,

(1) A sense of ignorance and a willingness to be taught.

---

[61] Stott, *The Message of the Sermon on the Mount*, (2020) 23-4.

It stands opposed to pride of intellect and to confidence in the conclusions of our own understandings. Where this state of mind prevails, this intellectual blindness is the consequence. Those who profess themselves to be wise become fools. It is only those who are sensible of their ignorance and of their insufficiency to discover truth and who are converted so as to be as little children, who have the Holy Ghost, who is the source of all true knowledge and one of the great blessings of the kingdom of God.

(2) A sense of unworthiness, as opposed to a spirit of self-righteousness.

It is a consciousness of guilt and ill-desert in the sight of God which leads the soul to cry, God, be merciful to me, a sinner. But when he is made sensible of the enormity of his guilt, and when he trembles at the wrath of God and renounces his own righteousness, then he receives the righteousness of Christ and becomes rich indeed.

(3) A sense of pollution, as opposed to self-complacency or a disposition to admire our own excellence and to regard ourselves as attractive in the sight of others.

To this is opposed a sense of vileness, which leads us to abhor ourselves and lay our mouths in the dust before God. To those who are thus poor in spirit, the Spirit comes and adorns them with all his heavenly grace.

(4) A sense of helplessness.

This is opposed to the conceit of our own power to change our hearts, to subdue sin, to secure holiness of heart and life... It is only those who are poor in spirit whom He helps.

(5) Poverty of Spirit is a sense of wretchedness, i.e., of the utter incompetency of the world to fill the desires of the soul.

Those who think themselves rich because possessed of this world's sources of happiness, and desire nothing more, God leaves in their contentment. But those who are sensible of their poverty, who hunger and thirst after God, He fills with Himself."[62]

Lastly, Sinclair Ferguson gave the following grace-filled explanation about the topic.

"Poverty of spirit is neither a financial nor a depressive condition...

What is poverty of spirit? By speaking of the poor 'in spirit,' Jesus underlines the fact that he is not speaking about a lack of material prosperity. That may lead to poverty in spirit, but it is not identical to it...

Jesus is describing the person who sees his spiritual bond-

---

[62] Charles Hodge, *Princeton Sermons: Outlines of Discourses*, Doctrinal and Practical, (London, UK: T. Nelson, 1879) 169-70.

age, is conscious of the debt of his sins (cf. Matt. 6:12), and knows that in himself he is dispossessed before God. All he can do is cry for mercy, and depend upon the Lord. No one can be a Christian without this spirit. Everyone who is a Christian has this spirit. It is the spirit of the prodigal son...

> *Nothing in my hand I bring,*
> *Simply to Thy Cross I cling;*
> *Naked, come to Thee for dress;*
> *Helpless, look to Thee for grace;*
> *Foul, I to the fountain fly;*
> *Wash me, Saviour, or I die.*
>
> A. M. Toplady

In the early chapters of Romans, Paul hints at how this new spirit is born... 'There is no one righteous, not even one; there is no one who understands, no one who seeks God. All have turned away, they have together become worthless; there is no one who does good, not even one' *(Rom. 3:10-12).*

What is the result of taking this divine indictment seriously, and applying it to ourselves as we think of the judgment seat of God and his verdict on our lives'? Paul does not leave it to our imagination: every mouth will be shut and silenced, and the whole world—ourselves included—will be condemned as guilty before God (*Rom. 3:19*)...

When God leads us to see that this is our real condition before him, and we recognise this to be so, then poverty of spirit is born in our hearts. Undeceived at last, we see that our only hope is in the Lord. We are poor men and women in ourselves, with no righteousness of our own to plead before God. We are bankrupt, debtors in his court. Our plea must be for mercy...

If you would be rich and possess a kingdom, you must... become poor in spirit."[63]

All of the above help us to better understand the meaning of being poor in spirit and they also touch our hearts! This is what it means to be poor in spirit. It is why I believe the following verses best exemplify the difference between the blessed, who are poor in spirit, and the cursed, who are rich in spirit.

"And Levi made him a great feast in his house, and there was a large company of **tax collectors** and others reclining at table with them. And **the Pharisees** and their scribes grumbled at his disciples, saying, 'Why do you eat and drink with tax collectors and sinners?' And Jesus answered them, **'Those who are well have no need of a physician, but those who are sick.**

---

[63] Ferguson, *Sermon on the Mount*, (1987) 15-8.

I have not come to call the righteous but sinners to repentance.'" (Luke 5:29-32)

Those who are poor in spirit, like the tax collector, know of their spirit's terminal illness; the fact that they are sinners. Oppositely, those rich in spirit, like the Pharisees, do not know their illness or their sin and they live deludedly thinking they are righteous. Thus, they do not sincerely realize nor understand the severity of the necessity for repentance and that they absolutely need their spiritual doctor Jesus. So, they neither repent nor believe.

Although both are mentioned in the verse above, Jesus later brings them up again as the main protagonists in the parable of "The Pharisee and the Tax Collector."

"He also told this parable to some who trusted in themselves that they were righteous, and treated others with contempt: Two men went up into the temple to pray, one a Pharisee and the other a tax collector. The Pharisee, standing by himself, prayed thus: 'God, I thank you that I am not like other men, extortioners, unjust, adulterers, or even like this tax collector. I fast twice a week; I give tithes of all that I get.' But the tax collector, standing far off, would not even lift up his eyes to heaven, but beat

his breast, saying, 'God, be merciful to me, a sinner!' I tell you, this man went down to his house justified, rather than the other. For everyone who exalts himself will be humbled, but the one who humbles himself will be exalted."
(Luke 18:9-14)

This parable clearly shows us who is poor in spirit and blessed and who is rich in spirit and cursed. The rich in spirit are like the Pharisee in this passage. In other words, they are people who are intoxicated in their own self-righteousness. They are people who, like the Pharisee above, mistakenly believe that they have satisfied everything with the standards they set up for themselves. They are prideful people who believe that because they have money, honor, knowledge, and faith, they lack nothing. That is why they boast while praying, lifting up their heads saying, "God I thank you that I am not like other men, extortioners, unjust, adulterers, or even like this tax collector. I fast twice a week; I give tithes of all that I get."

On the other hand, those who are poor in spirit are like the tax collector. How did the tax collector pray? He stood far off, and would not even lift up his eyes to heaven, and beat his breast, crying out, "God, be merciful to me, a sinner" and repented. Whose prayer did God hear and who did God call righteous? It was the prayer of the tax collector! Like Jesus proclaimed in the beatitudes, this parable also vividly shows us that heaven is for those who are poor in spirit. Therefore, through this parable, I hope you can seriously reflect on whether you are like the tax collector or the Pharisee.

And I am sure those of you reading this book believe in Jesus. However, not all of you are actually Christians, for there are both Pharisees and Christians among you. In the end, the Pharisee will go to hell and the Christian will enter heaven.

Have you realized by now what the primary characteristic is that differentiates the two? It is to be poor in spirit. In other words, it is whether you know yourself or not. A person who is not poor in spirit cannot have true repentance. A person who is not poor in spirit also cannot have true faith. These types of people, even if they believe in Jesus, will become Pharisees. The more diligently they believe, the more they will become Pharisees. For if you are not poor in spirit, believing in Jesus will be of no use, and having an earnest faith life will be useless. They will never be able to become a Christian. The more they try, the more they will be like a Pharisee. In short, all effort made without being poor in spirit is in vain. Therefore, all of you must become poor in spirit without fail.

The first step in christianity is thus being poor in spirit. There is nothing that can substitute this and it is shown clearly in the beatitudes. For apart from the Lord's prayer, the beatitudes are the most well-known verses in the Bible, and the first of them is to be poor in spirit. Thomas Watson said the following about the importance of this beatitude.

> "Why does Christ here begin with the poverty of spirit? Why is this put in the forefront? I answer, Christ does it to show that **poverty of spirit is the very basis and foundation of all the other graces that follow**. You may as well **expect fruit to grow without a root, as the other graces without this**."[64]

Lloyd-Jones also talked about the absolute importance of being poor in spirit as follows.

> "'**Blessed are the poor in spirit … It is not surprising that this is the first, because it is obviously, as I think we shall see, the key to all that follows**. There is, beyond any question, a very definite order in these Beatitudes. Our Lord does not place them in their respective positions haphazardly or accidentally; there is what we may describe as a spiritual logical sequence to be found here … **It is the fundamental characteristic of the Christian and of the citizen of the kingdom of heaven, and all the other char-**

---

[64] Thomas Watson, *The Beatitudes: An Exposition of Matthew 5: 1-12*, (London, UK: Banner of Truth Trust, 1971) 42.

acteristics are in a sense the result of this one."[65]

Being poor in spirit precedes even repentance and faith. Many think that Christianity starts with faith. However, this is not true. Before faith is repentance (Mark 1:15, Acts 20:21, Heb. 6:1). And before repentance is being poor in spirit.[66] What God looks for when he chooses those to be saved is this poor in spirit heart (I will completely confirm this point through the Bible in the future when I write a detailed book on predestination). Therefore, there is nothing that precedes being poor in spirit.

As evidence, as I have already explained, being poor in spirit is to open one's eyes (Acts 26:17-18). Jesus opens our eyes "so that they may turn from darkness to light and from the power of Satan to God (meaning repentance), that they may receive forgiveness of sins and a place among those who are sanctified by faith in me." Therefore, we can clearly see that being poor in spirit precedes repentance and faith.

---

[65] Lloyd-Jones, *Studies in the Sermon on the Mount*, (1959) 42.

[66] It may look like a contradiction of sequence and order to have being poor in spirit as the seedbed where repentance and faith grow from while also making the previous argument that the one who repents and believes is the beatitude person. But this is not in conflict with one another. For the beatitudes are not just characteristics that those who are saved possess after receiving salvation. They are characteristics that describe the attributes (which are linked to salvation) one had even before being saved.

Additionally, if you look in the beatitudes, those who mourn come after the poor in spirit (Matt. 5:4). It is the same in Isaiah 66:2.

> KJV "But to this man will I look, even to him that is poor and of a contrite spirit, and trembleth at my word."

Therefore, being poor in spirit precedes repentance!

Moreover, there is a synonym used in the Bible for the poor in spirit and that is the expression to be like a child. The reason the poor in spirit are blessed is because theirs is the kingdom of heaven. Jesus also says the following.

> "But when Jesus saw it, he was indignant and said to them, 'Let the **children** come to me; do not hinder them, f**or to such belongs the kingdom of God**.'" (Mark 10:14)

The promised blessing is the same. We can thus infer that being poor in spirit and being like a child hold equivalent meanings. Kathryn Kuhlman wrote as follows.

> **"The Kingdom of God belongs to the little children in exactly the same way the Kingdom of Heaven belongs to the poor in spirit. Its powers are theirs. You see, the poor in spirit, those**

who acknowledge their absolute nothingness in God's presence, can be likened to a little child: simple, unaffected, and teachable. It is when we possess the spirit like that of a little child that we are able to realize our nothingness and come to the knowledge that all our sufficiency is of God. Only then can we inherit His Kingdom. These two classes—the poor in spirit and those who possess the spirit of a little child—are one and the same in God's sight; and right here we find the key that unlocks the resources of the storehouse of the universe and the wealth of it all is ours."[67]

Being poor in spirit and being like a child are equal to one another. In Matthew 11:25, Jesus says the following.

"At that time Jesus declared, **'I thank you, Father, Lord of heaven and earth, that you have hidden these things from the wise and understanding and revealed them to little children'**"

Like so, Jesus said that the kingdom gospel will be hidden from the wise and understanding but revealed to little children. The kingdom gospel is only revealed to those who are

---

[67] Kuhlman, *In Search of Blessings*, (1989) 3-4.

poor in spirit and like little children. The gospel is received not as knowledge but as revelation for them. That is why they do not let what they hear fall in vain but are able to repent and believe. Therefore, being poor in spirit truly precedes repentance and having faith and is the key to all.

Through this, we can now understand why certain people do not repent even after listening and why certain people do not believe even after listening. It is because their spirit is not poor. This is the reason why people can listen at the same time, same place, and to the same sermon yet only some repent and believe while others do not. Thus, I believe there is nothing more frightening or fatal than becoming rich in spirit. Simply put, it is a curse. It is not an over-exaggeration to say so. For this is something in complete opposition to the blessing Jesus spoke of.

Thankfully, I have seen the poor in spirit heart inside the majority of our church members who have listened to The Sermon series I preached. I am continuing to see people further become poor in spirit as well. Praise God! Yet, this does not mean that I am saying all of you are poor in spirit.

Let me be straight forward and ask these critical questions to those of you who attend church. Do you not identify as a beatitude person? Do you lack the righteousness that exceeds that of the scribes and pharisees? Do you not walk the narrow path nor follow the will of the father? Are you instead intoxicated with having outward righteousness and being diligent in your religious duties? Do you thus believe there is nothing wrong with your faith, and are confident in going to heaven? If so, you are a person who is rich in spirit. In other words, if a person who lives against God's will does not ponder, nor mourn, nor tremble after reading this book on The Sermon, they are rich in spirit. There is no question about it. That person is not blessed but under a curse. If they continue to live like this and die, they will go to hell. Therefore I beg you to search yourself with this message and become poor in spirit. I pray all of you will become poor in spirit and truly start anew with this book on The Sermon.

2) Being Poor in Spirit and a Humble Heart

All of humanity has sinned and their hearts have become depraved. God rejects these blind and prideful people who do not know their own state. Yet, He gives grace to those who know their condition and become humble in heart.

> **"Toward the scorners he is scornful, but to the humble he gives favor."** (Proverbs 3:34)

"Therefore it says, **'God opposes the proud but gives grace to the humble.'**" (James 4:6)

"**God opposes the proud but gives grace to the humble.**" (1 Peter 5:5)

Like so, God gives grace to the humble. The grace of salvation is not an exception to this either. That is why when Jesus received the question, "who is the greatest in the kingdom of heaven", he called a child to him and put him in the midst of them and said "Truly, I say to you, unless you turn and become like children, you will never enter the kingdom of heaven. Whoever humbles himself like this child is the greatest in the kingdom of heaven" (Matt. 18:1-4).

Just as water flows downstream, all grace flows towards the humble. It is the same for the grace of salvation. Therefore, to receive salvation, you need to know yourself and become humble in heart.

Because of this, many people mistake being poor in spirit for being humble. Certainly being poor in spirit and humility have an intimate relation with one another. However, humility does not equal being poor in spirit. Thomas Watson explains this very well.

"What is the difference between poverty of spirit and humility? These are so alike that they have been taken one for the other. Chrysostom, by 'poverty of spirit', understands humility. Yet I think there is some difference. They differ as the cause and the effect. Tertullian says, none are poor in spirit but the humble. He seems to make humility the cause of poverty of spirit. I rather think poverty of spirit is the cause of humility, for when a man sees his want of Christ, and how he lives on the alms of free grace, this makes him humble. He that is sensible of his own vacuity and indigence, hangs his head in humility with the violet. Humility is the sweet spice that grows from poverty of spirit."[68]

This is correct. Being poor in spirit is the root and humility is the fruit. In the end, humility stops with knowing your place. That is why humility cannot take credit or become a qualification. John Wesley said this.

"'Poverty of spirit', then, as it implies the first step we take in running the race which is set before us, is a just sense of our inward and outward sins, and of our guilt and helplessness. This some have monstrously styled 'the virtue of humility';

---

68 Watson, *The Beatitudes*, (1971) 42.

thus teaching us to be proud of knowing we deserve damnation. But our Lord's expression is quite of another kind; conveying no idea to the hearer but that of mere want, of naked sin, of helpless guilt and misery."[69]

Now you can understand the relationship between the poor in spirit and the humble! If so, then from now on, even if you become poor in spirit and as a result become humble in heart, do not grow prideful in your heart because of it. God gives grace to those who are humble. This word itself shows us that the grace that befalls those who are humble is just that: grace. Therefore, let us profess like Paul that all is through God's grace and give all the glory to God alone and become further humble.

3) The Important Meaning That is Incorporated in Being Poor in Spirit!

Being poor in spirit is the start of the beatitudes. As I have already explained, it is formed out of a burden of guilt and from deeply recognizing one's inner depravity. Being poor in spirit is confessing "Father I stretch my hands to thee no other

---

[69] Wesley, *The Sermons of John Wesley*, (2013) 480.

help I know" and lifting up your empty hands in front of God. Therefore, we need to know that from the beginning, the beatitudes and The Sermon were rejecting a legalistic view of salvation.

John Wesley, while preaching on The Sermon said this famous saying.

> "Christianity begins just where heathen morality ends."[70]

This is so true. The salvation in Christianity is thoroughly a salvation not by works but by grace. For not only is being called righteous made possible only through the grace of God, so also is winning against sin and doing the will of the father. Thus, I plead with you to remember that the beatitudes nor The Sermon are teaching salvation by works. At the same time, although we do not believe that the two are teaching 'salvation by works', we should not forget that they are emphasizing 'judgment by works.'

4) The Heaven Promised to Those Who Are Poor in Spirit

The beatitudes first introduce the mutual characteristics of

---

[70] Wesley, *The Sermons of John Wesley*, (2013) 480.

the blessed that God acknowledged. The latter half of each beatitude then explains the reason behind why they are blessed.

Why then are the poor in spirit blessed? They are blessed because theirs is the kingdom of heaven.

> "Blessed are the poor in spirit, **for theirs is the kingdom of heaven.**" (Matthew 5:3)

This "heaven" is not the heaven we will enter in the future. It is the heaven that comes out in Matthew 4:17 where it says, "Repent, for the kingdom of heaven is at hand." In other words, it is the heaven on earth and the heaven in the heart of the believer. Therefore, it has the same meaning as saying you are saved. Because of this, Douglas Hare said the following.

> **"Modern readers need to be reminded that Matthew's 'kingdom of heaven' is no more otherworldly than Luke's kingdom of God… The 'poor in spirit' are 'blessed' not only because of their future participation in God's kingdom but because of their present assurance of that blessedness."** [71]

Thus, the reason the poor in spirit are blessed is because they were accepted and acknowledged as the people of God.

---

[71] Hare, *Matthew*, (1993) 37.

There is something that we need to understand here before moving on. It is the fact that no matter who you are, if you are not poor in spirit, then God will never acknowledge you. People born into the church are not an exception. It is the same for elders, pastors, and even missionaries. That is why Arthur Pink said the following.

> "The very first thing said of Him in the N.T. is, 'thou shalt call His name Jesus, for He shall save His people (not 'from the wrath to come', but) from their sins' (Matt. 1:21). **Christ is a Savior for those realizing something of the exceeding sinfulness of sin, who feel the awful burden of it on their conscience, who loathe themselves for it, who long to be freed from its terrible dominion; and a Savior for no others. …**
>
> **Should the reader exclaim, I was not conscious of the heinousness of sin nor bowed down with a sense of my guilt when Christ saved me. Then we unhesitatingly reply, either you have never been saved at all, or you were not saved as early as you supposed.**"[72]

This is not an overstatement. It is utterly biblical and the truth. Therefore, when you are examining yourself, above all

---

[72] Arthur W. Pink, *Studies on Saving Faith*, (Bottom of the Hill, 2011) 10.

else, examine yourself with a poor in spirit heart. Through this, I hope you will never fool yourselves and will correctly know who you are and change to become real Christians.

5) The Key to Becoming Poor in Spirit

It is useless for a man to gain the whole world but forfeit his soul. How much more is this true for one's eternal life?

"Blessed are the poor in spirit, for theirs is the kingdom of heaven." (Matthew 5:3)

This verse shows us that those who are poor in spirit will enter heaven, but those who are not will not enter heaven. Therefore, we have no choice. We must desperately become one who is poor in spirit.

How then can we become poor in spirit when our hearts are currently filled to the brim with pride? Sinclair Ferguson said the following on this.

> "We have... basic spiritual needs... to come to understand ourselves, to discover what we really are in the presence of God. His word reveals this:
>
> *'Sharper than any double-edged sword, it penetrates even*

to dividing soul and spirit, joints and marrow; it judges the thoughts and attitudes of the heart. Nothing in all creation is hidden from God's sight. Everything is uncovered and laid bare before the eyes of him to whom we must give account.' (Heb. 4:12-13)

When God's word is expounded in the power of the Spirit, we are forced, under its influence, to see ourselves in all our sinfulness. Thus, discovering ourselves, we become poor in spirit, mourn for our sins, and become meek before God. That is what Jesus has taught us already in his words of blessing."[73]

One of the functions of the Word of God is that it uncovers us. That is how it shows us our reality. Therefore, if you desire to become poor in spirit, you need to throw away your prideful thoughts and pay close attention to the Word of God.

According to the Bible, the four particular passages below show us our current conditions and are effective in making us poor in spirit.

① Romans 1-3

In these three chapters, Paul exposed the sins of the gentiles, the Jews, and all of mankind. He allowed them to see their cur-

---

[73] Ferguson, *Sermon on the Mount*, (1988) 25-6.

rent state. Sinclair Ferguson said the following about this.

> "In the early chapters of Romans, Paul hints at how this new spirit [a heart of poverty] is born… 'There is no one righteous, not even one; there is no one who understands, no one who seeks God. All have turned away, they have together become worthless; there is no one who does good, not even one' (*Rom 3:10-12*).
>
> What is the result of taking this divine indictment seriously, and applying it to ourselves as we think of the judgment seat of God and his verdict on our lives'? Paul does not leave it to our imagination: every mouth will be shut and silenced, and the whole world - ourselves included - will be condemned as guilty before God (*Rom 3:19*)…
>
> When God leads us to see that this is our real condition before him, and we recognise this to be so, then poverty of spirit is born in our hearts. Undeceived at last, we see that our only hope is in the Lord … Our plea must be for mercy."[74]

We need to look more critically at these chapters. First, Paul pointed out the sins of the gentiles.

---

[74] Ferguson, *Sermon on the Mount*, (1987) 16-7.

"**For the wrath of God is revealed from heaven against all ungodliness and unrighteousness of men, who by their unrighteousness suppress the truth. For what can be known about God is plain to them,** because God has shown it to them. For his invisible attributes, namely, his eternal power and divine nature, have been clearly perceived, ever since the creation of the world, in the things that have been made. So they are without excuse. For although they knew God, they did not honor him as God or give thanks to him, but they became futile in their thinking, and their foolish hearts were darkened. Claiming to be wise, they became fools, and exchanged the glory of the immortal God for images resembling mortal man and birds and animals and creeping things. Therefore God gave them up in the lusts of their hearts to impurity, to the dishonoring of their bodies among themselves, because they exchanged the truth about God for a lie and worshiped and served the creature rather than the Creator, who is blessed forever! Amen. For this reason **God gave them up to dishonorable passions. For their women exchanged natural relations for those that are contrary to nature; and the men likewise gave up natural relations with women and were consumed with passion for one another,** men committing shameless acts with men and receiving in themselves the due penalty for their error. And since they did not see fit to acknowledge God, God gave them up to a debased mind to do what ought not to be done. **They were filled with all manner of unrighteousness, evil, covetousness, malice. They are full of envy, murder, strife, deceit, maliciousness. They are gossips, slanderers, haters of God, insolent, haughty, boastful, inventors of evil, disobedient to parents, foolish, faithless, heartless, ruthless.** Though they know God's righteous decree that those who practice such things deserve to die, they not only do them but give approval to those who practice them." (Romans 1:18-32)

As shown, the sins of the gentiles are a variety of ethical sins, including idol worship and homosexuality. Homosexuality, which is abominable, is not the only sin. As humans who are a creation of the Creator God, committing idolatry is committing a cardinal sin against the 1st and 2nd commandment from the 10 Commandments. Moreover, not believing in Jesus itself is a grave sin.

> **"concerning sin, because they do not believe in me."** (John 16:9)

Not only this, but who can really say that they have never committed any of the ethical sins that are listed in verses 29-

31? No one can say so. Therefore, all gentiles are sinners. That is why Paul simply wrote in Galatians 2:15, the "gentile sinners."

Paul also portrayed the sins of Jews as follows.

> "But if you call yourself a **Jew** and rely on the law and boast in God and know his will and approve what is excellent, because you are instructed from the law; and if you are sure that you yourself are a guide to the blind, a light to those who are in darkness, an instructor of the foolish, a teacher of children, having in the law the embodiment of knowledge and truth— **you then who teach others, do you not teach yourself? While you preach against stealing, do you steal? You who say that one must not commit adultery, do you commit adultery? You who abhor idols, do you rob temples? You who boast in the law dishonor God by breaking the law. For, as it is written, 'The name of God is blasphemed among the Gentiles because of you.'"** (Romans 2:17-24)

The Jews had the law and were very proud of this fact. However, they failed to keep the law. As shown in the prayers of the Pharisee and the tax collector, they somewhat kept the letter of the law. That is, they cleaned their outside (actions). They did not keep the mind of the law. Their inside (heart) was dirty.

This is a bit of a digression, but there is no one who can abide by all things written in the book of the law (Gal. 3:10). Because of this, there is no one declared righteous by the works of the law (Rom. 3:20, Gal 2:16, 3:11). The Jews were not an exception to this. Therefore, everyone is a sinner. Not only the gentiles, but also the Jews.

Thereafter, Paul specified the sin of all humankind.

> "What then? Are we Jews any better off? No, not at all. For we have already charged that **all, both Jews and Greeks, are under sin, as it is written: "None is righteous, no, not one; no one understands; no one seeks for God. All have turned aside; together they have become worthless; no one does good, not even one."** "Their throat is an open grave; they use their tongues to deceive." **"The venom of asps is under their lips."** "Their mouth is full of curses and bitterness." "Their feet are swift to shed blood; in their paths are ruin and misery, and the way of peace they have not known." **"There is no fear of God before their eyes."'**
> (Romans 3:9-18)

"None is righteous, no, not one!" This is the proclamation of God who searches the heart and tests the mind with His fiery eyes. So, how can we dare deny this? We cannot. We must acknowledge it.

There is no need to explain all of this one by one. For at the end it says, "[t]here is no fear of God before their eyes." This one verse is enough. God said, through the prophet Jeremiah, "know and see that it is evil and bitter ... the fear of me is not in you" (Jer. 2:19). Yet, humanity fears people seeing them but does not fear God watching them (differing from Joseph). That is why they live sinning various sins when other people are not looking. Thus, are we sinners or not sinners? We are sinners. All of mankind is a sinner. We must realize this, for that is when we can be poor in spirit.

② The 10 Commandments

Previously, I said that being poor in spirit is "to open one's eyes," which is what Jesus said to Paul (Acts 26:15-18). Being poor in spirit is opening the eyes to accurately see one's state.

But what makes our eyes open? They open because of the commandments of the law.

> "**The law of the LORD** is perfect, reviving the soul; the testimony of the LORD is sure, making wise the simple; the precepts of the LORD are right, rejoicing the heart; **the commandment of the LORD is pure, enlightening the eyes.**" (Psalm 19:7-8)

For one of the main functions of the law is to make us realize our sin.

"For by works of the law no human being will be justified in his sight, **since through the law comes knowledge of sin.**" (Romans 3:20)

"for sin indeed was in the world before the law was given, but **sin is not counted where there is no law.**" (Romans 5:13)

"Did that which is good [the law], then, bring death to me? By no means! It was sin, producing death in me through what is good, **in order that sin might be shown to be sin, and through the commandment might become sinful beyond measure.**" (Romans 7:13)

Like so, the law allows us to realize our sin. The Bible records these exemplary real examples.

"**And all the people gathered as one man into the square before the Water Gate. And they told Ezra the scribe to bring the Book of the Law of Moses that the L**ORD **had commanded Israel.** So Ezra the priest brought the Law before the assembly, both men and women and all who could understand what they heard, on the first day of the seventh month. And he read from it facing the square before the Water Gate from early morning until midday, in the presence of the men and the women and those who could understand. And the ears of all the people were attentive to the Book of the Law ... And Ezra opened the book in the sight of all the people ... as he opened it all the people stood ... **They read from the book, from the Law of God, clearly, and they gave the sense, so that the people understood the reading... all the people wept as they heard the words of the Law.**" (Nehemiah 8:1-9)

"**While they were bringing out the money that had been brought into the house of the Lord, Hilkiah the priest found the Book of the Law of the Lord given through Moses. Then Hilkiah answered and said to Shaphan the secretary, 'I have found the Book of the Law in the house of the Lord.'** And Hilkiah gave the book to Shaphan. Shaphan brought the book to the king, and further reported to the king, 'All that was committed to your servants they are doing. They have emptied out the money that was found in the house of the Lord and have given it into the hand of the overseers and the workmen.' Then Shaphan the secretary **told the king, 'Hilkiah the priest has given me a book.' And Shaphan read from it before the king. And when the king heard the words of**

the Law, he tore his clothes." (2 Chronicles 34:14-19)

Let me say something very important here. The act of the law making us deeply realize our sin is necessary to save our souls. For Jesus Himself said the following.

"And Jesus answered them, '**Those who are well have no need of a physician, but those who are sick. I have not come to call the righteous but sinners to repentance.**'" (Luke 5:31-32)

Paul also said this, which has the same meaning.

"**Why then the law? It was added because of transgressions... But the Scripture imprisoned everything under sin,** so that the promise by faith in Jesus Christ might be given to those who believe. Now before faith came, we were held captive under the law, imprisoned until the coming faith would be revealed. **So then, the law was our guardian until Christ came, in order that we might be justified by faith.**" (Galatians 3:19, 22-24)

Let me be straightforward with you. Even Jesus was not able to make these people, who believed they were righteous, repent. Then, how can we do so? It is impossible. Therefore, before pastors hastily preach the gospel, they should first work on having people realize their sins through the law. Thus, they need to help people truly repent and believe in the gospel instead of just having them repeat a salvation prayer, like a parrot with their lips.

Yet, unfortunately, the majority of pastors only talk about the cross, atonement, grace, faith, confession of faith, assurance of salvation, etc. They do not talk at all or only minimally about realizing your sins through the law. That is why the church is full of fake believers and there is even a growth of fake pastors as well.

Arthur Pink in *Studies on Saving Faith*, realized this current state of the church and lamented.

> "Just as the world was not ready for the New Testament before it received the Old; just as the Jews were not prepared for the ministry of Christ until John the Baptist had gone before Him with his clamant call to repentance, so the unsaved are in no condition today for the Gospel till the Law be applied to their hearts, for 'by the law is the knowledge of sin' (Rom. 3:20). It is a waste of time to sow seed on ground which has never been ploughed or spaded! To present the vicarious sacrifice of Christ to those whose dominant passion is to take their fill of sin, is to give that which is holy unto the dogs.

The nature of Christ's salvation is woefully misrepresented by the present-day 'evangelist.' He announces a Savior from Hell, rather than a Savior from sin. And that is why so many are fatally deceived, for there are multitudes who wish to escape the Lake of fire who have no desire to be delivered from their carnality and worldliness. The very first thing said of Him in the N.T. is, 'though shalt call His name Jesus, for He shall save His people (not 'from the wrath to come,' but) from their sins' (Matt. 1:21). Christ is a Savior for those realizing something of the exceeding sinfulness of sin, who feel the awful burden of it on their conscience, who loathe themselves for it, and who long to be freed from its terrible dominion; and a Savior for no others. …

Should the reader exclaim, I was not conscious of the heinousness of sin nor bowed down with a sense of my guilt when Christ saved me. Then we unhesitatingly reply, Either you have never been saved at all, or you were not saved as early as you supposed. … But to think that one may be saved by Christ whose conscience has never been smitten by the Spirit and whose heart has not been made contrite before God, is to imagine something which has no existence whatever in the realm of fact."[75]

---

[75] Pink, *Studies on Saving Faith*, (2011) 9-10.

John Stott made the same critique.

"And the law must still be allowed to do its God-given duty today. **One of the great faults of the contemporary church is the tendency to soft-pedal sin and judgment. Like false prophets we 'heal the wound of God's people lightly' (Je. 6:14; 8:11).** This is how Dietrich Bonhoeffer put it: 'It is only when one submits to the law that one can speak of grace... I don't think it is Christian to want to get to the New Testament too soon and too directly.' **We must never bypass the law and come straight to the gospel. To do so is to contradict the plan of God in biblical history...**

So in our modern evangelism we cast our pearls (the costliest pearl being the gospel) before swine. **People cannot see the beauty of the pearl, because they have no conception of the filth of the pigsty. No man has ever appreciated the gospel until the law has first revealed him to himself. It is only against the inky blackness of the night sky that the stars begin to appear, and it is only against the dark background of sin and judgment that the gospel shines forth...**[76]

We cannot come to Christ to be justified until we have first been to Moses to be condemned."[77]

---

[76] John R. W. Stott, *The Message of Galatians*, (Downers Grove, IL: Inter-Varsity Press, 1968) 93.
[77] Ibid., 102.

I couldn't agree more on this point. Therefore, we need to first, through the law, make them realize their sin to feel for themselves the need for repentance and the need for a savior. That is when they will repent when you tell them to repent. They will pay the cost of the disciple when you tell them to pay the cost. They will obey when you tell them to receive Jesus as King and obey Him. We will not have to plead with them but instead it will be like what happened in Acts and they will ask "brothers, what shall we do?" or "sirs, what must I do to be saved?" and will beg you for the way to be saved.

If you want to become a true Christian who is poor in spirit, read the 10 commandments in Exodus 20 carefully. Then you will realize why you are a sinner. And read the 10th commandment most carefully.

> "**You shall not covet** your neighbor's house; **you shall not covet** your neighbor's wife, or his male servant, or his female servant, or his ox, or his donkey, or anything that is your neighbor's." (Exodus 20:17)

Because the Pharisees did not observe this verse, they mistakenly believed that they were righteous and did not realize their sins.

"He also told this parable to some who **trusted in themselves that they were righteous, and treated others with contempt:** 'Two men went up into the temple to pray, one a Pharisee and the other a tax collector. **The Pharisee, standing by himself, prayed thus: 'God, I thank you that I am not like other men, extortioners, unjust, adulterers, or even like this tax collector. I fast twice a week; I give tithes of all that I get.'"** (Luke 18:9-12)

"Woe to you, scribes and Pharisees, hypocrites! For you clean the outside of the cup and the plate, but inside they are full of **greed** and self-indulgence." (Matthew 23:25)

On the other hand, Paul who was also a Pharisee and prided himself in being flawless in front of the law, deeply realized that he was a sinner.

"What then shall we say? That the law is sin? By no means! **Yet if it had not been for the law, I would not have known sin. For I would not have known what it is to covet if the law had not said, 'You shall not covet.'"** (Romans 7:7)

The 10th commandment supplies us with a clue that the 10 commandments are not just for our actions but rather commandments for our heart and mind. For example, the physical act of murder is not the only way one can murder. Hating someone is also equivalent to murder.

> "**Everyone who hates his brother is a murderer**, and you know that no murderer has eternal life abiding in him." (1 John 3:15)

Therefore, through the 10th commandment, you need to correctly understand the meaning of each commandment, and examine yourself accordingly. Then, you are bound to become poor in spirit.

③ The Sermon on the Mount

The law helps us realize our sin. However, there is something that shows us our sins more clearly and shockingly than the law. It is the Sermon on the Mount. It is especially the teachings of Jesus that reveal the fundamental purpose and spirit of the commandments of the law.

> "**You have heard that it was said to those of old, 'You shall not murder; and whoever murders will be liable to judgment.' But I say to you that everyone who is angry**

with his brother will be liable to judgment; whoever insults his brother will be liable to the council; and whoever says, 'You fool!' will be liable to the hell of fire. You have heard that it was said, 'You shall not commit adultery.' But I say to you that everyone who looks at a woman with lustful intent has already committed adultery with her in his heart. If your right eye causes you to sin, tear it out and throw it away. For it is better that you lose one of your members than that your whole body be thrown into hell. And if your right hand causes you to sin, cut it off and throw it away. For it is better that you lose one of your members than that your whole body go into hell. It was also said, 'Whoever divorces his wife, let him give her a certificate of divorce.' But I say to you that everyone who divorces his wife, except on the ground of sexual immorality, makes her commit adultery, and whoever marries a divorced woman commits adultery. Again you have heard that it was said to those of old, 'You shall not swear falsely, but shall perform to the Lord what you have sworn.' ... Let what you say be simply 'Yes' or 'No'; anything more than this comes from evil. You have heard that it was said, 'An eye for an eye and a tooth for a tooth.' But I say to you, Do not resist the one who is evil. But if anyone slaps you on the right cheek, turn to him the other also. And if anyone would sue you and take your tunic, let him have your cloak as well. And if anyone forces you to go one mile, go with him two miles. Give to the one who begs from you, and do not refuse the one who would borrow from you. You have heard that it was said, 'You shall love your neighbor and hate your enemy.' But I say to you, Love your enemies and pray for those who persecute you, so that you may be sons of your Father who is in heaven. For he makes his sun rise on the evil and on the good, and sends rain on the just and on the unjust." (Matthew 5:21-45)

Indeed, who can stand in front of this Word and say they are sinless? Who can dare call themselves righteous? Take this Word as a mirror and examine yourselves. All the self-righteous acts you boasted of will fall crumbling down. That is how, like the tax collector, you will profess, "God, be merciful to me, a sinner." Moreover, not only should you read this passage, you should also read this book attentively till the end. And pay special attention to the section on Matthew 5:21-48. For there will be nothing better than this to make you poor in spirit. Therefore, I hope you realize how great a blessing this book series is for you all.

④ The Verses That Show One's Inner Depravity!

There is a saying that says, "a person is a sinner not because they sin, but because they are a being that cannot help but sin." I agree. That is why throughout the Bible it says that man is "slave to sin". Humans have not only committed sins, but they are deeply depraved on the inside. The Bible says the following about how severe this depravity is.

> "**The heart is deceitful above all things, and desperately sick**; who can understand it?" (Jeremiah 17:9)

Have you ever seen a dead rat rotting? It rots permeating a foul odor and there are even maggots swarming inside the body. Yet, the heart of man is more rotten than this rat. Jesus frankly exposed the human heart in the following manner.

> "And he said, 'What comes out of a person is what defiles him. **For from within, out of the heart of man, come evil thoughts, sexual immorality, theft, murder, adultery, coveting, wickedness, deceit, sensuality, envy, slander, pride, foolishness.** All these evil things come from within, and they defile a person.'" (Mark 7:20-23)

As written, the maggots that continue to rise up in the rotten hearts of man are the maggots of "evil thoughts." In our hearts, we constantly have the sexual immorality maggot, theft maggot, murder maggot, adultery maggot, coveting maggot, wickedness maggot, deceit maggot, sensuality maggot, envy maggot, slander maggot, pride maggot, and the foolishness maggot rise up inside of us. With our own strength, we cannot fathom overcoming these wicked thoughts that never stop coming up from inside us. It is written clearly in the writings of Paul.

> **"For those who live according to the flesh set their minds on the things of the flesh, but those who live according to the Spirit set their minds on the things of the Spirit. For to set the mind on the flesh is death**, but to set the mind on the Spirit is life and peace. For the mind that is set on the flesh is hostile to God, for it does not submit to God's law; indeed, it cannot. **Those who are in the flesh cannot please God."**
> (Romans 8:5-8)

This is also expressed more gruesomely in the previous chapter in the confession of Paul about his experience before conversion.

"For we know that the law is spiritual, but I am of the flesh, sold under sin. For I do not understand my own actions. **For I do not do what I want, but I do the very thing I hate.** Now if I do what I do not want, I agree with the law, that it is good. So now it is no longer I who do it, but sin that dwells within me. For I know that nothing good dwells in me, that is, in my flesh. For I have the desire to do what is right, but not the ability to carry it out. For I do not do the good I want, but the evil I do not want is what I keep on doing. Now if I do what I do not want, it is no longer I who do it, but sin that dwells within me. ...Wretched man that I am! Who will deliver me from this body of death?" (Romans 7:14-24)

In the same chapter, Paul even wrote that the law aggravates the sin inside of us to commit crimes.

"What then shall we say? **That the law is sin?** By no means! Yet if it had not been for the law, I would not have known sin. For I would not have known what it is to covet if the law had not said, 'You shall not covet.' But **sin, seizing an opportunity through the commandment, produced in me all kinds of covetousness.** For apart from the law, sin lies dead." (Romans 7:7-8)

To put it simply, people will listen to sermons that tell you to not do something and will be stimulated to commit that very sin. That is the type of being we are. Thus, you can grasp the depth of the depravity of the human heart!

I believe the following verse best expresses this corruption of man.

> **"Can the Ethiopian change his skin or the leopard his spots? Then also you can do good who are accustomed to do evil."** (Jeremiah 13:23)

The confession of Paul discussed above is not something that can only be experienced before one's conversion. There might be a difference in degree, but even those who are saved can experience this. That is why, as it is recorded in Romans 8:23, all Christians groan inwardly as we wait eagerly for the redemption of our bodies. Thus, we can see the depravity of man and how deep the root of sin is.

Beloved, do you still believe that people are not sinners? Do you still believe that people do not need to repent and that they do not need a savior? We must repent and absolutely need to have a savior. Therefore, I hope you realize this and lay down your prideful hearts and become poor in spirit.

There is just one more thing that I would like to add. We

need to sincerely ask the Holy Spirit, who is the Counselor, for help.

> "Nevertheless, I tell you the truth: it is to your advantage that I go away, for if I do not go away, the Helper will not come to you. But if I go, I will send him to you. And **when he comes, he will convict the world concerning sin and righteousness and judgment**" (John 16:7-8)

One of the reasons the Holy Spirit came upon this earth was to help us realize our sin. Thus, we need to cry out and ask the Spirit to work powerfully to let us realize our sin through the four points I have introduced to you thus far. If you do so, you will all become poor in spirit.

Lastly, I want to end this explanation on the poor in spirit by warning the rich and comforting the poor.

In the prayers of the Pharisee and the tax collector, the tax collector prayed thus.

> "But the tax collector, standing far off, would not even lift up his eyes to heaven, but beat his breast, saying, **'God, be merciful to me, a sinner!'**" (Luke 18:13)

Tax collectors, during this period, generally took the job because of the money and thus most of them were rich. However, as we see in this parable, the tax collector here did not focus on his wealth. He focused on his sin and ethical failings. That is what the rich must do. Wake up quickly from the false stability that your wealth gives you. And instead, look straightforward at the grave danger you are in because of your sin.

Kathryn Kuhlman in the book In Search of Blessings, says the following about the tax collector.

> "He did not look upon his neighbor, but saw his own sins. That man may have possessed great material wealth…but he realized that he lacked something which God alone could supply. Thus, **the poverty which is a key to God's kingdom, is the realization that even though we may possess all things, all things are nothing without God. If you can get to the place where you can realize that all things are nothing without God—no matter what you have, though you may possess all that this world counts as riches—then you have learned the secret of being numbered among the poor in spirit, those who possess all things through Jesus Christ.**"[78]

Therefore, focus not on what you have but what you do

---

[78] Kuhlman, *In Search of Blessings*, (1989) 6-7.

not have. In other words, focus not on your wealth, but on how spiritually wretched, pitiful, poor, blind, and naked you are. Remember that without God, your riches mean nothing. Hence, I hope you become poor in spirit and through inheriting heaven, that you become the true rich.

Now I would like to say a few words for the poor.

The people of this world focus on the rich. However, God is more interested in you than in the rich. Therefore, do not dwell on your misfortunes. You are far more favorable in front of God than the rich. If you look in Phillip Yancey's book, the following excerpt expresses this very well.

> "Various scenes in the Gospels give a good picture of the kind of people who impressed Jesus. A widow who placed her last two cents in the offering. A dishonest tax collector so riddled with anxiety that he climbed a tree to get a better view of Jesus. A nameless, nondescript child. A woman with a string of five unhappy marriages. A blind beggar. An adulteress. A man with leprosy. Strength, good looks, connections, and the competitive instinct may bring a person success in a society like ours, but those very qualities may block entrance to the kingdom of heaven. Dependence, sorrow, repentance, a longing to change—these are the gates to God's kingdom.
>
> 'Blessed are the poor in spirit,' said Jesus. One commentary

translates that **'Blessed are the desperate.'** With nowhere else to turn, the desperate just may turn to Jesus, the only one who can offer the deliverance they long for. Jesus really believed that a person who is poor in spirit, or mourning, or persecuted, or hungry and thirsty for righteousness has a peculiar 'advantage' over the rest of us. Maybe, just maybe, the desperate person will cry out to God for help. If so, that person is truly blessed...

God's partiality [is] toward the poor and the disadvantaged. *Why would God single out the poor for special attention over any other group?* I used to wonder. **What makes the poor deserving of God's concern?** I received help on this issue from a writer named Monika Hellwig, who lists the following 'advantages' to being poor:

1. The poor know they are in urgent need of redemption...

3. The poor rest their security not on things but on people.

4. The poor have no exaggerated sense of their own importance, and no exaggerated need of privacy...

7. The poor can wait, because they have acquired a kind of dogged patience born of acknowledged dependence...

10. The poor can respond to the call of the Gospel with a certain abandonment and uncomplicated totality because they have so little to lose and are ready for anything."[79]

---

[79] Philip Yancey, *The Jesus I Never Knew*, (Grand Rapids, MI: Zondervan, 1995) 114-5.

So, what do you think? Is it not a great advantage? Therefore, to all those who are poor, have low self-esteem, are frustrated, and feel unfortunate, do not place in vain this amazing merit that you all have. Use it to become poor in spirit. Currently, you may be jealous of the rich. Yet, in the future, as the parable of the rich man and Lazarus shows us, the rich will eternally envy you.

As you all well know, I am not smart and I was not studious. Thus, I had to rely on God and I was able to receive the wisdom that God gave me. As a result, every week I am experiencing the privilege of preaching sermons that shame even the wisest people (1 Cor. 1:27). The God that I have experienced is a master of reversals. God not only turns blessings into curses but also turns poverty and curses into blessings without any difficulty. Therefore, do not despair because you are poor but instead become poor in spirit. I pray that you are blessed to experience not just comebacks in your life but also spiritual comebacks.

2. AM I ONE WHO MOURNS?

"**Blessed are those who mourn, for they shall be comforted.**" (Matthew 5:4)

After Martin Luther led the religious reformation with the slogan "faith alone", a strange trend of disregarding repentance and only emphasizing faith emerged. As a result, those who cry or mourn have disappeared from the church. I believe John Stott's criticism of this is truly fair.

> "**I fear that Christians who make much of grace sometimes thereby make light of sin.** There is not enough sorrow for sin among us."[80]

According to the main passage of this chapter, a Christian is one who mourns. Without mourning, the person cannot be a Christian. Therefore, the church must once again restore their

---

[80] Stott, *The Message of the Sermon on the Mount*, (2020) 25.

heart of mourning.

1) The Exact Meaning of Mourning

On the basis of Luke 6, many scholars interpret mourning as the tears of those who are poor and unfortunate. For example, Scot McKnight wrote the following.

> "Those who 'mourn' both grieve in their experiences of tragedy, injustice, and death, and reach out to others in grief and compassion when they experience injustice, sin, evil, tragedy, and death. In other words, they suffer and they love those who suffer. ...
>
> The meaning of this beatitude depends on what these blessed people are mourning about. **Are they mourning for their loved ones? Israel's condition in exile or oppression? Injustice they have experienced? The lack of love, peace, holiness, and justice in the land? Or, as so many have claimed, are they mourning over their own sins?** The answer to this set of questions is found by exploring the historical context. We must begin with Isaiah 61:1-4 (in the context of the hope in chs. 40-66)....
>
> -verses omitted-
>
> **This text clearly suggests that the mourners are those who

are grieved over both Israel's and their own exile."[81]

Like so, there are surprisingly many scholars who believe that mourning comes from the lament of one's unfortunate circumstances. On the other hand, David Turner wrote the following.

> "People mourn over many different misfortunes, but the most likely reasons for mourning here are sin…"[82]

Out of the two, which then is correct? I am certain that the latter is correct. Those who "mourn" in our main passage of this chapter are not mourning because of misfortune or poverty like those in Luke, but rather mourning over sin. As Paul said, they are caught up in "godly grief" (2 Cor. 7:10) and mourning. The evidence for this is in the next three points.

① The Characteristics of Poverty in the Beatitudes

What does the first beatitude, to be poor, mean? In Matthew, it is not the poverty of material things but of the spirit. If this is the case, we must understand mourning to be of the same

---

[81] McKnight, *Sermon on the Mount*, (2013) 40-1.
[82] Turner, *Matthew*, (2008) 150.

nature. Sinclair Ferguson explained this well.

> "Jesus is speaking about life in the kingdom of God. **The poverty he describes is in a man's spirit, not his pocket. Similarly, the grief Jesus describes is man's mourning over his own sinfulness; it is regret that he has proved a disappointment to the Lord.**"[83]

② The Order of the Beatitudes

"Blessed are **the poor in spirit**, for theirs is the kingdom of heaven. Blessed are **those who mourn**, for they shall be comforted." (Matthew 5:3-4)

Like so, those who mourn come after those who are poor in spirit.

Yet, where does mourning come from? Does it suddenly fall from the sky? No. It comes from being poor in spirit.

As I have already explained, poverty of the heart is deeply recognizing one's sins and inner depravity. Therefore, when one becomes poor in spirit, the heart of mourning will naturally arise inside them. Lloyd Jones wrote the following on this topic.

---

[83] Ferguson, *Sermon on the Mount*, (1987) 18.

"To 'mourn' is something that follows of necessity from being 'poor in spirit'. It is quite inevitable. As I confront God and His holiness, and contemplate the life that I am meant to live, I see myself, my utter helplessness and hopelessness. I discover my quality of spirit and immediately that makes me mourn. I must mourn about the fact that I am like that."[84]

Rev. Dong-won Lee also said the following.

"A man who sees himself through God's eyes cannot be arrogant any longer. He cannot help but become poor. And mourning begins with the recognition of this poverty. The poverty of the heart leads one to a grieving heart."[85]

Therefore, the mourning that comes after becoming poor in spirit is not a general sense of mourning. It signifies a mourning due to one's sins.

③ The Parallelism with Isaiah 66:2

KJV "...but to this man will I look, even to **him that is poor**

---

[84] Lloyd-Jones, *Studies in the Sermon on the Mount*, (1959) 58.
[85] Dong-won Lee, *Be Like This*, (in Korean) (Seoul, Korea: Nachimvan Publishing, 1995) 35.

and of a contrite spirit, and trembleth at my word."

I believe that not only the first and second beatitude, but the third beatitude as well is also portrayed in this verse chronologically. The "poor" in this verse is equivalent to being poor in spirit. And like this poverty, it also shows those with a "contrite spirit." To be "contrite" (to feel extreme remorse) is not a general sense of mourning but more so a mourning over one's sins. Therefore, this is surely defining mourning as mourning due to one's sins.

Thomas Watson explained that to go into heaven, "we must go through the valley of tears".[86] This is true. Take a look at Isaiah chapter 6. Isaiah went into the temple and after witnessing the glory of God, he found himself to be unholy and said, "woe is me! For I am lost; for I am a man of unclean lips..." (Isa. 6:5a) and he mourned.

Look at the woman in Luke 7. This woman wiped the feet of Jesus with her tears (38).

Look at the prodigal son in Luke 15. Before he returned to his father, he confessed the following. "I will arise and go to my father, and I will say to him, 'Father, I have sinned against heaven and before you. I am no longer worthy to be called

---

[86] Watson, *The Beatitudes*, (1971) 59.

your son.'" (18-19a).

Look at the tax collector in Luke 18. He beat his chest while confessing and crying out, "God, be merciful to me, a sinner" (13).

Look in Acts 2. The three thousand, who were born again on the day of Pentecost, also were cut to the heart and mournfully asked, " ...Brothers, what shall we do?" (Acts 2:37).

Lastly, take a look at Romans 7. After realizing his sin through the law, Paul cried out, "Wretched man that I am! Who will deliver me from this body of death?" (Rom. 7:24).

Being poor in spirit leads us to be mournful, and mourning leads us to true repentance and faith. However, there are many who have only repeated a profession of faith and have never mourned over their sins or repented. I pray that you all will not be like those people and will instead become those who mourn.

Some might read my words and say, "I have already mourned and been saved." Yet, "those who mourn" in this verse is in the present tense and nonrestrictive. Mourning does not end right after a sinner repents of their sins and becomes a Christian. It continues on after that. Lloyd Jones wrote the following on this.

> **"Now this is not only true at conversion; it is something that continues to be true about the Christian.** He finds himself guilty of sin, and at first it casts him down and makes him

mourn. But that in turn drives him back to Christ; and the moment he goes back to Christ, his peace and happiness return and he is comforted. So that here is something that is fulfilled at once. The man who mourns truly is comforted and is happy; **and thus the Christian life is spent in this way, mourning and joy, sorrow and happiness, and the one should lead to the other immediately."**[87]

For example, let us take a look at Apostle Paul. In Romans 7, he mourned, painfully crying out because of his sins. In Romans 8, he made the following confession, having been saved through Christ.

"There is therefore now no condemnation for those who are in Christ Jesus. For the law of the Spirit of life has set you free in Christ Jesus from the law of sin and death." (Romans 8:1-2)

Yet, that is not the end. There is still a danger of perishing because of sin.

"So then, brothers, we are debtors, not to the flesh, to live according to the flesh. **For if you live according to the flesh**

---

[87] Lloyd-Jones, *Studies in the Sermon on the Mount*, (1959) 60.

you will die, but if by the Spirit you put to death the deeds of the body, you will live. For all who are led by the Spirit of God are sons of God." (Romans 8:12-14)

Not only this, but Paul continued to grieve over the sinful nature that was still inside of himself even after being born again and freed from the shackles of sin.

"For we know that the whole creation has been groaning together in the pains of childbirth until now. **And not only the creation, but we ourselves, who have the firstfruits of the Spirit, groan inwardly as we wait eagerly for adoption as sons, the redemption of our bodies.**" (Romans 8:22-23)

Therefore, mourning due to sin continues forever until the redemption of our bodies and does not end after being born again. A Christian is one who mourns their entire life, not one who mourned at one point in history. Jesus is saying that this kind of person is the one who is blessed.

2) Another Meaning of Mourning

We first mourn because of our sin and inner depravity.

Even after being born again, we live mourning our entire lives. However, we do not only mourn for our sins. We mourn for the sins of our parents, siblings, partner, children, relatives, friends, neighbors, etc., just as much as we do for our own sins.

> "And the LORD said to him, **'Pass through the city, through Jerusalem, and put a mark on the foreheads of the men who sigh and groan over all the abominations that are committed in it.'"** (Ezekiel 9:4)

When we look at churches in our country and around the world today, do you not see that we need to do the same? A true Christian is like this person. Because of this, Lloyd Jones said the following.

> "The man who is truly Christian is a man who mourns also because of the sins of others. He does not stop at himself. He sees the same thing in others. He is concerned about the state of society, and the state of the world, and as he reads his newspaper he does not stop at what he sees or simply express disgust at it. He mourns because of it, … He mourns because of the sins of others. Indeed, he goes beyond that and mourns over the state of the whole world as he sees the moral muddle and unhappiness and suffering of mankind, and reads of wars

and rumours of wars. He sees that the whole world is in an unhealthy and unhappy condition. He knows that it is all due to sin; and he mourns because of it."[88]

This fact appears in various places in the Bible.

"My eyes shed streams of tears, because people do not keep your law." (Psalm 119:136)

"Oh that my head were waters, and my eyes a fountain of tears, that I might weep day and night for the slain of the daughter of my people!" (Jeremiah 9:1)

"For many, of whom I have often told you and now tell you even with tears, walk as enemies of the cross of Christ." (Philippians 3:18)

"and if he rescued righteous Lot, greatly distressed by the sensual conduct of the wicked (for as that righteous man lived among them day after day, he was tormenting his righteous soul over their lawless deeds that he saw and heard)" (2 Peter 2:7-8)

---

[88] Lloyd-Jones, *Studies in the Sermon on the Mount*, (1959) 59.

Like this, a true Christian will not only mourn for their sins, but will also mourn for the sins of others. And like Paul, they will pray again and again with a broken heart for the salvation of others.

"Brothers, my heart's desire and prayer to God for them is that they may be saved." (Romans 10:1)

Therefore, ask yourself. Do you have this mourning inside of you? You must! Without fail! For only a person who has this will be a beatitude person, that is, a true Christian. To say it differently, only these people will have all their tears washed away by the Lord and enter the kingdom of heaven.

3) God Does Not Desire Cheap Tears.

I think I need to talk a little bit about myself here. Since I was young, I liked people like St. Francis who cried in the church. I was most envious of those who cried and repented for their sins, who cried in thanksgiving of God's love and grace, and those who cried and prayed for the salvation of the souls of others. I believe I was more inclined to feel this way because I was not a person who could easily cry like those above.

I highly valued and had a high opinion of those who cried and prayed. And perhaps that is why God allowed me to meet Pastor Ok-kyung Kim. But after experiencing many different kinds of people, I realized that not everyone who cries a lot is like Pastor Kim. Kathryn Kuhlman said the following in relation to this.

> **"There are men and women whose tears can flow as easily as water spouting from an open faucet. But long ago I learned that there are different kinds of tears.**
>
> Some are shed because of jealousy. I'm sure you are aware that the first weapon a jealous person will use is tears. In situations like that, I find I have to check myself for it is my first impulse to confront them with the fact that I know **their crying is only a sham and a weapon to gain their own way.**
>
> **Then there are tears of self-pity. Those are the people who have lived a lifetime of feeling sorry for themselves and have worked hard to gain sympathy on every side.**
>
> **Yes, I have found that nothing can mean so little as tears, and nothing can mean so much as tears."** [89]

Therefore, what is important is not just the act of shedding tears and crying. This fact is clearly shown in the next verse.

---

[89] Kuhlman, *In Search of Blessings*, (1989) 11-2.

"For you know that afterward, when he desired to inherit the blessing, **he was rejected**, for he found no chance to repent, **though he sought it with tears**." (Hebrews 12:17)

The reason God did not forgive Esau even though he cried and pleaded, was because his goal was to be blessed. Esau was not sad about his sin but upset because he lost his blessing. That is why he cried and pleaded. And as a result, he lost the chance to repent. God is not fooled by our tears. The Prophet Joel said this.

"'Yet even now,' declares the LORD, **'return to me with all your heart, with fasting, with weeping, and with mourning; and rend your hearts and not your garments.'** Return to the LORD your God..." (Joel 2:12-13a)

Therefore, we must not just cry, but return to God with all our hearts. In other words, we must have broken hearts that rend us.

Thomas Watson said the following important words.

"There may be sorrow where there are no tears. The vessel may be full though it wants vent. It is not so much the weeping

eye God respects, as the broken heart."[90]

Benny Hinn also said this.

"[Jesus] wasn't talking about an emotional mourning or a physical mourning. He was talking about a spiritual mourning, brokenness before the Lord. David declared, 'A broken and a contrite heart... thou wilt not despise.' (Ps. 51:17 KJV) David was repentant and brokenhearted over his sin."[91]

Surprisingly, "to mourn" does not mean to cry tears. In the Greek, "to mourn" is "pentheo" which means "to mourn, lament". Moreover, the Oxford Dictionary definition of "to mourn" is not to cry, but rather "to feel deep sorrow or regret for." To give a familiar example, let us take a look at 1 Kings 21.

"And when Ahab heard those words, he tore his clothes and put sackcloth on his flesh and fasted and lay in sackcloth and **went about dejectedly.** And the word of the LORD came to Elijah the Tishbite, saying, 'Have you seen how Ahab has humbled himself before me? Because he has humbled himself be-

---

[90] Watson, *The Beatitudes*, (1971) 80.
[91] Benny Hinn, *Biblical Road to Blessings,* (Nashiville, TN: Thomas Nelson Inc, 1997) 86.

fore me, I will not bring the disaster in his days; but in his son's days I will bring the disaster upon his house.'" (1 Kings 21:27-29)

Among these, verse 27 has been translated as the following in different translations.

NIRV "When Ahab heard what Elijah had said, he tore his clothes. He put on the rough clothing people wear when they're sad. He went without eating. He even slept in his clothes. **He went around looking sad.**"

NASB "Yet it came about, when Ahab heard these words, that he tore his clothes and put on sackcloth and fasted, and he lay in sackcloth and **went about despondently.**"

See, Ahab did not cry tears. Instead, he not only tore his clothes but also tore his heart. He mourned with a broken heart. When he did so, God saw it and had compassion for him. Thus, no matter what sin you have sinned, it will be ok. Nor does it matter how much you have sinned. If you go forth with a broken heart and repent, the God who had mercy on Ahab will also have mercy on you. Therefore, I pray that you will not only cry, but repent with a grieving and broken heart, and be forgiven and transformed.

4) The Heavenly Comfort That Will Be Given to Those Who Mourn!

Jesus broke social convention when he said blessed are those who mourn. The reason he then gave for such people being blessed was the comfort they would receive.

If so, what exactly is the kind of comfort that will be given to those who mourn?

Before I explain this, there is something I need to put into order first. When you read the beatitudes, the promise statements of 5:3 and 5:10, "for theirs is the kingdom of heaven," are the same and are in the present tense. On the other hand, verses 4-9 that are in between, have promise statements that are in the future tense. The reason v. 3 and v.10 use the present tense is because the kingdom of heaven was at hand, and the disciples were already in possession of it (Matt. 4:17). It is also showing us that through the above inclusio passage, verses 4-9 that talk about the second to seventh blessings, are also related to the kingdom of heaven and thus salvation. Douglas Hare wrote the following on this.

> "'Theirs is the kingdom of heaven,' an assurance granted both to the poor and to the persecuted (v. 10), brackets the main group of beatitudes and is perhaps to be considered as implic-

it in all of them."[92]

Moreover, Dr. Yong-eui Yang said this.

"Through the 'inclusio' structure that wraps the paragraph on the beatitudes within a kingdom of heaven theme (v.3, v.10), it strongly implies that its entire focus is set on the kingdom of heaven."[93]

Sinclair Ferguson also said the following.

"Jesus himself makes this plain by beginning and ending the Beatitudes with the same promised blessing: 'Theirs is the kingdom of heaven' (v. 3 and 10). In verses 4-9 this chief blessing is further explained and illustrated in a series of six specific blessings: comfort (v. 4), inheriting the earth (v. 5), being filled (v. 6), receiving mercy (v. 7), seeing God (v. 8), and being called sons of God (v. 9). In its simplest terms, Jesus' teaching means this: his disciples have already – here and now – entered into the kingdom."[94]

---

[92] Hare, *Matthew*, (1993) 37.
[93] Yang, *How Will You Read the Book of Matthew?*, (2011) 91.
[94] Ferguson, *Sermon on the Mount*, (1987) 45.

Apart from these scholars, many others also hold similar assertions. And this is correct. The promise statements in the second to seventh beatitudes are explanations of the "heaven" that is present in the promise statements of the first and eighth beatitude. However, different from the promise statements of the first and eighth beatitude that are in the present tense, these are in the future tense. Therefore, these promises point to entering the kingdom of heaven in the future and thus are of our ultimate salvation.

This is reminiscent of the promises that were made to the overcomers in the seven churches of Asia. As I explained in detail in my sermon series on Revelations, they were all entirely promises about ultimate salvation. Although expressed differently, they all meant our ultimate salvation. It is the same for the beatitudes. The promise statements in the beatitudes all point to our ultimate salvation.

It is incredibly important that we understand this. For why was it important to understand the meaning of the promise for the overcomers in Revelation 2 and 3? It was because only by understanding this promise could we then have the truth, the essence of salvation, clearly revealed to us: that only overcomers can go into heaven. As a result, we can then give this vitally important and powerful teaching to believers that they must become overcomers.

The beatitudes are exactly the same. If we do not realize that through the inclusio structure of the first and eighth beatitude, the promise statements of the second to seventh blessings are about our ultimate salvation, the beatitudes will simply stop at being nothing more than morals. But if we do realize this, the beatitudes will not just be an ethical teaching, but will clearly be revealed as portraying the saved. Now it is no longer the case that we nonchalantly try to become a beatitude person and if it does not work out, we shrug our shoulders. Instead, we must become a beatitude person at all costs. It becomes vitally important and the message of the beatitudes becomes a double-edged sword. This is what pierces our hearts and makes us repent. It is the reason why it is so vitally important to correctly understand the promises of the second to seventh blessings.

Thus, we need to know, in more detail, why the promises in verses 4-9 are in the future tense. We need to do so, at the very least, to set a standard for how to interpret these promises.

Many scholars, on the basis of the promise statements in the second to seventh beatitudes being in the future tense, interpret them as holding a future-oriented meaning. For example, Dr. Yong-eui Yang wrote the following.

"The concluding parts of the first (v. 3) and last beatitude

(v. 10), which make an 'inclusio' structure, are in the present tense. Yet, all the other statements are in the future tense. **If all eight blessings are relevant to the kingdom of heaven, you can see that the difference of tenses between these apodoses reflect the tense temporal relations of the kingdom of heaven. In other words, the apodoses that create the "inclusio" are referring to the privilege of the kingdom of heaven that a disciple currently enjoys. Meanwhile, the other apodoses are referring to the future prize that the kingdom of heaven guarantees."**[95]

To make such an interpretation is fairly plausible and immaculate, for the promises in the first and eighth beatitudes are in the present tense and the promises in the second to seventh beatitudes are in the future tense. Thus, I have no wish to oppose this interpretation.

Nevertheless, I believe that on the basis of the inclusio structure of the first and eighth beatitude, the promises in the second to seventh beatitudes hold both the meaning of the present and the future. In other words, they hold the meaning of salvation that has already been given and the meaning of salvation that has not yet come. It is more beneficial to interpret

---

[95] Yang, *How Will You Read the Book of Matthew?*, (2011) 91-2.

it in this manner. Herman Ridderbos had the same thought as myself.

> "True, the second halves of the following Beatitudes put the blessings of the kingdom in the future tense; nevertheless verses 3 and 10 explicitly state that the kingdom already is the possession of those whom Jesus pronounces blessed. The verses that follow will show that He did not merely mean that his possession was already stored up in heaven (cf. v. 12). On the contrary, the initial manifestation of salvation was already present on earth through Jesus' work (11:1-6; 12:26; Luke 17:21), and it was even within people's reach (11:12)."[96]

That is why I believe the promise statements in the second to seventh beatitudes point to both the salvation that is currently enjoyed in this world, as well as the salvation that has not yet come that we will enjoy in the future. I believe that we must interpret each promise statement of the beatitudes with a focus on these two points. Therefore, I want to explain to you "for they shall be comforted" from these two aforementioned viewpoints.

---

[96] Ridderbos, *Matthew*, (1987) 88.

① A Level of Comfort "Already" Given

What exactly is the comfort that those who mourn will receive in this world? Arthur Pink wrote the following.

> "**They shall be comforted.**' This gracious promise receives its fulfillment, first, in that Divine consolation which immediately follows a sound **conversion** (i.e. one that is preceded by conviction and contrition), namely **the removal of that conscious load of guilt which lies as an intolerable burden on the conscience.**"[97]

Moreover, John Stott said this.

> "We should experience more 'godly sorrow' of Christian penitence (2 Cor. 7:10), like the sensitive and Christlike eighteenth-century missionary to the American Indians David Brainerd, who wrote in his journal on 18 October 1740:
>
> 'In my morning devotions my soul was exceedingly melted, and bitterly mourned over my exceeding sinfulness and vileness.'
>
> Tears like this are the holy water which God is said to store in his bottle (Ps. 56:8).

---

[97] Pink, *An Exposition of the Sermon on the Mount*, (2011) 20.

> **Such mourners, who bewail their own sinfulness, will be comforted by the only comfort which can relieve their distress, namely the free forgiveness of God.**
>
> **'The greatest of all comfort is the absolution pronounced upon every contrite mourning sinner.'(Lenski, p. 187)"**[98]

This is true. Conversion and the forgiveness of sins are the very comfort that those who mourn can receive on this earth.

I believe that the latter of these is most intricately and beautifully expressed in David's Psalms on repentance.

> "**Blessed is the one whose transgression is forgiven, whose sin is covered. Blessed is the man against whom the LORD counts no iniquity**, and in whose spirit there is no deceit. For when I kept silent, my bones wasted away through my groaning all day long. For day and night your hand was heavy upon me; my strength was dried up as by the heat of summer. (Selah) **I acknowledged my sin to you, and I did not cover my iniquity; I said, "I will confess my transgressions to the LORD," and you forgave the iniquity of my sin.** (Selah)" (Psalm 32:1-5)

---

[98] Stott, *The Message of the Sermon on the Mount*, (2020) 25.

"Have mercy on me, O God, according to your steadfast love; according to your abundant mercy **blot out my transgressions. Wash me thoroughly from my iniquity, and cleanse me from my sin!** For I know my transgressions, and my sin is ever before me…Behold, I was brought forth in iniquity, and in sin did my mother conceive me…**Purge me with hyssop, and I shall be clean; wash me, and I shall be whiter than snow. Let me hear joy and gladness; let the bones that you have broken rejoice. Hide your face from my sins, and blot out all my iniquities.** Create in me a clean heart, O God, and renew a right spirit within me. Cast me not away from your presence, and take not your Holy Spirit from me. **Restore to me the joy of your salvation, and uphold me with a willing spirit…The sacrifices of God are a broken spirit; a broken and contrite heart, O God, you will not despise."**

(Psalm 51:1-17)

This is the comfort given to those who mourn. Therefore, I hope you all enjoy this comfort by mourning and repenting and confessing.

On the other hand, the word "comfort" in Greek is *parakaleo* and it means "to call", "to invite", "to advise", "to discipline", "to encourage", "to implore", and "to beseech". In the Bible research program Biblelex 9, it explains the word as follows.

"Parakaleo means to call (summon), to invite, to ask. In Acts 28:2, parakaleo means 'to call (to oneself), to summon': 'The native people showed us unusual kindness, for they kindled a fire and welcomed us all, because it had begun to rain and was cold.'

In Acts 28:14, parakaleo has a more special meaning, 'to invite': 'There we found brothers and were invited to stay with them for seven days. And so we came to Rome.'

Similarly, the word shows an invitation to the gospel or missions ministry in Acts 16:9; 8:31; 13:42."

In this aspect, Pastor Dong-won Lee's assertions also have a point.

"This word [comfort] is a very interesting word as it is combined with the preposition 'beside' and the verb 'to call.' [It means] 'to be called beside someone and to stand by them.'

The Lord called the Holy Spirit the Helper. The word helper holds the very same meaning. The Holy Spirit, the one who is called to stand with us! The Holy Spirit that Jesus sent is the very one who is right beside us.

Here, the word 'comfort' is used as the same word. Beloved, do you experience the Lord beside you? Do you discover the true comfort of the Lord?

> When a soul faces his sin, and sincerely mourns because of this, the presence of the Lord is right there. You will find the Lord of forgiveness, healing and grace drawing near you...
>
> The author of this Psalm tells us that 'The Lord is near the brokenhearted and saves the crushed in spirit.'"[99]

This is true. The Lord is near the brokenhearted. He will never scorn them.

Think about the heart of parents for a child who did wrong. Many times children do not realize their wrongs even if they are scolded. Thus, the worry of the parents deepens. For what the parents desire is not to admonish the child but rather that the child becomes upright. However, imagine that the child deeply realizes their wrongs and mourns. Is there anything that would bring more delight or more joy to the parents? This is what the parents desperately desired. Would the parents then scorn and distance themselves from this child who deeply realized their sin and mourned? No, they would embrace them. God is the same.

Sin, however, blocks the path between God and people.

> "but your iniquities have made a separation between you

---

99   Lee, *Be Like This*, (1995) 37-8.

and your God…" (Isaiah 59:2a)

Sin not only takes away the presence of God from people, but it also takes away glory, honor, and peace. One becomes filled with the feeling of being alone and of being rejected by God. But if we mourn, God draws near to us. God forgives us of our sins and we can feel that He is with us.

> "For thus says the One who is high and lifted up, who inhabits eternity, whose name is Holy: **"I dwell in the high and holy place, and also with him who is of a contrite and lowly spirit, to revive the spirit of the lowly, and to revive the heart of the contrite."** (Isaiah 57:15)

Therefore, the greatest comfort given to those who mourn is God Himself. Thus, you must mourn and repent if you desire God. I pray that by doing so, you will all be blessed and receive forgiveness of your sins and God with it.

② The Level of Comfort That Has "Not Yet" Come

David Turner said that "those who mourn now will receive future comfort through the anointed servant of Isa. 61."[100] Ac-

---

[100] Turner, *Matthew*, (2008) 151.

cording to the Scriptures, one of the duties of the Messiah is to comfort.

> "The Spirit of the Lord God is upon me, because the Lord has anointed me to bring good news to the poor; he has sent me to bind up the brokenhearted, to proclaim liberty to the captives, and the opening of the prison to those who are bound; to proclaim the year of the Lord's favor, and the day of vengeance of our God; **to comfort all who mourn**; to grant to those who mourn in Zion—to give them a beautiful headdress instead of ashes, the oil of gladness instead of mourning, the garment of praise instead of a faint spirit; that they may be called oaks of righteousness, the planting of the Lord, that he may be glorified." (Isaiah 61:1-3)

The Messiah is one who comforts. That is why this verse exists.

> "Now there was a man in Jerusalem, whose name was Simeon, and this man was righteous and devout, **waiting for the consolation of Israel**, and the Holy Spirit was upon him." (Luke 2:25)

But the Messiah is not just a comforter in the present. He also comforts us in the future. In other words, those who mourn will not only be comforted in the present, but will also be comforted in the future. To say it differently, they will not only receive comfort in this world, but also receive comfort in the afterlife.

Then what exactly is the comfort that those who mourn will receive in the future? This comfort is the very comfort that is shown in the parable of the rich man and Lazarus.

> "But Abraham said, 'Child, remember that **you in your lifetime received your good things**, and Lazarus in like manner bad things; **but now he is comforted here**, and you are in anguish.'" (Luke 16:25)

Arthur Pink also cited this verse while explaining the comfort that those who mourn receive.

> "**'Comfort' is when we leave this world and are done with sin forever. Then shall 'sorrow and sighing flee away.' To the rich man in hell, Abraham said of the one who had begged at his gate, 'now he is comforted'(Luke xvi, 25)."**[101]

Let us compare this verse to Luke 6:24.

---

[101] Pink, *An Exposition of the Sermon on the Mount*, (2011) 21.

"**But woe to you** who are rich, **for you have received your consolation.**"

If this is the case, then we can understand that the comfort that those who mourn will enjoy is in effect actually heaven.

On the other hand, there is a place that better explains the comfort that those who mourn receive. It is in the Book of Revelations.

> "Therefore they are before the throne of God, and serve him day and night in his temple; and he who sits on the throne will shelter them with his presence. They shall hunger no more, neither thirst anymore; the sun shall not strike them, nor any scorching heat. For the Lamb in the midst of the throne will be their shepherd, and he will guide them to springs of living water, **and God will wipe away every tear from their eyes.**"
> (Revelation 7:15-17)

> "Then I saw a new heaven and a new earth, for the first heaven and the first earth had passed away, and the sea was no more. And I saw the holy city, new Jerusalem, coming down out of heaven from God, prepared as a bride adorned for her husband. And I heard a loud voice from the throne saying, "Behold, the dwelling place of God is with man. **He will dwell with**

them, and they will be his people, and God himself will be with them as their God. **He will wipe away every tear from their eyes, and death shall be no more, neither shall there be mourning, nor crying, nor pain anymore**, for the former things have passed away." (Revelation 21:1-4)

Praise God! This is the very comfort that those who mourn will receive in the future. Dr. Yong-eui Yang said the following.

> "When the kingdom of heaven is completed, God will remove all sin, suffering, death and wipe away every tear from their eyes (Rev. 21:4). Then the disciples 'who mourn' will receive true comfort from God."[102]

Just as we might wipe the tears of another to comfort them, when the time comes, God will personally wipe all our tears away. He will give us eternal joy. Is this not the most perfect comfort? Those who mourn will receive this kind of perfect comfort. This is why Jesus said blessed are those who mourn.

However, although those who mourn will receive this amazing comfort, those who do not mourn will forever be miserable, weeping and gnashing their teeth (Matt. 22:13, 24:51, 25:30).

---

[102] Yang, *How Will You Read the Book of Matthew?*, (2011) 93.

Because of this, Jesus in Luke 6 used such strong language like "woe to you!" to warn us of the following.

> "And he lifted up his eyes on his disciples, and said: 'Blessed are you who are poor, for yours is the kingdom of God. 'Blessed are you who are hungry **now**, for you shall be satisfied. 'Blessed are you who weep **now,** for you shall laugh. 'Blessed are you when people hate you and when they exclude you and revile you and spurn your name as evil, on account of the Son of Man! Rejoice in that day, and leap for joy, for behold, your reward is great in heaven; for so their fathers did to the prophets. 'But **woe to you** who are rich, for you have received your consolation. 'Woe to you who are full **now**, for you shall be hungry. '**Woe to you who laugh now, for you shall mourn and weep**." (Luke 6:20-25)

What we need to focus on here is the word "now." Are you someone who mourns "now?" Or are you someone who laughs from drunkenness on the world? I hope you become one who mourns "now" when you are still alive and have the chance.

> **"Be wretched and mourn and weep. Let your laughter be turned to mourning and your joy to gloom."** (James 4:9)

We must realize our sins and become poor in spirit to mourn "now." I pray that you will not weep or gnash your teeth forever either. Instead, I pray that you will be blessed and God Himself will wipe all the tears from your eyes and comfort you.

3. AM I MEEK?

"Blessed are the meek, for they shall inherit the earth."

(Matthew 5:5)

I will explain the third beatitude by dividing it into two sections.

1) "Blessed Are the Meek"

If you look in Luke 6, a portion of the beatitudes is recorded there.

> "And he lifted up his eyes on his disciples, and said: 'Blessed are you **who are poor,** for yours is the kingdom of God.' 'Blessed are you **who are hungry** now, for you shall be satisfied.' 'Blessed are you **who weep** now, for you shall laugh.'" (Luke 6:20-21)

Those who are "poor," "hungry," and those who "weep" are

all actually experiencing such things in their lives. More than a few scholars use this as a stepping stone to interpret the beatitudes. Thus, they interpret the meek as those who accept living in these situations and succumbing to them. They believe that the meekness Jesus talked of is "submission to God's will." In other words, it is to "carry ourselves calmly, without swelling or murmuring, under the dispensations of providence."[103]

"It is the LORD. Let him do what seems good to him." (1 Samuel 3:18)

They believe that meekness is confessing in the above manner. On the other hand, they claim that to respond like Jonah is the opposite of meekness.

"Yes, I do well to be angry, angry enough to die." (Jonah 4:9)

This interpretation is incredibly persuasive, for it is based on Luke 6. So, it is equally confusing to know which is correct. It makes us question whether our original interpretation or this new one is correct. This is why I must explain this point further.

---

[103] Watson, *The Beatitudes*, (1971) 105.

First, the understanding of Luke 6 in itself is correct. Jesus did speak to those who were actually poor, hungry, and mourning. However, this message was not for all who are poor, all who are hungry, or all who are mourning. This was a message Jesus spoke to the disciples, who were amongst the poor, hungry, and mourning, but those who also correctly responded to His words. To put it simply, Jesus spoke in such a manner because so many of His disciples were in these situations. Therefore, the poor are not just those who are physically poor, but rather those who have become poor in spirit due to their poverty. This is the same for the other beatitudes.

Thus, the Gospel of Matthew and the Gospel of Luke are not in contradiction with one another. Rather, the Gospel of Matthew accurately reveals the intention of Jesus' words written in Luke. Through this, we can see how the interpretation of the scholars that I introduced above is erroneous.

So, with this in mind, let us figure out who exactly are the meek. I believe that there are two meanings for "the meek" in the beatitudes.

① Meekness Towards Other People

Jesus talked about "the meek" in the third beatitude. The Oxford Dictionary defines meekness as "**being quiet, gentle, and** easily imposed on."

Thomas Watson also defined it as the following.

> "**Meekness is a grace whereby we are enabled by the Spirit of God to moderate our passion… [b]y nature the heart is like a troubled sea, casting forth the foam of anger and wrath. Now meekness calms the passions.**"[104]

This is the fundamental meaning of being meek. It holds the same meaning when we look at the original language. "Meek" in Greek is "praus", meaning "meek," "kind," "humble," and "compassionate." Therefore, to be meek is to be gentle and mild towards others.

A Christian is not only poor in spirit and one who mourns, but also meek towards others. And there are three reasons why meekness is bound to be a characteristic of a true Christian.

a) A Christian is a beatitude person who has been saved through repentance and faith (Matt. 5:1-12).

The third beatitude is to be "meek" (Matt. 5:5). I will explain this further at a later time, but being poor in spirit and mournful beget meekness. Therefore, a true Christian is meek.

---

[104] Watson, *The Beatitudes*, (1971) 106.

b) **A Christian has righteousness that exceeds that of the scribes and Pharisees (Matt. 5:20).**

Having righteousness that exceeds that of the scribes and Pharisees means one is different from those who only knew and tried to keep the letter of the law. It means one understands the mindset of the law that Jesus taught. In other words, one knows and keeps the base objective and correct meaning (Matt. 5:17). Jesus, while explaining the commandment to not murder, said the following.

> "You have heard that it was said to those of old, 'You shall not murder; and whoever murders will be liable to judgment.' But I say to you that **everyone who is angry with his brother will be liable to judgment**; whoever insults his brother will be liable to the council; and whoever says, 'You fool!' will be liable to the hell of fire." (Matthew 5:21-22)

A Christian lives following after this Word. Therefore, a true Christian is meek.

c) **A Christian is one who bears the fruits of the Spirit (Gal. 5:22-23).**

There are desires of the flesh, even inside a Christian that make "becoming angry" possible (Gal. 5:16-17, 20). However, a Christian acts following the Spirit and not the flesh. They live bearing the fruits of the Spirit. And one of the fruits of the Spirit is to be meek.

> "But the fruit of the Spirit is love, joy, peace, longsuffering, gentleness, goodness, faith, **meekness**, temperance: against such there is no law." (Galatians 5:22-23, KJV)

Therefore, a true Christian is meek.

Yet, "the meek" did not become meek naturally. Therefore, those who are innately hot-tempered and far from meek cannot use this as an excuse. Pastor Dong-won Lee said the following.

> "Someone might say, 'Pastor, by nature, I am not meek.' **Well, was Moses a meek man by nature?** No! He beat to death the Egyptian man who despised his people. Through this, we can see that he was not meek by nature. However, Moses became meek. **Was Paul meek by nature?** No, but he too became meek."[105]

Therefore, we cannot give the excuse that we were born with

---

[105] Lee, *Be Like This*, (1995) 49.

such a personality. Instead, we must become meek without fail.

Then, where does meekness come from if it is not innate?

It comes from the heart of being poor and from the heart of mourning. Sinclair Ferguson explained this well.

> **"Poverty of spirit and mourning over sin have a pervasive influence on our lives. Their immediate effect is to make us *meek*.**
>
> The word *meekness* is notoriously difficult to define. It is certainly not a lack of backbone... The meek man is the one who has stood before God's judgment, and abdicated all his supposed 'rights'. He has learned, in gratitude for God's grace, to submit himself to the Lord and to be gentle with sinners...[106]
>
> **When we know what we are before God, and look to him for grace and salvation, then we become poor in spirit; then we mourn for our sins; then, having seen ourselves as we really are, we bow to his will in all things. And as we experience the gentleness of his grace, we are meek and gentle with others."**[107]

Lloyd-Jones explained it in the following manner.

"What, then, is meekness? I think we can sum it up in this way.

---

[106] Ferguson, *Sermon on the Mount*, (1987) 21.
[107] Ferguson, *Sermon on the Mount*, (1987) 23-4.

> **Meekness** is essentially a **true view of oneself, expressing itself in attitude and conduct with respect to others. ... A man can never be meek unless he is poor in spirit. A man can never be meek unless he has seen himself as a vile sinner."**[108]

This is true. Thus, if one is not meek, it is because they do not know themselves. They do not know their place. In the end, it is an impertinent act to easily be angered. This is somewhat implied in the following verse.

> "Brothers, if anyone is caught in any transgression, you who are spiritual should restore him in a spirit of **gentleness. Keep watch on yourself, lest you too be tempted**." (Galatians 6:1)

Therefore, we must all realize our sins and become poor in spirit. We must also be aware of our sinfulness and become one who mourns. And on this foundation, we must all become one who treats others meekly.

② Meekness Towards God

I believe that we must be meek far more towards God than we are towards other people. When we listen to God's Word,

---

[108] Lloyd-Jones, *Studies in the Sermon on the Mount*, (1959) 68.

we must not be like the people who became angry after listening to Stephen's sermon.

> "Now when they **heard these things they were enraged**, and they ground their teeth at him… But they cried out with a loud voice and stopped their ears and **rushed together at him**. Then they **cast him out of the city and stoned him**. And the witnesses laid down their garments at the feet of a young man named Saul." (Acts 7:54, 57-58)

We must instead be like those who heard Peter's sermon and trembled in fear.

> "Now when **they heard this they were cut to the heart**, and said to Peter and the rest of the apostles, **'Brothers, what shall we do?'**" (Acts 2:37)

We see this important message when we look at Isaiah 66:2.

> "All these things my hand has made, and so all these things came to be, declares the LORD. But this is the one to whom I will look: **he who is humble and contrite in spirit and trembles at my word**."

Did you notice that it has the same structure as the beatitudes? That is why I believe trembling at God's Word is the ultimate meaning of being meek in the beatitudes.

As you all well know, the Israelites were continuously angry with the prophets who proclaimed the Word of God. They persecuted and killed the prophets. We must not become angry at the Word like them. Instead, we should receive it meekly.

> "The meek will He guide in judgment, and **the meek He will teach His way.**" (Psalm 25:9, MEV)

> "Therefore put away all filthiness and rampant wickedness and **receive with meekness the implanted word, which is able to save your souls.**" (James 1:21)

Like so, meekness is related to listening to the Word. Ultimately, meekness represents the ear to hear. The Israelites could not enter Canaan because they did not have the ear to hear.

> "**But to this day the LORD has not given you a heart to understand or eyes to see or ears to hear.**" (Deuteronomy 29:4)

In the same manner, those who are not meek or those who

do not have the ear to hear cannot receive the new heaven and new earth as their inheritance. Thus, this meekness is critically important.

Yet, in spite of this, most do not interpret the meek like I do. Many times, the explanation ends after simply discussing meekness towards others. Occasionally, there were a few who followed my interpretation. However, there are not many of them and I could only find four such people.

First, Thomas Watson said the following about being meek.

"**Flexibleness to God's Word: when we become pliable to all its laws and maxims. He is spiritually meek who … does not quarrel with the instructions of the Word, but with the corruptions of his heart**. Cornelius' speech to Peter savoured of a meek spirit: 'Now therefore we are all here present before God, to hear all things that are commanded thee of God' (Acts 10:33). How happy is it when the Word which comes with majesty is received with meekness! (James 1:21)."[109]

Moreover, Arthur Pink said the following.

"Godly sorrow softens the heart, so that it is made receptive to

---

[109] Watson, *The Beatitudes*, (1971) 105-6.

the entrance of the Word. Meekness consists in the spirit being made pliant, tractable, submissive, teachable."[110]

Lloyd-Jones also wrote the following about being meek.

"**[Meekness] also means that we are ready to listen and to learn; that we have such a poor idea of ourselves and our own capabilities that we are ready to listen to others.** Above all we must be ready to be taught by the Spirit, and led by the Lord Jesus Christ Himself. **Meekness always implies a teachable spirit.**"[111]

Lastly, Pastor Dong-won Lee wrote the following about meekness.

"**Our attitude must be meek when receiving the Word.**
    James 1:19-20 says, 'Know this, my beloved brothers, let every person be quick to hear, slow to speak, slow to anger; for the anger of man does not produce the righteousness of God.'
    Nowhere in history does it say the righteousness of God was achieved through anger. Thus, the Word says the anger of man does not produce the righteousness of God. This is to empha-

---

[110] Pink, *An Exposition of the Sermon on the Mount*, (2011) 23.
[111] Lloyd-Jones, *Studies in the Sermon on the Mount*, (1959) 70.

size the following verse.

> 'Therefore put away all filthiness and rampant wickedness and receive with meekness the implanted word, which is able to save your souls.' (v. 21)
>
> It is telling us that we need to receive the Word meekly."[112]

Yet, unfortunately, even these scholars, while enumerating the various meanings of meekness, explained things in a simple manner and glossed over it. No one accurately explained this as the key meaning of meekness. However, I believe this to be the key meaning of meekness and there are several reasons why.

a) First, it matches the order of Isaiah 66.

> "All these things my hand has made, and so all these things came to be, declares the LORD. But this is the one to whom I will look: **he who is humble and contrite in spirit and trembles at my word.**" (Isaiah 66:2)

God is the one who spoke these words and Jesus is God who came on this earth. Thus, He would not have spoken against this meaning. Therefore, I believe that meekness means the above.

---

[112] Lee, *Be Like This*, (1995) 45-6.

b) **This is the meaning of meekness in the Bible.**

"The meek will he guide in judgment, and **the meek will he teach his way**." (Psalm 25:9, KJV)

"Of his own will he brought us forth by the word of truth, that we should be a kind of firstfruits of his creatures. Know this, my beloved brothers: let every person be quick to hear, slow to speak, slow to anger; for the anger of man does not produce the righteousness of God. **Therefore put away all filthiness and rampant wickedness and receive with meekness the implanted word, which is able to save your souls**." (James 1:18-21)

Through verse 18, we see that to be 'quick to hear' in verse 19 is talking about the Word. However, it also says to be 'slow to anger' and conversely to 'receive with meekness the implanted word.' Therefore, the meaning of this verse is to not be angry when listening to the Word and to instead, receive it meekly.

Like so, the scriptures do not use 'meek' to simply mean a gentle characteristic but to rather be the correct attitude towards the Word. Since it is then even in the same order as Isaiah 66:2, is there any reason why we should not interpret 'the meek' to mean as much? There is no reason not to. Because of this, I believe that meekness is the act of correctly responding to God's Word.

c) The beatitudes before and after the meek are about God.

"The poor" and those "who weep" in Luke 6 are the "poor in spirit" and those who "mourn for one's sins" in Matthew 5. We have also seen that being poor in spirit is about God and mourning is also about God. Not only this, but to hunger and thirst for righteousness, which comes after meekness, is also towards God. He wishes for us to live a life that is righteous in God's eyes (Matt. 6:1). If this is true, being meek, which is in between these things, must also fundamentally be about God.

d) The context of Matthew's statements

In Luke 6, it simply described people's external conditions because it was usually the poor, the hungry, and the weeping who received the gospel. However, in Matthew 5, they were not dealing with their circumstances but rather why they were blessed. In other words, it is talking about why they were saved and why they will enter heaven.

And it is because they were poor of heart and because they mourned for their sins. I believe we need to thus look at being meek in the same vein of thought. Namely, just like how being poor in spirit and mourning are related to salvation, we need to view being meek as also being related to salvation. Thus, we must understand meekness as trembling in front of the Word of God.

e) This interpretation is highly probable.

The interpretation that those who realize their sins and become poor in spirit and mourn for their sins will then treat others meekly, is a natural way of thinking. And it is a correct interpretation. However, this is not the only natural interpretation.

Jesus said the following.

> "And Jesus answered them, **'Those who are well have no need of a physician, but those who are sick. I have not come to call the righteous but sinners to repentance.'"**
> (Luke 5:31-32)

I have said this before, but one becomes poor in spirit when they realize that they are a sinner. For the Pharisees who thought themselves to be righteous were the very ones who persecuted Jesus. They hated Jesus, rejected His words, found fault with Him and attacked Him. However, those who realized they were sinners, that is, the tax collectors and prostitutes, eagerly received Jesus' words. Therefore, it is not only natural to say that those who are poor in spirit and mournful will become meek. It is equally natural to say that the poor in spirit and mournful will fear and tremble in front of the Word of God and accept it.

Jesus said that He was useless to those who do not know that they are sinners. Even the Lord cannot do anything for such people. For not everyone receives the gospel when it is preached. The gospel is only effective for those who realize their sins. Only those who are actually poor in spirit and mournful can receive the gospel. That is why Paul said that the law will lead us to Christ (Gal. 3:24).

To those who have not realized their sins, the gospel is offensive and a heart of resistance rises up inside of them. However, if you have realized your sins through the law, you will keenly become aware of the need for Christ, the need for the gospel, and the need to repent and have faith. As a result, you will become meek in front of the gospel.

Read this carefully. Anyone who wants to be saved must not only be poor in spirit and mournful but also have this meekness where you tremble in front of the Word. This is what gives birth to repentance and faith. Therefore, I hope you all reflect upon yourselves and become one who meekly accepts God's Word.

2) "For They Shall Inherit the Earth!"

I explained this while dealing with the second beatitude, but the promise for the second to seventh beatitudes hold two meanings of ultimate salvation. The first is a "salvation that has already come" that we enjoy on this earth. The second is one we will enjoy in the afterlife as a "salvation that has yet to come". We must interpret the above with a focus on these two things.

① The Meaning of the Earth We Have 'Already' Received

God created mankind as a steward to reign over the world. He gave us control over the land and all the creations inside it.

> "Then God said, **'Let us make man** in our image, after our likeness. **And let them have dominion over the fish of the sea and over the birds of the heavens and over the livestock and over all the earth and over every creeping thing that creeps on the earth.'** So God created man in his own image, in the image of God he created him; male and female he created them. And God blessed them. And God said to them, **'Be fruitful and multiply and fill the earth and subdue it, and have dominion over the fish of the sea and over

the birds of the heavens and over every living thing that moves on the earth.'" (Genesis 1:26-28)

"When I look at your heavens, the work of your fingers, the moon and the stars, which you have set in place, what is man that you are mindful of him, and the son of man that you care for him? Yet you have made him a little lower than the heavenly beings and crowned him with glory and honor. **You have given him dominion over the works of your hands; you have put all things under his feet, all sheep and oxen, and also the beasts of the field, the birds of the heavens, and the fish of the sea, whatever passes along the paths of the seas.**" (Psalm 8:3-8)

"The heavens are the LORD's heavens, but **the earth he has given to the children of man.**" (Psalm 115:16)

However, man was not satisfied with these things and desired more. That is why he fell for the temptation of the snake. As a result, the land that was given to humans was naturally taken over by Satan. This is depicted well when Satan shows the glory of the world to Jesus and says "for it has been delivered to me" (Luke 4:6).

Thankfully, through the death on the cross, Jesus recovered

what Adam had lost. He proclaimed, "All authority in heaven and on earth has been given to me" (Matt. 28:18). When He returns, Jesus will actually requisition all the earth. Thus, He will reign as king for a thousand years with the saints. And afterwards, He will create a new heaven and a new earth for us. That is our inheritance.

We must understand the promise that we will receive the earth as our inheritance inside this bigger picture. Therefore, to inherit the earth means that we will go into the new heaven and new earth. However, Sinclair Ferguson said the following while explaining this.

> **"But even now, the Christian has a partial experience of this."**[113]

He then said the following as evidence.

> "'I tell you the truth, ... no one who has left home or wife or brothers or parents or children for the sake of the kingdom of God will fail to receive many times as much in this age and, in the age to come, eternal life' (Lk. 18:29).
> **This is what Jesus means when he says in the sermon that everything we need will be provided for us if we make the king-**

---

[113] Ferguson, *Sermon on the Mount*, (1987) 49.

dom and the righteousness of God our first priority (Matt. 6:33). Millions of Christians throughout the ages can bear witness to the certainty of his promise."[114]

This is correct. However, I cannot understand why Sinclair Ferguson cited Luke. For it is more effective to cite the verses in Matthew or Mark.

"And everyone who has **left houses** or brothers or sisters or father or mother or children or **lands**, for my name's sake, **will receive a hundredfold** and will inherit eternal life." (Matthew 19:29)

"Jesus said, 'Truly, I say to you, there is no one who has left **house** or brothers or sisters or mother or father or children or **lands**, for my sake and for the gospel, who will not **receive a hundredfold** now in this time, houses and brothers and sisters and mothers and children and **lands**, with persecutions, and in the age to come eternal life.'" (Mark 10:29-30)

Like so, the meek, namely the true disciples, will not only inherit the new heaven and the new earth that is to come but

---

[114] Ferguson, *Sermon on the Mount*, (1987) 50-1.

will also receive a home and land in this world as a blessing. To give a familiar example in the Bible, Isaac, who was known to be meek, inherited large lands.

> "And Isaac sowed in that land and reaped in the same year a hundredfold. The LORD blessed him, and the man became rich, and gained more and more until he became very wealthy. He had possessions of flocks and herds and many servants, so that the Philistines envied him. (Now the Philistines had stopped and filled with earth all the wells that his father's servants had dug in the days of Abraham his father.) But when Isaac's servants dug in the valley and found there a well of spring water, the herdsmen of Gerar quarreled with Isaac's herdsmen, saying, 'The water is ours.' So he called the name of the well Esek, because they contended with him. Then they dug another well, and they quarreled over that also, so he called its name Sitnah. **And he moved from there and dug another well, and they did not quarrel over it. So he called its name Rehoboth, saying, 'For now the LORD has made room for us, and we shall be fruitful in the land.'"** (Genesis 26:12-15; 19-22)

Moreover, a similar message is recorded in Psalms.

> "Be still before the LORD and wait patiently for him; fret not

yourself over the one who prospers in his way, over the man who carries out evil devices! **Refrain from anger, and forsake wrath! Fret not yourself;** it tends only to evil. For the evildoers shall be cut off, but those who wait for the LORD shall inherit the land. In just a little while, the wicked will be no more; though you look carefully at his place, he will not be there. **But the meek shall inherit the land and delight themselves in abundant peace.**" (Psalm 37:7-11)

Like so, those who receive the Word meekly will inherit the earth. In other words, by being blessed on this earth, they experience the type of the new heaven and new earth. This interpretation is in harmony with the meaning that meekness is receptively receiving the Word and obeying it. For the Bible continuously promises blessings for those who obey. Therefore, we must understand the promise of the "earth" for those who are meek to pertain to actual land or in other words, blessings.

The following situation happened during the last election. Elder Seung-gyu Kim, who was the Minister of Justice and the Director of the National Intelligence Service, came to my office with several people. What he told me then was so memorable that I recorded it to use later in a sermon. It was about the first president of our country, Dr. Syngman Rhee.

Dr. Syngman Rhee had been very smart since he was a child.

One day, a friend said to him, "Let's go to church!" Rhee asked him back, "Why do I need to go to church?" And this is how his friend responded.

> "We need to go to church to learn English. You're going to need to be good at English in order to succeed in this coming global era."

After thinking about it, it sounded right, so Rhee followed him to church and started to learn English. Rhee was so intelligent that in six months-time, he was at the level to teach others English.

Later in his life, Syngman Rhee was discovered attempting to make the country a republic whilst it was being ruled by Emperor Gojong. Because of this, he was sentenced to death and was imprisoned in jail.

The American missionaries, however, knew Rhee to be incredibly bright. They thought "if this person is transformed, he would be a major help to the evangelization of Korea." So, they sent him a Bible to read. Rhee then read that Bible and while in jail reading, he received the fire of the Holy Spirit. After receiving the Spirit, he realized that all the nations that had accepted Christianity were now well off and had become developed countries. So, he thought, "If our country wants to become well off, there needs to be more Christians," and he asked God for two things while imprisoned.

First, he asked for there to be more than one million Christians in the country.

At the time, our nation had 17 million to 18 million people living in it. 1 million would be around 7% of the population.

Second, he asked to be freed from prison and prayed to live and be delivered from within.

God listened to his prayers, and he was freed from prison. And after much tribulation, he became the first president of this country. When he started his first national assembly, he started it with a prayer to God. For he believed that the higher ups needed to believe in Jesus in order for those under them to believe, and for even more people to be able to believe in Jesus. Because of this, he filled more than 40% of the high offices with Christians. Rhee also stationed army chaplains in the army, police chaplains for police officers, and school chaplains for the schools, etc. He raised pastors everywhere for the gospel to spread and be evangelized in the country. As a result, by the time Dr. Syngman Rhee resigned from the presidency, South Korea had over 1.17 million Christians. Not only did God give him the 1 million Christians he asked for, but God gave him 170,000 more.

What is most important to note is that if South Korea had been communized, then we would have become like North

Korea, would have lost the freedom of religion, and would have become the poorest and most miserable country. It is due to Dr. Syngman Rhee that we were not communized. Through all this, our country was able to become a democratic republic. Praise God!

After telling me this story, Elder Seung-gyu Kim said, "This country financially prospered proportionally to the growth of Christians." He explained how our country continued to grow in this manner until we no longer envied others. However, Kim mourned the fact that now, our country is facing many hardships since the churches became corrupt, politicians and media turned anti-Christian, and the left-wing political party took over.

There is a reason why I have introduced this story to you. It is to show you that if you properly believe in Jesus, in the end you will be blessed. This is not only shown throughout the history of Israel in the Old Testament, but also in the history of Europe, the history of the Puritans and the U.S., and the history of South Korea. This is the clear truth.

On the other hand, some people might unfortunately read my words and think "he is still caught up in prosperity theology!" You might then be displeased with me. That is why I believe I need to explain a little more for you.

The Bible, for the most part, says that Jesus died nailed on the cross for our sins. However, in the following verses it says that He was hanged on a tree to redeem us from a curse. Moreover, it says the purpose was "so that… the blessing of Abraham might come to the Gentiles."

> **"Christ redeemed us from the curse of the law by becoming a curse for us**—for it is written, 'Cursed is everyone who is hanged on a tree'—**so that in Christ Jesus the blessing of Abraham might come to the Gentiles**, so that we might receive the promised Spirit through faith." (Galatians 3:13-14)

This is also prophesied about in Genesis 12:3.

> "I will bless those who bless you, and him who dishonors you I will curse, and **in you all the families of the earth shall be blessed**."

Paul said the following about this verse.

> **"And the Scripture, foreseeing that God would justify the Gentiles by faith, preached the gospel beforehand to Abraham, saying, 'In you shall all the nations be blessed.'"** (Galatians 3:8)

Surprisingly, Paul said that Genesis 12:3 is the gospel. And he equated "blessing" (Abraham's blessing), with righteousness and not with material blessings. In light of this fact, the "curse" is also not what we were thinking it to mean. What Paul envisioned as the curse was not poverty, illness, or destruction: the opposite of material blessings. Rather, it was the condemnation of sin and the ruin that comes because of it: the opposite of the blessing of Abraham, which is righteousness. Therefore, we need to understand the curse in verse 13 with this context. In other words, Jesus was not hanged on a tree to solve poverty, illness, or destruction. We need to realize that He was hanged on the cross to solve the condemnation of sin, which is the opposite of righteousness. Verses 13-14 are the written record of this.

> **"Christ redeemed us from the curse of the law by becoming a curse for us—for it is written, 'Cursed is everyone who is hanged on a tree'—so that in Christ Jesus the blessing of Abraham might come to the Gentiles,** so that we might receive the promised Spirit through faith."

Therefore, we should not take this verse as evidence for "the gospel of blessing" the way the Full Gospel denomination has done. That would be unbiblical. In my opinion, the Full Gospel Church has participated in the prosperity gospel. It is not because other people have labeled them so, but because the famous Full Gospel pastors themselves show us this fact with their actions and their fruit.

Currently, many scholars and pastors harshly condemn prosperity theology and the prosperity gospel. One of the most classic books on this is Christianity in Crisis by the renowned heresy hunter, Hank Hanegraaff. There is another book that was published after this titled, Throw Away the Gospel of Greed: Dissecting the Health and Wealth Gospel. This book was edited and compiled by Dr. Seyoon Kim and has the writings of not only Hank Hanegraff, but also Gordon Fee, Douglas Moo, Dennis Hollinger, and David Larsen. They attack the Full Gospel-like prosperity gospel and also lump together even Pastor Kenneth Hagin's teachings on blessings that he made based on the Bible. They severely bash him, making him out to be a heretic or cult leader.

Certainly, the prosperity gospel is wrong. Prosperity theology also has its issues. However, to denounce them to this extent is too extreme and has lost equilibrium.

In my opinion, both sides have lost balance. However, since we have already discussed the prosperity gospel and prosperity theology, I want to take this time to talk about the scholars who condemn them.

We are now in the time of the New Testament and not the Old Testament. The Old Testament was an era of types and signs, while the New Testament is a time for fulfilling them.

Moreover, all of the beatitudes that Jesus taught were internal and spiritual blessings (Matt. 5:3-12). Because of this, many scholars believe that the blessings in the New Testament are all like the beatitudes and have become spiritual blessings. We see this clearly in the scholars' interpretations of 1 Peter 3:10. These thoughts have led them to view material wealth as taboo and vulgar. However, this is not the correct perspective. So, in order to set this right, I have even written a book titled, A Balanced Teaching on Riches!

Still, I would like to give a more complete explanation on this to you. In the time of the Old Testament, God gave blessings to those who obeyed (Deut. 28). Everyone agrees with this point. The problem arises in the fact that many now believe that in the New Testament, this is no longer the case. For example, Gordon Fee said the following.

> **"In the full biblical view wealth and possessions are a zero value for the people of God. Granted that often in the Old Testament—but never in the New—possessions are frequently related to a life of obedience."[115]**

Then, is there really no relationship between obedience and

---

[115] Gordon D. Fee, *The Disease of the Health and Wealth Gospels* (Costa Mesa, CA: The Word for Today, 1979), 4.

material blessings in the New Testament? This is not the case. God continues to bless those who are obedient, even today. Apostle Paul also acknowledged this.

> "'Honor your father and mother' (this is **the first commandment with a promise), 'that it may go well with you and that you may live long in the land.'"** (Ephesians 6:2-3)

"The first commandment with a promise" that Paul referenced is the 5th commandment of the ten commandments.

> "'Honor your father and your mother, **that your days may be long in the land that the LORD your God is giving you.'"** (Exodus 20:12)

Did Paul say that this promise is no longer relevant in the New Testament era? No. By saying, "that it may go well with you and that you may live long in the land," he showed that this promise is still effective. Therefore, the promises for blessings in the Old Testament are still effective for Christians of the New Testament.

There is still a more indisputable and perfect piece of evidence than the above. It is Matthew 5:17.

> "Do not think that I have come to abolish the Law or the Prophets; I have not come to abolish them but to fulfill them."

I will explain this in more detail when discussing Matthew 5:17-20, but the Bible says that the law was abolished (Eph. 2:15). Yet, it also says that it is perfect (James 1:25). The law is at the same time abolished and made perfect. It is not that a part of the law was abolished, but that the moral, civil, and ceremonial laws were all abolished and all made perfect. It is vitally important that we understand this. Because many believe that the law was abolished, they mistakenly think the law is irrelevant to them. Thus, we must remember that the law was not abolished but fulfilled.

What should we do then, now that the law has been made perfect? Naturally, we must keep it. Jesus said the following.

> "Therefore whoever relaxes one of the least of these commandments and teaches others to do the same will be called least in the kingdom of heaven, but **whoever does them** and teaches them will be called great in the kingdom of heaven. **For I tell you, unless your righteousness exceeds that of the scribes and Pharisees, you will never enter the kingdom of heaven.**" (Matthew 5:19-20)

Like so, after saying He came to fulfill the law, He told us to keep it. That is why we must keep the law in the way Jesus interpreted it for us in Matthew 5:21-48.

Now, let me ask you a question. According to Jesus, the law was not abolished but fulfilled. If this is so, would the blessings for those who keep the law and the curses for those who do not have disappeared? Certainly not!

This is common sense! Think about it. If the law was not abolished, how can the principle of blessings and curses recorded in Deuteronomy 28 be abolished? Jesus needed to have abolished the law for them to have been abolished. Consequently, those who keep the moral law that Jesus fulfilled will not only enter heaven but will also receive the blessings on this earth. Moreover, those who do not keep it, will not only go to hell but will also receive curses on this earth. This is because the law has not been abolished and the promise for the blessing and warning for the curse are still effective. Beloved, this is the truth that the scriptures are really talking about.

Therefore, to teach that "if you do not live by God's Word, you will be cursed. But, if you live by God's Word, you will be blessed. Thus, you need to live by God's Word," is not the prosperity gospel nor prosperity theology. This is the original truth that the Bible talks of and is, therefore, an utterly biblical sermon.

Beloved, do not ever misunderstand the difference between the Old and New Testament.

> **"Do not think that I have come to abolish the Law or the Prophets; I have not come to abolish them but to fulfill them."** (Matthew 5:17)

If this is true, nothing changes fundamentally. The Old Testament functioned under a theonomy and so did the New Testament (Matt. 5:17-20, 1 Cor. 9:20-21). In other words, those who did not live by the Word could not receive ultimate salvation in the Old Testament, and it was the same in the New (i.e. 1 Cor. 9:27, 10. That is why it said, as an "example"). Thus, the patterns for obedience and blessings and disobedience and curses were the same in the Old and New. Therefore, if we obey, we will be blessed and if we disobey, we will be cursed not only in the old generation but also in the new generation. The next verse drives the final wedge for this argument.

> "For if anyone is a hearer of the word and not a doer, he is like a man who looks intently at his natural face in a mirror. For he looks at himself and goes away and at once forgets what he was like. But the one who looks into the perfect law, **the law of liberty, and perseveres, being no hearer who forgets but a doer**

who acts, he will be blessed in his doing." (James 1:23-25)

Jesus did not come to abolish the law but to fulfill it. And the law that Jesus fulfilled is this "perfect law, the law of liberty" (25). Additionally, Apostle James said that those who keep this law will be blessed. This is a decisive passage that shows that even in the New Testament era, those who obey will be blessed and those who disobey will be cursed. Therefore, we must believe that this is so and teach accordingly.

Yet, even if this is true, it is wrong to overly emphasize blessings and constantly talk about blessings in every sermon. If you desire to teach biblically, then you must have the gospel truth as your main message. We must preach and teach like Paul did in Ephesians 6:2-3, focusing on justification as the main message and then secondarily discussing blessings. We must preach that "Jesus did not come to abolish the law but to fulfill it. Thus, we must keep the law. And those who do will not only receive ultimate salvation but also receive blessings on this earth. Therefore, you must obey." This type of sermon is completely biblical. It is absolutely not wrong to say so. It is rather more wrong to overly belittle and speak negatively about blessings. Do scholars honestly desire to be poor? If they too, enjoy an increase of income and desire to be well off, why do they denounce blessings so? Why do they view blessings solely in a negative manner? Does that make them more righteous? It is petty self-righteousness and a perverted intellect from a theological error. Thus, do not by any means be swayed by their words without discerning them.

Beloved believers, let us all believe that those who obey the scriptures will not only receive ultimate salvation but also the blessings on this earth. And let us bear this in mind as we become those who are meek and listen to the Word and obey to actually be the ones to enjoy this blessing and receive it.

② **The Meaning of the Earth That We Have "Not Yet" Received**

There are two meanings for meekness. One, is a meekness towards others. This has an intimate relationship with ultimate salvation.

The second, is meekness towards God. We can see this right away when we compare the first three beatitudes to Isaiah 66:2. This too, once again has an intimate relationship with one's ultimate salvation. Accordingly, the fact that the meek inherit the earth signifies that they will receive the ultimate salvation.

The Israelites received Canaan as their inheritance. This is a type of heaven. Thus, to receive the earth as one's inheritance is not simply to receive a large land like Isaac did. It means that only those who are meek can receive the kingdom of God as their inheritance.

I explained it in detail while preaching on Revelations, but heaven is not realized in the heavens but on earth. Therefore, the meek inheriting the earth means inheriting the new heaven and new earth.

I am ashamed to say this, but I did not know this until relatively recently. I did not figure this out until I started planning out this message on the Sermon on the Mount. Thankfully, the scholars understood the meaning of receiving the earth as inheritance before I did. I would like to introduce several of these writings to you.

First, Herman Ridderbos wrote the following about the earth the meek will inherit.

> "It is they [the meek], not those whose motto is that the strong get their way, who will inherit the earth. This promise contains the important truth that the blessings of the kingdom will not only be heavenly and spiritual but also earthly and material. When the kingdom of heaven finally comes in glory, it will come on the earth (Rev. 21:2)."[116]

Dr. Yong-eui Yang also said the following about the earth the

---

[116] Ridderbos, *Matthew*, (1987) 89.

meek will inherit.

> "The apodosis of the third beatitude (v. 5) also clearly shows that the kingdom of God the disciples enjoy is looking towards a futuristic completion. The 'earth' here primarily refers to the territory of Israel. However, in the current context that is dealing with the fulfillment of the Messianic reign, it looks to be referring to the renewed land/inheritance (i.e. 19:27-29). If so, then the promise of the earth could mean in it of itself an eschatological reign of God (i.e. Isa. 61:7). In this case, the promise of the apodosis of the third beatitude looks to be referencing that 'the meek' will inherit the earth when the kingdom of God is fulfilled."[117]

The Chokmah Commentary also wrote the following about the earth the meek will inherit.

> "The real meaning of 'the meek will inherit the earth' that Jesus mentioned is like how the Israelites in the Old Testament according to the promise of God (Gen. 15:18), went into the land of Cannan. The believers in the New Testament will thus also enter the new heaven and new earth (Isa. 66:22; Rev. 21:1),

---

[117] Yang, *How Will You Read the Book of Matthew?*, (2011) 94.

which is the apex of the kingdom of the Messiah. In this world, those who are strong and aggressive, those who ignore the laws, and are disorderly possess the earth. But the inheritance of heaven will be given to those who obey the will of God and are meek (Psalm 37:1, 11, 22, 34)."[118]

Lastly, This is what Pastor Dong-won Lee said about the earth the meek will inherit.

"God has a plan of redemption for the earth, just as He does for humankind. The earth will be restored. The Bible references many times the promise of God of how the earth will be restored.

'The righteous shall inherit the land and dwell upon it forever.' (Ps. 37:29)

'Blessed are the meek, for they shall inherit the earth.' (Matt. 5:5).

The eternal inheritance that we will receive on the final day is the restored earth that has qualitatively been made new. We will live in the land that has the completely restored creation design and glory of God. For we currently live in a world, looking at a heaven and earth that has also been corrupted due to the

---

[118] Byoung-do Kang, *Matthew (in Korean)*, The Chokmah Commentary, (Seoul, Korea: Christian Wisdom Publishing Company, 1990) 226.

sin and corruption of man. When we look closely at nature, we see bloody fights even between animals and the earth growing thorns and thistles. The universe is filled with moanings and groanings of pain. For when man became depraved and was cursed, nature was cursed with him. However, when the plan for the redemption of humanity is completed, the cursed universe will also be completely made new qualitatively. The universe will no longer be influenced by sin or Satan and will be restored to a state of glory that perfectly reveals God's glory. That is when the promise Apostle Paul made to us in Romans 8:19 and on will be realized.

'For the creation waits with eager longing for the revealing of the sons of God' (v. 19).

It is that even the creations will look forward to the moment when Jesus returns, and us believers are glorified through God's grace. 'For the creation was subjected to futility, not willingly, but because of him who subjected it, in hope that the creation itself will be set free from its bondage to corruption and obtain the freedom of the glory of the children of God' (vv. 20-21).

Even nature is eagerly awaiting Jesus' second coming, when everything will be restored.

'For we know that the whole creation has been groaning together in the pains of childbirth until now' (v. 22).

Stand still and listen. To the sounds of the birds crying and not singing. To the sounds of the animals roaring in pain. To the sounds of anguish that the universe is also groaning with us. And when the day of our mourning ends, the day of mourning for nature too will end. Let us hope for the day when redemption is completed and everything is restored. For the day where the new heaven and new earth is qualitatively made completely new and we can meet again."[119]

We can now be sure that the land promised to the meek refers to the ultimate salvation, the new heaven and the new earth!

However, we cannot help but become serious the moment we realize this. For this means that if we are not meek, we cannot enter heaven.

Kathryn Khulman said the following.

"I must admit that not many people earnestly desire to be meek. Be honest with yourself; look yourself directly in the face, and you (like most of us) will have to say, 'I do not want to be meek!' We do not seek to acquire the meekness of a lamb, but rather prefer the qualities of a mighty tiger. Watch something. We all

---

[119] Dong-won Lee, *Final Fight, Final Victory*, (Seoul, Korea: Nachimvan Publishing, 1980) 241-2.

have the tendency to shy away from the word 'meekness.'"[120]

This is the truth! However, meekness is not simply a virtue. It is an indispensable necessity. For those who are not meek cannot enter the kingdom of heaven. This is clearly shown in the teachings of Jesus.

> "You have heard that it was said to those of old, 'You shall not murder; and whoever murders will be liable to judgment.' **But I say to you that everyone who is angry with his brother will be liable to judgment; whoever insults his brother will be liable to the council; and whoever says, 'You fool!' will be liable to the hell of fire.**" (Matthew 5:21-22)

Jesus, while interpreting the 6th commandment, explained how it is not only murder to actually kill a person but it is also murder when we curse and get angry at another. When we compare this with the previous verse (v. 20), we can see that this means such people cannot enter heaven.

Is this not shocking? Therefore, we must be afraid if we get angry easily. And we must repent and fix our ways.

Paul's words also show us that those who are not meek

---

[120] Kuhlman, *In Search of Blessings*, (1989) 19.

cannot enter heaven. 'Anger' is included in the list of sins that send us to hell (Gal 5:19-21). On the other hand, 'Meekness' is included in the list of fruits that those who are saved bear (Gal. 5:22-23). Those who get angry cannot enter heaven. Only those who are meek can enter heaven. Therefore, we must not look at becoming angry as a small sin. We must instead acknowledge its severity and quickly repent and fix ourselves.

Meanwhile, I explained that meekness is not only something we do towards others but also towards God. There are largely two responses for how people take in the Word. They either tremble or become angry (the opposite of being meek). Many, when faced with a message that exposes themselves, respond like those who listened to Stephen's sermon in anger and gnash their teeth. They throw stones at the preacher. Only a minority tremble in fear because of the Word, like those who heard Peter' sermon did. Yet, it is only people like those few who will be saved. Therefore, we must use this as a touchstone to fairly assess ourselves.

Let me be straightforward and ask this question. Which group are you currently in? Are you in the group that listens to the Word with a heart of trepidation and examines themselves to repent? Or are you in the group that is angry at the preacher, complaining and criticizing them? If you are in the latter, you must be afraid. For it means that you are not poor in spirit nor one who mourns. Thus, it means that you are not one who is meek in front of God's Word. In other words, it means that you are not saved. Such a reaction shows that you do not have the ear to hear and is self-revealing that you are headed to hell. Thus, I pray you will repent as soon as possible and turn around from your old ways.

4. AM I ONE WHO HUNGERS AND THIRSTS FOR RIGHTEOUSNESS?

"Blessed are those who hunger and thirst for righteousness, for they shall be satisfied." (Matthew 5:6)

Hunger and thirst are one of the most urgent and fundamental desires for a human being. Hunger requires us to eat, while thirst requires us to drink. Food and drink are not a luxury but essentials for survival. In the same way, righteousness is not a luxury but a necessity. Just as our physical lives rely on what we eat and drink, our spiritual lives rely on desiring righteousness and being satisfied.

Sin, however, brings death to our souls.

"For the wages of **sin** is **death**" (Romans 6:23)

"Then desire when it has conceived gives birth to **sin**, and **sin** when it is fully grown brings forth **death**." (James 1:15)

Oppositely, righteousness brings life to our souls.

"For to set the mind on the flesh is **death**, but to set the mind on the Spirit is **life** and peace... For if you live according to the flesh you will die, but if **by the Spirit you put to death the deeds of the body, you will live**." (Romans 8:6; 8:13)

Therefore, what we must have and absolutely need is righteousness.

I want you to remember this and carefully read the explanations on righteousness. I pray that through this, you may all hunger and thirst for righteousness and be blessed.

1) What Is the Righteousness Jesus Spoke of?

Sinclair Ferguson asserted that there are three different meanings of the righteousness Jesus spoke of in this verse.

"The righteousness we seek (our relationship to God being what it ought to be) has three dimensions.

First, it is provided for us by Jesus himself. We have sinned, but God made Christ to become sin for us, so that in him (through faith) we might receive righteousness (2 Cor. 5:21). This is the centre of the gospel. We lack righteousness, but God provides it for us. ...

It has a second aspect. We cannot welcome Christ as our Saviour (as Luther did) without being willing for him to be precisely that – Saviour. As such, he saves us from sin's power and its influence. He not only brings pardon, but he works in us to make us live in our right relationship with God. ...

It is one of the great tragedies of the church today that we have come to believe in what Dietrich Bonhoeffer called 'cheap grace' – a Saviour who leaves us much as we were, instead of actually saving us from sin.

Sometimes this distinction has been justified by speaking of 'carnal' Christians and 'spiritual' Christians, as Paul seems to do in 1 Corinthians 3:1-4. ...

The third aspect of God's righteousness for which we long involves our seeking to see it established everywhere. ... In the world in which we live, we are to encourage moral integrity and right relationships, both by the work of evangelism, and by all we do to reform society and bring it into conformity to Christ's teaching. The work of evangelism and missions and the task of social reformation are not to be thought of as alternatives for the Christian. They go together."[121]

---

[121] Ferguson, *Sermon on the Mount*, (1987) 28-9.

There are no issues in the first and second concepts here. For even though justification is not the main point of this verse, it is, at the very least, implied in this message. What is a problem, however, is whether the third concept is actually incorporated in this verse or not.

Contrary to our expectations, Douglas Hare strongly claims that the meaning of the righteousness in the verse is this third meaning.

> "It is customary to regard 'righteousness' here as a reference to personal ethics (hence the TEV rendering: 'Happy are those whose greatest desire is to do what God requires'). There is much to be said in favor of this understanding. The First Gospel places heavy emphasis on personal righteousness (see 5:20, 7:21-4). ...
>
> The metaphors of hungering and thirsting seem more apt with reference to a righteousness that is not subject to our willing and doing, the righteousness of God. Here we should think ... of God's saving righteousness as proclaimed by the prophets. 'My righteousness [RSV: 'deliverance'] draws near speedily, my salvation has gone forth' (Isa. 51:5). Isaiah 51:1 must be understood in the same way: 'Listen to me, you that pursue righteousness [RSV: 'deliverance'], you that seek the Lord' (NRSV). It is not their own righteousness that is the object of their yearning

but God's.

If it is correct to understand the beatitude in this way ('Blessed are those who yearn for the manifestation of God's saving righteousness'), **the distance between Luke's version and Matthew's is greatly diminished. In the Lukan parallel it is clear that this beatitude, like the first, refers to those who are literally hungry. The corresponding woe promises the well-fed that they will exchange places with the undernourished (Luke 6:21, 25). Like Luke, Matthew yearns for the establishment of social justice.**

Among those who long for God to set things right are both those who themselves suffer hunger pangs and those who mourn over an inequitable distribution of goods and services that allows millions to starve on a planet capable of providing food sufficient for all. 'How blest are those who hunger and thirst to see right prevail; they shall be satisfied' (NEB)."[122]

This is very unexpected! But like so, there are many scholars who interpret the meaning of hungering and thirsting for righteousness to mean those who are waiting for social justice to be established as an extension of "the poor" and "the weeping" in Luke 6.

---

[122] Hare, *Matthew*, (1993) 39-40.

Moreover, this kind of interpretation has substantial appeal to it. For it allows the division to be made that the beatitudes are simply about the poor and alienated who are saved, and the verses after it are about how those people should live. If this is true, it would be in harmony with the low standards of the modern church. It would also allow one to feel much more at peace.

However, I do not believe that "to hunger and thirst for righteousness" can ever mean the above. For we have already revealed that the real meaning of the message "blessed are the poor" in Luke is shown in the expression "blessed are the poor in spirit." And we also revealed that when we compare the weeping to those who are "poor and of a contrite spirit," in the parallel verse in Isaiah 66:2, we see that it is not talking about crying over being poor and struggling but rather mourning over sins. I've also already explained that the meek too are shown in Isaiah 66:2 as those who tremble at God's Word. In other words, they are those who have the ear to hear. Therefore, in this context, those who "hunger and thirst for righteousness" should not be viewed as those who desire social justice issues to be expanded upon, but rather as those who desire a righteous character and life.

Thankfully, many scholars interpret the "righteousness" in this verse to not be about social righteousness (justice) but about individual righteousness (holiness). First, this is what Lloyd-Jones wrote.

> "[Righteousness] also means of necessity **a desire to be free from the power of sin. Having realized what it means to be poor in spirit and to mourn because of sin within, we naturally come to the stage of longing to be free from the power of sin.**"[123]

> "To hunger and thirst after righteousness is nothing but the longing to be positively holy. I cannot think of a better way of defining it."[124]

John Stott also said the following.

> "**Moral righteousness is a righteousness of character and conduct which pleases God.** Jesus goes on later to contrast this Christian righteousness with Pharisaic righteousness (20). The latter was an external conformity to rules; the former is an inner righteousness of heart, mind and motive. **For this we should hunger and thirst.**"[125]

---

[123] Lloyd-Jones, *Studies in the Sermon on the Mount*, (1959) 78.
[124] Lloyd-Jones, *Studies in the Sermon on the Mount*, (1959) 79.
[125] Stott, *The Message of the Sermon on the Mount*, (2020) 28.

And Dr. Yong-eui Yang said the following.

"The **'righteousness'** that Matthew suggested as the **subject of desire for the disciples** is a gift of the Messianic reign of Jesus. It refers to **the conduct in accordance with the will of God, which appears on the basis of a new personal relationship between God and the disciple.** (i.e. 5:20; 6:33; 7:21). The **characteristic of a disciple** under the reign of God is that **he actively anticipates and prays that the will of God will be fulfilled in his life and relationship (6:33)**. Therefore, when a disciple really hungers and thirsts for 'righteousness' like so, it confirms his identity as a disciple and such confirmation becomes a necessary condition for his happiness."[126]

I believe that this interpretation is correct.

Think about it. According to the context of Matthew, the beatitude people are those who have repented (Matt. 4:17). So, would these people be solely focused on social justice? Is this not a topic that many who have not repented are also interested in?

Also, the beatitudes portray what kind of person will be blessed and inherit the kingdom of heaven. They portray

---

[126] Yang, *How Will You Read the Book of Matthew?*, (2011) 94-5.

the characteristics of the saved. This then shows not only the characteristics of the saved, but also the conditions for their ultimate salvation. If so, can we really say that mourning over social irregularities and desiring perfect justice to occur are conditions and evidence for being saved? It is rather highly unnatural to connect these as a direct relation to one's salvation.

Above all else, the focus of The Sermon is not social justice. Certainly "righteousness" is one of the main themes of The Sermon, for the concept of "righteousness" comes up periodically in it. Christians are at times persecuted for righteousness sake (5:10). We must also have righteousness that exceeds that of the scribes and Pharisees (5:20). We must practice righteousness in front of God (6:1). And we must especially seek the kingdom of God and righteousness, believing that God will provide all that we need (6:33). However, all of these things are not about social justice but rather points to the righteousness that helps us live according to the Word of God. Because of this, I firmly believe that the "righteousness" in this verse is not about social justice but rather about the righteousness that should be visible in the characteristics and lives of believers.

2) What Exactly Does It Mean to Hunger and Thirst?

"To hunger" and "to thirst" are not only basic physical desires, but are extremely strong desires. Several summers ago, I went hiking in the middle of a heat wave. The person who was holding all our water, however, could not follow my pace and lost his way. So, I hiked up and down four hills by myself, sweating buckets in the boiling humid heat. I was so parched that I couldn't wait any longer and I drank four times from a dirty puddle in a dried up valley stream.

Thankfully, for the most part, our country is not a country that lacks water. There are not many times when we are stuck feeling thirsty. Israel, however, is a different story. I visited Israel once, but chose a bad season to visit and went in the middle of their summer. Their heat is of a different level from the heat in our country. I felt as if I had jumped inside a steam oven. As I felt the sweltering, scorching heat, I was able to newly understand the meaning of Jesus crying out on the cross, "I am thirsty."

Yet, it was much worse during Jesus' time. At the time in Palestine, one felt hunger and thirst daily. Water was scarce, and at times, they were short of provisions as well. That is why Jesus purposefully used these words and used this reference to show how we should desire righteousness. He shows us how much we should hunger and thirst for this. Therefore, it should be a great challenge to all of us.

Beloved, do you know why so many people ask, "I have

hungered and thirsted for righteousness, but why am I still not satisfied?" It is because they did not truly hunger or thirst for righteousness or have not hungered enough. Thomas Watson gave the following criticism.

> "*The carnal man's objection*. I have (says he) hungered after righteousness, yet am not filled. You say you hunger and are not satisfied? Perhaps God is not satisfied with your hunger."[127]

Smith Wigglesworth said the following.

> "... **when you long to be holy, when you long to be pure, then and only then will the law of the Spirit of life make you free from the law of sin and death.**"[128]

John Stott also said the following.

> "Again and again Scripture addresses its promises to the hungry. God 'satisfies the thirsty and fills the hungry with good things' (Ps. 107:9). **If we are conscious of slow growth, is the**

---

[127] Watson, *The Beatitudes*, (1971) 140.
[128] Albert Hibbert, *Smith Wigglesworth: The Secret of His Power* (Tulsa, OK: Harrison House, 1982) 19-20.

reason that we have a jaded appetite?"[129]

You cannot be satisfied with just becoming hungry or thirsty. You must truly and fully hunger and thirst for righteousness.

Then, what exactly is truly and fully hungering and thirsting for righteousness? To motivate and help you all, I want to introduce a few explanations on this.

First, John Wesley organized hungering and thirsting for righteousness as the three following points.

> "'Blessed are they which do hunger and thirst after' this; in order to fully to understand which expression we should observe, **first, that hunger and thirst are the strongest of all our bodily appetites. In like manner this hunger in the soul, this thirst after the image of God, is the strongest of all our spiritual appetites when it is once awakened in the heart; yea, it swallows up all the rest in that one great desire to be renewed after the likeness of him that created us.**
>
> **We should, secondly, observe that from the time we begin to hunger and thirst those appetites do not cease, but are more and more craving and importunate till we either eat and drink, or die. And even so, from the time that we begin to hunger and**

---

[129] Stott, *The Message of the Sermon on the Mount*, (2020) 29.

thirst after the whole mind which was in Christ these spiritual appetites do not cease, but cry after their food with more and more importunity. Nor can they possibly cease before they are satisfied, while there is any spiritual life remaining.

We may, thirdly, observe that hunger and thirst are satisfied with nothing but meat and drink. If you would give to him that is hungry all the world beside, all the elegance of apparel, all the trappings of state, all the treasure upon earth, yea thousands of gold and silver; if you would pay him ever so much honour, he regards it not; all these things are then of no account with him. He would still say, 'These are not the things I want; give me food, or else I die.' The very same is the case with every soul that truly hungers and thirsts after righteousness. He can find no comfort in anything but this: he can be satisfied with nothing else. Whatever you offer beside, it is lightly esteemed; whether it be riches, or honour, or pleasure, he still says, 'This is not the thing which I want. Give me love or else I die!'"[130]

Thomas Watson said the same thing.

"Hunger is satisfied with nothing but food. Bring a hungry man flowers, music; tell him pleasant stories; nothing will content

---

[130] Wesley, *The Sermons of John Wesley*, (2013) 491-2.

him but food. …

And to use Basil's expression, the hungry soul is almost distracted till it enjoys the thing it hungers after."[131]

Michael Wilkins also said the following.

"Persons who 'hunger and thirst' are in dire need. They will perish if they are not filled. Such is the passion of those who desire righteousness."[132]

And more than the others, I was most moved by the words of Kathryn Kuhlman.

"Through the years I have observed that one will never find God until God becomes the deepest desire of that individual.

One gets exactly what he is looking for! He will see what he wants to see. He will find in life what he really wants to find.

Jesus knew human nature; therefore, He could say,

'Blessed are they which do hunger and thirst after righteousness: for they shall be filled.'

Thirst is a strong word and when a human soul thirsts for God, that soul will be filled with God. Not only will he find God

---

[131] Watson, *The Beatitudes*, (1971) 128.
[132] Wilkins, *Matthew*, (2004) 207.

> for himself, but he will bring God's Kingdom on Earth.
>
> This is very real to me for I cannot remember a time in my life when every atom of my being did not cry out for God. You speak of physical hunger, and I'll admit that I have been physically hungry for food; but I tell you of a truth, I have never known a physical hunger as great as my hunger for spiritual things."[133]

This is a truly shocking confession that really challenges us! Therefore, do not give up after making a bit of an attempt. Be like Kathryn Kuhlman and become one who has stronger hunger than the hunger of the flesh and a stronger thirst than the thirst of the flesh.

Meanwhile, the Bible often says that people are made holy through faith. Thus, as we become one who hungers and thirst for righteousness, we must firmly believe in the Lord's promise that we will be satisfied and be filled.

There are plenty of messages on this promise that have been given to us.

> **"For he satisfies the longing soul, and the hungry soul he fills with good things."** (Psalm 107:9)

---

[133] Kuhlman, *In Search of Blessings*, (1989) 29-30.

"Blessed are those who hunger and thirst for righteousness, for they shall be satisfied." (Matthew 5:6)

"He has filled the hungry with good things," (Luke 1:53)

God never lies. That is why Thomas Watson says that "God never bids us seek him 'in vain.'"[134] And the words of Dr. Tozer on this that "every man is as holy and as full of the Spirit as he wants to be,"[135] is now a famous saying.

The wonderful man of God, John G. Lake, also confidently said the following words.

"And the *hunger of a man's soul must be satisfied.* It must be satisfied. It is a law of God; that law of God is in the depth of the spirit."[136]

Lloyd-Jones said the following as if he guaranteed it.

"For if we do hunger and thirst we shall be filled. There is no qualification at all, it is an absolute statement, it is an absolute

---

[134] Watson, *The Beatitudes*, (1971) 136.
[135] A. W. Tozer, *Born After Midnight*, (Chicago, IL: Moody Publishers, 1959) 10.
[136] John G. Lake, *Living in God's Power*, (New Kensington, PA: Whitaker House, 2012) 174.

promise—'Blessed are they which do hunger and thirst after righteousness: for they shall be filled.'"[137]

This is correct. Therefore, we should not only hunger and thirst for righteousness, but also believe that we will be satisfied. That is how all of you can be filled with righteousness and be satisfied.

He Binds the Broken Hearted

You bind the broken hearted
You heal the wounded soul
Father of all heaven
We give You full control
Come have Your way in us, O Lord
Come set our spirits free
O Father send revival
And start the work in me

Lord, I hunger, thirst for Your righteousness
Father come and fill me once again
Lord, I hunger, thirst for Your righteousness

---

[137] Lloyd-Jones, *Studies in the Sermon on the Mount*, (1959) 87.

Fill me with Your oil and Your wine

Fill me with Your Spirit
I want to see Your face
To live in Your presence
Know Your glory and Your grace
It's not my will but Yours I choose
To follow to the end
So mold me, yes, and make me
Let a new day begin

Lord, I hunger, thirst for Your righteousness
Spirit come and fill me once again
Lord, I hunger, thirst for Your righteousness
Fill me with Your oil and Your wine
You bind the broken hearted
You heal the wounded soul
Father of all heaven
We give You full control
Come have Your way in us, O Lord
Come set our spirits free
O Father send revival
And start the work in me

Lord, I hunger, thirst for Your righteousness
Spirit come and fill me once again
Lord, I hunger, thirst for Your righteousness
Fill me with Your oil and Your wine

Lord, I hunger, thirst for Your righteousness
Spirit come and fill me once again
Lord, I hunger, thirst for Your righteousness
Fill me with Your oil and Your wine
Fill me with Your oil and Your wine
Fill me with Your oil and Your wine

3) Why Must We Become One Who Hungers and Thirst for Righteousness?

There are mainly two reasons why we must hunger and thirst for righteousness without fail.

① If we do not hunger and thirst for righteousness, we cannot truly be happy.

Sinclair Ferguson said, "already we know that the kingdom of God consists of righteousness *(Rom. 14:17)*."[138] Heaven con-

---

[138] Ferguson, *Sermon on the Mount*, (1987) 50.

sists of "a heaven that has come inside of us" and "a heaven that we will enter." Meanwhile, the Bible says the following about the heaven that has come inside of us.

> "For the **kingdom of God** is not a matter of eating and drinking but of **righteousness** and peace and joy in the Holy Spirit." (Romans 14:17)

The Bible also says the following about the heaven we will enter.

> "waiting for and hastening the coming of the day of God, because of which the heavens will be set on fire and dissolved, and the heavenly bodies will melt as they burn! But according to his promise we are waiting for **new heavens and a new earth in which righteousness dwells.**" (2 Peter 3:12-13)

Did you pay attention to the fact that both are on the foundation of "righteousness?" It is not heaven if there is no righteousness. Thus, a human being can never become happy without righteousness.

For example, what did Jesus promise to those who hunger and thirst for righteousness? He promised satisfaction. The subject of the verbs to hunger and thirst is righteousness, making the subject of satisfaction also a satisfaction of righteousness. Therefore, we need righteousness to truly be satisfied. This truth is clearly shown in the following verses.

> "and to keep **the commandments and statutes of the LORD, which I am commanding you** today **for your good?"** (Deuteronomy 10:13)

> **"There will be tribulation and distress for every human being who does evil,** the Jew first and also the Greek, **but glory and honor and peace for everyone who does good**, the Jew first and also the Greek." (Romans 2:9-10)

Thus, if you desire happiness, you must hunger and thirst for righteousness.

Meanwhile, our minds were darkened by the depravity of humanity.

> "… but they became futile in their thinking, **and their foolish hearts were darkened**." (Romans 1:21)

> "Now this I say and testify in the Lord, that **you must no longer walk as the Gentiles do, in the futility of their minds. They are darkened in their understanding**, alienated from

the life of God **because of the ignorance that is in them**, due to their hardness of heart." (Ephesians 4:17-18)

This is why even though everyone desires happiness, they turn their eyes towards sin, instead of righteousness. They do not desire righteousness and desire only happiness itself. Thus, they cannot earn the happiness that they desire and instead become miserable. Lloyd-Jones explained this well in the following manner.

> "'Blessed are they which do hunger and thirst after righteousness.' What does it mean? Let me put it negatively like this. **We are not to hunger and thirst after blessedness; we are not to hunger and thirst after happiness. But that is what most people are doing. We put happiness and blessedness as the one thing that we desire, and thus we always miss it; it always eludes us. According to the Scriptures happiness is never something that should be sought directly; it is always something that results from seeking something else.** ...
>
> They are trying to find happiness, they are making it their goal, their one objective. But they do not find it because, **whenever you put happiness before righteousness, you will be doomed to misery.** That is the great message of the Bible from beginning to end. They alone are truly happy who are seeking to

be righteous. **Put happiness in the place of righteousness and you will never get it.**

The world, it is obvious, has fallen into this primary and fundamental error, an error which one could illustrate in many different ways. Think of a man who is suffering from some painful disease. Generally the one desire of such a patient is to be relieved of his pain, and one can understand that very well. No-one likes suffering pain. The one idea of this patient, therefore, is to do anything which will relieve him of it. Yes; but if the doctor who is attending this patient is also only concerned about relieving this man's pain he is a very bad doctor. His primary duty is to discover the cause of the pain and to treat that. Pain is a wonderful symptom which is provided by nature to call attention to disease, and the ultimate treatment for pain is to treat the disease, not the pain. So if a doctor merely treats the pain without discovering the cause of the pain, he is not only acting contrary to nature, he is doing something that is extremely dangerous to the life of the patient. The patient may be out of pain, and seems to be well; but the cause of the trouble is still there.

Now that is the folly of which the world is guilty. It says, 'I want to get rid of my pain, so I will run to the pictures, or drink, or do anything to help me forget my pain.' But the question is, What is the cause of the pain and the unhappiness and the wretchedness? They are not happy who hunger and thirst af-

ter happiness and blessedness. No. 'Blessed are they which do hunger and thirst after righteousness: for they shall be filled.'"[139]

A human being's happiness differs from that of an animal and depends on righteousness. Unless a person hungers and thirsts for righteousness, they will not be able to become happy, even on this earth. This is the reason why we must hunger and thirst for righteousness. Thus, I pray that all of you firmly set your hearts to hunger and thirst for righteousness.

② If you do not hunger and thirst for righteousness, you will not find eternal happiness.

The beatitudes are the characteristics of true Christians. Even if you diligently attend church, you are not a true Christian if you do not hunger and thirst for righteousness. Lloyd-Jones said the following.

> "I do not know of a better test that anyone can apply to himself or herself in this whole matter of the Christian profession than a verse like this."[140]

---

[139] Lloyd-Jones, *Studies in the Sermon on the Mount*, (1959) 75-6.
[140] Lloyd-Jones, *Studies in the Sermon on the Mount*, (1959) 74.

This is true. This verse is the greatest litmus test for knowing whether you are a true Christian or not. This fact is well represented in John Stott's writings.

> "Already in the Virgin Mary's song, the Magnificat, the spiritually poor and the spiritually hungry have been associated, and both have been declared blessed. For God 'has filled the hungry with good things but has sent the rich away empty' (Luke 1:53). The implications of this general principle are spelt out. **God satisfies those who *hunger and thirst for righteousness.* Such spiritual hunger is a characteristic of all God's people, whose supreme ambition is not material but spiritual. Christians are not like others, engrossed in the pursuit of possessions; what they have set themselves to 'seek first' is God's kingdom and righteousness (Matt. 6:33)."**[141]

This fact is also well represented in Pastor Dong-won Lee's writings.

> "Who hungers and thirsts? ... Those who are alive. Dead bodies do not feel hunger or thirst. It is the same spiritually. The unsaved, who are outside of Christ and dead spiritually, do not

---

[141] Stott, *The Message of the Sermon on the Mount*, (2020) 28.

have the hunger and thirst for God's righteousness. Yet, there is an earnest longing of righteousness in those who have been given a new life in Christ. ...

The life of a person without the confession 'I want to live righteously!' cannot be called a life renewed in Christ. Even an evildoer can desire heaven. But only the righteous can desire righteousness."[142]

Differing from worldly people, true Christians desire righteousness. This is one of their most prominent characteristics. Whoever does not hunger and thirst for righteousness is thus not a Christian. Then, where will these people go? Not surprisingly, they will be in Hell.

If you do not hunger and thirst for righteousness, it is not only in this world that you will fail to achieve happiness. You will be eternally disconnected from it. There is not a more absolute reason for why we must hunger and thirst for righteousness. This is enough! Therefore, I pray that you all will become those who hunger and thirst for righteousness.

4) If You Are Hungry and Thirsty for Righteousness, Can You Enter Heaven Without Being Satisfied?

---

[142] Lee, *Be Like This*, (1995) 52–3.

One is not a Christian, even if they say they believe in Jesus, if they only desire the things of this world and do not hunger or thirst for righteousness. They are spiritually dead like a non-believer. Pastor Dong-won Lee said the following in relation to this.

> "Who hungers and thirsts?
>
> First, those who are alive.
>
> Dead bodies do not feel hunger or thirst. It is the same spiritually. The unsaved, who are outside of Christ and dead spiritually, do not have the hunger and thirst for God's righteousness. But there is an earnest longing of righteousness in those who have been given a new life in Christ.
>
> Second, those who are healthy.
>
> What are the signs that show we are sick? The first sign of sickness is a loss of appetite. But when we regain our health, the first thing we feel is an appetite. Like so, when sin falls upon a Christian and they become sick, they lose spiritual interest. …
>
> The life of a person without the confession 'I want to live righteously!' cannot be called a life renewed in Christ. Even an evildoer can desire heaven. But only the righteous can desire righteousness."[143]

---

[143] Lee, *Be Like This*, (1995) 52–3.

This is true. However, it is a message that if wrongly interpreted can confuse people to think that all those who simply desire to be righteous are then those who are saved. The words of Arthur Pink that "Christ pronounces 'blessed' not those who *are full* of righteousness, but those who 'hunger and thirst' *after it*,"[144] follow this vein of thought. Although true, it can cause confusion and misunderstanding.

It is also true that "they will be satisfied" is in the future tense. That is why Dr. Yong-eui Yang wrote the following.

> "The apodosis of the fourth blessing also guarantees a futuristic reward. 'Fullness' is the characteristic of the Messianic reign. ... When the kingdom of God is ultimately completed, the disciples will experience fullness without the need to be hungry or thirsty for the righteousness of God anymore. It is because in those days, God's righteousness will be overflowing in the disciples' lives and all their relationships (Rev. 7:15-17; 22:1-5)."[145]

Arthur Pink also wrote the following.

> "In the day to come we shall be 'filled' with Divine holiness, for we shall be made 'like Him' (1 John iii, 2). Then shall we be

---

[144] Pink, *An Exposition of the Sermon on the Mount*, (2011) 28.
[145] Yang, *How Will You Read the Book of Matthew?*, (2011) 95.

done with sin for ever."[146]

Because of these writings, it is even easier to misunderstand and think that if you just desire to become more righteous, you will be saved. The wrongful interpretation of Romans 7 further fans the flames.

Such thoughts have long since filled the church. Yet, can we really be saved and enter heaven with just the desire to be righteous, when we are not actually righteous? This is not the case. For as Romans 7 shows us, even those who have not been converted can still desperately wish to do good works.

> "For I know that nothing good dwells in me, that is, in my flesh. **For I have the desire to do what is right, but not the ability to carry it out.** For I do not do **the good I want,** but the evil I do not want is what I keep on doing. Now if I do what I do not want, it is no longer I who do it, but sin that dwells within me." (Romans 7:18-20)

Furthermore, to "be satisfied", like that of the feast, represents heaven. And this heaven has already started inside of us. In other words, salvation has aspects of the "already"

---

[146] Pink, *An Exposition of the Sermon on the Mount*, (2011) 27.

and "not yet." Because of this, the satisfaction that those who hunger and thirst for righteousness will receive is not only enjoyable in the afterlife, but also in the present. In other words, you must live a righteous life to be a Christian, even if that life is not perfect. There is no room for doubt when we look at the following verses.

> **"For I tell you, unless your righteousness exceeds that of the scribes and Pharisees, you will never enter the kingdom of heaven."** (Matthew 5:20)

> **"Not everyone who says to me, 'Lord, Lord,' will enter the kingdom of heaven, but the one who does the will of my Father who is in heaven."** (Matthew 7:21)

Therefore, "the satisfaction of righteousness," along with "hungering and thirsting for righteousness," must become an important touchstone of salvation.

Lloyd-Jones explained in great detail how we can use the satisfaction of righteousness as a test to examine ourselves.

> "We must surely ask ourselves questions such as these: **Are we filled? Have we got this satisfaction? Are we aware of this dealing of God with us? Is the fruit of the Spirit being manifest-**

ed in our lives? Are we concerned about that? Are we experiencing love to God and to other people, joy and peace? Are we manifesting long-suffering, goodness, gentleness, meekness, faith and temperance?** They that do hunger and thirst after righteousness shall be filled. They are filled, and they are being filled.

Are we, therefore, I ask, enjoying these things? Do we know that we have received the life of God? Are we enjoying the life of God in our souls? Are we aware of the Holy Spirit and all His mighty working within, forming Christ in us more and more? If we claim to be Christian, then we should be able to say yes to all these questions.

Those who are truly Christian are filled in this sense. **Are we thus filled? Are we enjoying our Christian life and experience? Do we know that our sins are forgiven? Are we rejoicing in that fact, or are we still trying to make ourselves Christian, trying somehow to make ourselves righteous? Is it all a vain effort? Are we enjoying peace with God? Do we rejoice in the Lord alway[s]? Those are the tests that we must apply.** If we are not enjoying these things, the only explanation of that fact is that we are not truly hungering and thirsting after righteousness. For if we do hunger and thirst we shall be filled."[147]

---

[147] Lloyd-Jones, *Studies in the Sermon on the Mount*, (1959) 87.

Beloved, ask this question to yourself in all honesty. And if you are not satisfied, you must be fearful.

Meanwhile, the Bible wrote the following about the eternal future of those who live experiencing this fullness of righteousness.

> "Therefore they are before the throne of God, and serve him day and night in his temple; and he who sits on the throne will shelter them with his presence. **They shall hunger no more, neither thirst anymore; the sun shall not strike them, nor any scorching heat.**" (Revelation 7:15-16)

Of course, this is a message about real hunger and thirst. Yet, where does hunger and thirst come from? Such a desire did not exist in Eden or in heaven. Rather, it was created due to the sins of man. As a result, if a person hungers and thirsts for righteousness and lives righteously, they will not only gain satisfaction but will also be completely free from such things. Praise the Lord!

Moreover, the Bible wrote the following about the eternal future of those who do not know the satisfaction of righteousness.

> "and in Hades, being in torment, he lifted up his eyes and saw

Abraham far off and Lazarus at his side. And he called out, **'Father Abraham, have mercy on me, and send Lazarus to dip the end of his finger in water and cool my tongue, for I am in anguish in this flame.'"** (Luke 16:23-24)

This is the opposite result, but because sin (which is the basic cause for hunger and thirst) was not dealt with by hungering and thirsting for righteousness, a physical hunger and thirst will forever be rampant upon them.

Thomas Watson wrote the following.

> "If we do not thirst here we shall thirst when it is too late. If we do not thirst as David did—'My soul thirsteth for God' (Psalm 42:2)—we shall thirst as Dives did for a drop of water (Luke 16:24). They who do not thirst for righteousness shall be in perpetual hunger and thirst."[148]

Therefore, we must choose wisely. Thankfully, we are still given the opportunity to choose. However, sooner than we think, that chance will disappear and will never come again. Thus, I pray you will choose the right choice today.

Now, I would like to say a few words for those who are satis-

---

[148] Watson, *The Beatitudes*, (1971) 133.

fied because of righteousness. I believe that you are in need of the words of John Stott.

> "**Yet our hunger will never be fully satisfied in this life, nor our thirst fully quenched.** It is true that we receive the satisfaction which the Beatitude promises. But our hunger is satisfied only to break out again. Even the promise of Jesus that whoever drinks of the water he gives 'will never thirst' is fulfilled only if we keep drinking (John 4:13-14; 7:37). Beware of those who claim to have arrived, and who look to past experience rather than to future development! **Like all the qualities included in the Beatitudes, hunger and thirst are perpetual characteristics of the disciples of Jesus, as perpetual as poverty of spirit, meekness and mourning.**"[149]

Thus, do not be satisfied with your past or present hunger and thirst for righteousness. Instead, become one who continues to faithfully hunger and thirst for righteousness.

Lastly, if you look in Proverbs 27:7, it says the following.

> "One who is full loathes honey, **but to one who is hungry everything bitter is sweet.**"

---

[149] Stott, *The Message of the Sermon on the Mount*, (2020) 29.

Thomas Watson said the following citing this verse.

> "He that spiritually hungers tastes the promises sweet, nay tastes a reproof sweet. 'To the hungry soul every bitter thing is sweet' (Proverbs 27:7). A bitter reproof is sweet. He can feed upon the myrrh of the gospel as well as the honey."[150]

This is the very characteristic of our church members. Beloved, do you know why our members receive rebukes and reprimands with delight? It is because of the unique characteristics of our church. From the beginning, people who were hungry and thirsty for righteousness, in other words, those who desired to live by the Word congregated here. That is why most of our church members receive words of praise and criticism alike as sweet honey to their lips.

Yet, it is not only those at other churches, but also a minority of our members as well who do not receive the Word with delight. It is because they do not have a desire for righteousness inside of them. That is why they are not touched by messages that emphasize the need to repent, to have true faith, to be born again, to seek after holiness, to pray, and to fear being forsaken. They are not blessed by these words for they do not

---

[150] Watson, *The Beatitudes*, (1971) 128.

have the desire to live righteously.

This is what true pastors feel most sensitively and worry about. When Kathryn Kuhlman was alive, she too recognized this issue arising amongst her congregation. This is what she sincerely said.

> "**When I stand on the platform behind the pulpit, I am very sensitive to the congregation. You would be surprised if you knew how I watched the faces of the people to whom I minister, and the variety of expressions I see.** At the start of a service, some are quiet in thought. Others are in prayer and seem hardly conscious of their surroundings. Some are chatting away with those around them, observing their clothes, watching those who come in as they are seated.
>
> **There are some whose faces beam; I can see from their expressions that they are unaware of those about them—their focus is upon God. Then, when I begin to bring my message, there are some that I would compare to blotters or sponges, for they 'hear' with all their senses and soak up every word that I say.**
>
> There are others, however, who sit there utterly unresponsive. I am sure that they could not tell you what the sermon was about.
>
> **What really makes the difference? It is simply this—there are**

some who thirst after righteousness and hunger for God; they truly desire spiritual food.

On the other hand, there are those who are indifferent and expect the Lord to 'put it into their pocket' without any effort on their part."[151]

I too am very sensitive to the expressions and reactions of my audience. And I feel pain because of these souls and deeply worry for them. It is because I know very well what the result of such an attitude will bring about. As you well know, a characteristic of the sheep is to hear and follow the voice of their shepherd. However, we must have a desire for righteousness to have the ear to hear open. And you must have the ear to hear for faith to form, and faith is then necessary for change to occur. Just as one without a poor in spirit heart has no hope, one who does not hunger or thirst for righteousness has no hope spiritually. Thus, if any of you are like this, you must be afraid. I pray that you will repent and truly become one who hungers and thirsts for righteousness.

---

[151] Kuhlman, *In Search of Blessings*, (1989) 29.

5. AM I MERCIFUL?

"Blessed are the merciful, for they shall receive mercy."
(Matthew 5:7)

'Blessed are the merciful' comes after those who hunger and thirst for righteousness. That is why Sinclair Ferguson said the following.

> "Instead he intends that we should be turned away from ourselves to his righteousness, and finding his righteousness, we should be turned toward others in their need of mercy."[152]

The very characteristic that differentiates a Christian from a hypocrite is to not only be righteous, but also merciful to others!

The scribes and the Pharisees in the Bible are model hypo-

---

[152] Ferguson, *Sermon on the Mount*, (1987) 26.

crites. They had the very righteousness that Jesus condemned (Matt. 5:20). In other words, they were only righteous in their outward appearances and were not righteous in the inside. Yet, they still believed themselves to be righteous and despised others. It is exactly as Jesus depicted in the prayer of the Pharisee and the tax collector.

> "He also told this parable to some **who trusted in themselves that they were righteous, and treated others with contempt:** 'Two men went up into the temple to pray, one a **Pharisee** and the other a tax collector. **The Pharisee**, standing by himself, prayed thus: 'God, I thank you that I am not like other men, extortioners, unjust, adulterers, or even like this tax collector. I fast twice a week; I give tithes of all that I get.'" (Luke 18:9-12)

They believed themselves to be righteous and were not merciful towards sinners. This is shown extremely well in the following verses.

> "Early in the morning he came again to the temple. All the people came to him, and he sat down and taught them. The scribes and the Pharisees brought a woman who had been caught in adultery, and placing her in the midst they said to him, '**Teacher, this woman has been caught in the act of adultery. Now**

in the Law, Moses commanded us to stone such women. So what do you say?'" (John 8:2-5)

The above is a good representation of their character. That is why Jesus said the following to them.

> "Woe to you, scribes and Pharisees, hypocrites! For you tithe mint and dill and cumin, and have **neglected the weightier matters of the law: justice and mercy and faithfulness.**" (Matthew 23:23)

> "**Go and learn what this means: 'I desire mercy, and not sacrifice.'** For I came not to call the righteous, but sinners." (Matthew 9:13)

Christians, however, are different from these people. As those who hunger and thirst for righteousness, Christians are then satisfied. They are actually righteous. Yet, they also do not despise the sinners. They have mercy on them. They are like Jesus and not like the scribes and Pharisees.

> "And as they continued to ask him, he stood up and said to them, **'Let him who is without sin among you be the first to throw a stone at her.'** ... Jesus stood up and said to her, **'Woman,**

where are they? Has no one condemned you?' She said, 'No one, Lord.' And Jesus said, 'Neither do I condemn you; go, and from now on sin no more.'" (John 8:7, 10-11)

Therefore, through this message, we must honestly examine ourselves and question, "who am I?" Inspect yourselves to see whether you are a hypocrite or a Christian. I pray thus, that you all become true Christians who are righteous, yet, also merciful to others.

1) What Is Mercy?

"Mercy" is usually defined as feeling pity towards the poor and providing aid to them.

> "Whoever despises his neighbor is a sinner, but blessed is **he who is generous to the poor.**" (Proverbs 14:21)

Sinclair Ferguson said the following.

> **"Showing mercy to the poor and needy is a touchstone and hallmark of a true conversion to Christ."**[153]

---

[153] Ferguson, *Sermon on the Mount*, (1987) 33.

Does this sound too extreme? It truly is not. As evidence, think about the parable of the sheep and the goat. When you do, you will realize that this is not an extreme statement at all.

Paul wrote the following about giving alms to the poor.

> "He who supplies **seed** to the sower and **bread for food** will supply and multiply your seed for sowing and increase the harvest of your righteousness." (2 Corinthians 9:10)

In the earnings that God gives us, there are "seed... and bread for food". Thus, giving alms is not a choice but a duty. Nevertheless, many take their earnings all for themselves. Consequently, they become destitute.

> **"One gives freely, yet grows all the richer; another withholds what he should give, and only suffers want. Whoever brings blessing will be enriched and one who waters will himself be watered."** (Proverbs 11:24-25)

Thus, I want you to make a decision from here on out to give a portion of your earnings regularly to the poor. I pray that through this, you will all receive abundant blessings.

Meanwhile, the word "mercy" also holds a deeper spiritual meaning. Charles Finney said the following.

"Mercy, considered as a phenomenon of the will, is a disposition to pardon crime. It consists in willing the pardon and the well-being of one who deserves punishment. It is a goodwill viewed in relationship to one who deserves punishment."[154]

There are also many verses in the Bible that show this meaning of mercy.

"Have mercy on me, O God, according to your steadfast love; **according to your abundant mercy blot out my transgressions.**" (Psalm 51:1)

"Yet **he, being compassionate, atoned for their iniquity** and did not destroy them; he restrained his anger often and did not stir up all his wrath." (Psalm 78:38)

"let the wicked forsake his way, and the unrighteous man his thoughts; let him return to the LORD, **that he may have compassion on him**, and to our God, **for he will abundantly pardon.**" (Isaiah 55:7)

"To the LORD our **God belong mercy and forgiveness**, for

---

[154] Charles G. Finney, *Principles of Love*, (Minneapolis, MN: Bethany House Publishers, 1986) 72.

we have rebelled against him" (Daniel 9:9)

"She conceived again and bore a daughter. And the LORD said to him, 'Call her name No Mercy, **for I will no more have mercy on the house of Israel, to forgive them at all.**'" (Hosea 1:6)

"For I will be merciful toward their iniquities, and I will remember their sins no more." (Hebrews 8:12)

This is the meaning of the "merciful" mentioned in the beatitudes. As evidence, this meaning is in harmony with the very context of the beatitudes. For the poverty in the beatitudes is not a material poverty but a poverty of the spirit. Mourning is also not due to poverty and hardships but instead a mourning for one's sins. Meekness too does not come from acclimating to gentleness due to poverty and harsh situations. It is rather about becoming meek in front of the Word that insists on repentance. Hungering and thirsting for righteousness is also not about social justice but instead about desiring to live righteously by the will of God. If this is all true, then can the meaning of mercy suddenly simply be about pitying the poor? Sinclair Ferguson said the following.

"You cannot choose which beatitudes you want to be true of your life, and leave the others to one side. **The Beatitudes come as a whole, not as a series of options.** Every Christian is intended to show every grace. **One beatitude flows into the next, as we have already seen: the poor in spirit mourn for their sins, and as a result are marked by the meekness of those who know the truth about themselves in the presence of God. Such men and women hunger and thirst for righteousness, and receive it. Since they have been filled only because of the Lord's mercy to them, they become merciful to others."** [155]

Therefore, the "merciful" in the beatitudes are truly about those who are merciful to the sinners and those who wish to forgive them. This is the mercy that God desires from us.

2) Mercy Is Not a Choice but a Mandatory Obligation!

Kathryn Kuhlman said the following deeply moving words.

"As human beings, we draw back from the thought of God's justice, and are reluctant to think of Him in terms of justice. All of us pray for His mercy and we long for His mercy to be

---

[155] Ferguson, *Sermon on the Mount*, (1987) 35-6.

poured out upon us in fullest measure. It is not His justice that we seek but His mercy.

Without mercy—we are sunk. Every one of us has sinned and come short of God's glory, and the only prayer that you and I can pray [is,] 'God be merciful to me a sinner.' Why? Because without His mercy, there is nothing left but justice, and justice demands God's judgment because we are sinners."[156]

Pastor Dong-won Lee also said a similar message.

"What will we plead for when we meet God?
First, we might ask God to be generous towards us, since we have made many mistakes. When we do, the Lord will then ask us the following question.
'While living on the earth, how many times have you shown mercy to others?'
What we will need the most when we meet the Lord face to face on Judgment Day, will be the mercy of God."[157]

Do these words not resonate with you? You and I both desperately need God's mercy. We need to also look at the fact that this is what Jesus said.

---

[156] Kuhlman, *In Search of Blessings*, (1989) 33-4.
[157] Lee, *Be Like This*, (1995) 67–8.

"Blessed are the merciful, for they shall receive mercy." (Matthew 5:7)

You can see now why it is an obligation and not a choice to be merciful. We must have mercy for others and forgive them. For, we are all in absolute need of being shown this mercy.

This is expressed a bit differently in the Bible.

"and forgive us our debts, as we also have forgiven our debtors." (Matthew 6:12)

"For if you forgive others their trespasses, your heavenly Father will also forgive you, but if you do not forgive others their trespasses, neither will your Father forgive your trespasses." (Matthew 6:14-15)

"Then his master summoned him and said to him, 'You wicked servant! I forgave you all that debt because you pleaded with me. **And should not you have had mercy on your fellow servant, as I had mercy on you?**' And in anger his master delivered him to the jailers, until he should pay all his debt. **So also my heavenly Father will do to every one of you, if you do not forgive your brother from your heart.**" (Matthew 18:32-35)

These verses are a different expression of the fifth beatitude. The fact that we must be merciful to be shown mercy is to say that we must forgive in order to be forgiven. Therefore, we have no other choice. We must be merciful to others and forgive them.

If this is so, then what is the mercy God will give to those who are merciful?

First, it is the forgiveness of sins. When diving deeper, it is the ultimate salvation. Arthur Pink said the following.

> "The one who shows mercy to others gains thereby: 'the merciful man doeth good to his own soul' (Prov. 11:17)...
>
> [H]e receives mercy from God: 'with the merciful Thou wilt show Thyself merciful' (Ps. 18:25)—contrast 'he shall have judgment without mercy that hath showed no mercy' (James. 2:13). **Mercy will be shown to the merciful in the Day to come (see 2 Tim. 1:16, 18; Jude 21).**"[158]

Scot McKnight also said the following.

> "James said the same thing in other words: Speak and act as those you are going to be judged by the law that gives freedom,

---

[158] Pink, *An Exposition of the Sermon on the Mount*, (2011) 32.

because judgment without mercy will be shown to anyone who has not been merciful. Mercy triumphs over judgment. (Jas 2:12-13) **To the merciful is promised divine mercy at the judgment, that is, entrance into the kingdom."** [159]

Dr. Yong-eui Yang also said this.

"The apodosis 'for they shall receive mercy' is proclaiming that the currently joyful disciples, due to their merciful actions, will receive the conclusive and eternal mercy of God at the last judgment. When a disciple shows mercy even to his enemy, he is doing the will of God. This is then clearly a condition to enter the complete Kingdom of God at the last Judgment (i.e. 7:21). Yet, one must remember that the amount of mercy a disciple shows will never be enough to ask for one's salvation through it. For only by receiving the mercy of God can one enter the perfect Kingdom of God." [160]

This is the very meaning of the promise that the Lord gave to the merciful. To receive mercy is thus not to simply receive forgiveness, but to also enter heaven. Yet, many people become confused because of this.

---

[159] Mcknight, *Sermon on the Mount*, (2013) 45.
[160] Yang, *How Will You Read the Book of Matthew?*, (2011) 95.

They might ask, 'Does God really only have mercy on us when we are merciful, and only forgive us when we forgive others? If that is true, doesn't that mean that we are saved, not by grace, but by works? Is this really Jesus' intent when he spoke?'

Many scholars have tried to answer this question. Yet, many of them have given an incredibly doubtful answer. For example, Arthur Pink wrote the following about this verse.

> "Having received mercy from the Lord, the saved sinner now exercises mercy unto others. **It is not that God requires us to be merciful in order to obtain His mercy**—that would be to overthrow the whole scheme of grace—but **having been made the recipient of His wondrous grace. I cannot now but act graciously toward others.**"[161]

This message, in general, is correct. We are not trying to overthrow grace, nor are we saying we show mercy in exchange for receiving mercy. Yet, it is also true that this verse is still saying that we must be merciful to be treated with mercy by God. Therefore, the explanation above is unbalanced.

John Stott also said the following on this verse.

---

[161] Pink, *An Exposition of the Sermon on the Mount*, (2011) 29-30.

"'For if you forgive other people when they sin against you, your heavenly Father will also forgive you (Matt 6:14).' **This is not because we can earn mercy by mercy or forgiveness by forgiveness, but because we cannot receive the mercy and forgiveness of God unless we repent, and we cannot claim to have repented of our sins if we are unmerciful towards the sins of others. Nothing moves us to forgive like the sense of wonder that we have ourselves been forgiven. Nothing proves more clearly that we have been forgiven than our own readiness to forgive."** [162]

To be honest, I do not understand why these scholars cannot accept Jesus' words as is and instead have to think in a tiresome manner and explain things so tediously. This is unnecessary. Unfortunately, we see this kind of phenomenon appear in Sinclair Ferguson's writing as well.

"This presents us with something of a problem. Does Jesus mean that we will receive mercy only if we ourselves are merciful? **Certainly that is his meaning.**" [163]

It is fine up to here. He explained it very well. The problem

---

[162] Stott, *The Message of the Sermon on the Mount*, (2020) 31.
[163] Ferguson, *The Sermon on the Mount*, (1987) 30.

is what comes after.

> "Being merciful is the **natural** result of receiving Christ and experiencing the grace of God. **If we are not merciful, we cannot have received Christ's mercy**, and therefore cannot look forward to receiving his mercy in the last judgment.
>
> There is really no problem in what Jesus says about mercy. This manner of speaking occurs later in his teaching: Those who forgive the sins of others will be forgiven (Matt. 6:14). **This does not mean that we merit forgiveness by forgiving others, but rather, that unless we forgive others, there is no evidence that we ourselves have been forgiven.**
>
> A similar point is made in the parable about the unmerciful servant (Matt. 18:21-35). A merciful person cannot be forgiven a debt of a million pounds and then demand that someone who owes him a few pounds must repay him. **Of course, people can act like this (the servant in the parable, for example). But if they do they have not begun to grasp the privilege that has been extended to them. So it is in the kingdom of God."**[164]

This explanation is all over the place and has no backbone. Why in the world does this phenomenon occur? It is because

---

[164] Ferguson, *The Sermon on the Mount*, (1987) 30.

so many scholars have been fooled by the false doctrine of 'once saved, always saved' and are trying to match everything to it.

Once again, these types of explanations are not necessary. To go further, they are unbiblical. For in Matthew 18, **it was not as if the servant who owed ten thousand talents was not ever forgiven of his debt because he later did not have mercy on his fellow servant and forgive the debt of 100 denarii. He really had been forgiven of it all.** However, he did not have mercy on others as he had been given mercy. And that is why the unforgiving servant ended up in jail. The fact that he did not show mercy to another was not evidence for him not having ever been saved. Instead, it shows that once saved is not always saved and that he was forsaken. Jesus is warning us of exactly this in his parable. It is the same for the fifth beatitude.

Therefore, remember this. We must be merciful to others for we have been shown mercy. We must forgive others just as we have been forgiven. If we do not do this, we will be like the unforgiving servant and receive a judgment without mercy and will be forsaken. This is not a new or strange assertion. This is a very biblical and classic truth that many servants of God have been proclaiming since long ago.

Puritan theologian Thomas Watson said the following.

"A man may as well go to hell for not forgiving—as for not

believing."[165]

D. L. Moody, a famous evangelist, also said the following.

"Notice that when you go into the door of God's kingdom, you go in through the door of forgiveness."[166]

And Bishop John Ryle also said the following.

"All ideas of heaven in which forgiveness has not a place, are castles in the air and vain fancies. Forgiveness is the way by which every saved soul enters heaven. Forgiveness is the only title by which he remains in heaven. ... Surely an unforgiving soul in heaven would find his heart completely out of tune. Surely we know nothing of Christ's love to us but the name of it, if we do not love our brethren."[167]

There are also many other testimonies that show that those who are not merciful and do not forgive cannot enter heaven. I

---

[165] Thomas Watson, *The Lord's Prayer*, (London, UK: The Banner of Truth Trust, 1960) 184.
[166] D.L. Moody, *Prevailing Prayer: What Hinders It?*, (Chicago, IL: J.L. REGAN & CO., 1884) 60.
[167] Seung-woo Byun, *Christians Going to Hell*, (Seoul, Korea: Grace Publishing, 2008) 258.

would like to introduce a few of them to you.

① A Philippine Pastor's Testimony

This pastor "had resisted the call of God on his life several years because of his business success. He was making a large amount of money. His disobedience eventually caught up with him, and he was rushed to the hospital because of heart failure.

He died on the operating table and found himself outside the gates of heaven. Jesus was standing there and dealt with him about his disobedience. The man pleaded with the Lord that if He would extend his life, he would serve Him.

The Lord consented. Before sending him back to his body, the Lord showed him a vision of hell. He saw his wife's mother burning in the flames of hell.

He was amazed. She had said the 'sinner's prayer,' confessed to being a Christian, and had attended church. 'Why is she in hell?' he asked the Lord.

The Lord told him that **she had refused to forgive a relative and therefore could not be forgiven.**" [168]

② Angelica Zambrano's Testimony

---

[168] John Bevere, *The Bait of Satan*, (Lake Mary, FL: Charisma House, 2004) 123-4.

Let me introduce to you a part of sister Angelica's testimony.

"In Hell, people are tormented with the memories of what they did on Earth. Those who had known the Lord were tormented twofold.

The Lord said, 'There is no other opportunity [for those here]; there is still opportunity for those who are alive.'

I asked Him, 'Lord, why is my great-grandmother here? I don't know if she ever knew you. Why is she here in hell, Lord?'

He replied, '**Daughter, she is here because she failed to forgive. … Daughter, he who does not forgive, neither will I forgive him.**'

I asked, 'Lord, but You do forgive, and You are merciful.'

And He answered, '**Yes, Daughter, but it is necessary to forgive, because they have not forgiven many people, and that is why many people are in this place, because they failed to forgive…Go and tell humanity that it is time to forgive, and especially My people, for many of My people have not forgiven. Tell them to rid themselves of grudges, of resentment, of that hatred in their hearts, for it is time to forgive! If death were to surprise that person who has failed to forgive, that person may go to hell.**'"[169]

---

[169] Daum Beloved Church, (2008, November 2). Prepare to Meet Your God! http://cafe.daum.net/Bigchurch/Lul5/1278

③ Victoria Nehale's Testimony

Next, is a part of the testimony by sister Victoria.

"It was a place of utmost darkness ... it was hotter than the hottest of fires. ...

The place was filled with flies of all sizes—green, black, and grey flies. Every conceivable kind of fly was there. In addition, there were also short, thick, black worms everywhere, climbing on everything. ... The place was filled with the most disgusting stench; there are no words to describe the intensity of the stench in that place. The smell was almost like rotten meat but was a hundred times worse than the most decaying meat I have ever smelled in my entire life. The place was filled with the noise of wailing and gnashing of teeth, as well as of demonic, evil laughter.

The worst thing about this place is that it was filled with people. There were so many people that they could not be numbered. ... They were divided into many different groups. Even if they were in the groups, it was not possible to estimate the number of people in any single group because the groups were extremely large. The man led me to one of the groups on the eastern side of the place. He looked at me and said:

'Victoria, this is a group of people who refused to forgive

others. I told them many times in many different ways to forgive others but they rejected me; I have forgiven them all their sins but they refused to forgive others. Their time ran out and they found themselves here. They will be here for all eternity; they are eating the fruits of their labor for ever and ever.'"[170]

④ Carmelo Brenes' Testimony

I want to introduce to you a part of Carmelo Brenes' testimony titled, "Christians That Wound Up in HELL," which is very similar to the title of my first book, *Christians Going to Hell*.

"In Hell, we saw many who thought they were living holy while on Earth, but now they were just begging for mercy and another chance. My soul ached so much for them. We saw a woman who was acting like she was reading the Word of God, and preaching about John 3:16.

She said: 'For God so loved the world that he gave his one and only Son, that whoever believes in Him shall not perish but have eternal life.'

Jesus said she was there **'Because she could not forgive her**

---

[170] Victoria Nehale, *A Friendly Reminder: Time is Fast Running Out!* (Author-Publishers, 2008) 29-31.

husband; she never managed to forgive her husband' (Matt 6:14-15). This woman had been shepherding an evangelical church for 35 years, but now in Hell, she is begging for one more chance to forgive her husband.

The [B]ible warns us[.]

'Settle matters quickly with your adversary who is taking to you court. Do it while you are still with him on the way, or he may hand you over to the judge, and the judge may hand you over to the office, and you may be thrown into prison' (Matt. 5:25) and **'Blessed are the merciful, for they will be shown mercy'** (Matt. 5:7).

If you are someone who cries in the presence of the Lord, you are still under grace and mercy. But if you feel that you cannot cry anymore, or pray anymore, if you have stopped your prayer life, you are in great danger. **Forgiveness is something special, and that woman never forgave. After 35 years of hard work for God, she lost it all in the end. Meditate on this, and make sure you forgive all. How do you want to spend eternity?"**[171]

Beloved, if you do not forgive others, you will never be able to enter heaven. No one is an exception to this. Therefore, I pray that you all be wise and forgive everyone you have not

---

[171] Daum Beloved Church, (2011, November 9). Christians that wound up in HELL, https://cafe.daum.net/Bigchurch/Lul5/1286

forgiven while you still have the chance.

3) Anyone Can Be Merciful and Forgive Others!

Do you all wish to be merciful and forgive others now? Thus, I want to show you practical methods on how you can actually forgive others.

The key is the cross. The cross not only gives us the obligation to forgive, but it also gives us the key to be able to forgive. John Stott said the following.

> **"Nothing moves us to forgive like the sense of wonder that we have ourselves been forgiven."** [172]

This is true! Therefore, the key to forgiveness is not through the sin of others, but through my own sin. It is to focus on the forgiveness I have received, rather than the forgiveness I need to give. When we do this, we will be able to easily have mercy on others and forgive them.

A long time ago, I went to America for church related reasons and I visited Kona, Hawaii and was able to go to YWAM and visit their University of the Nations. As soon as I landed

---

[172] Stott, *The Message of the Sermon on the Mount*, (2020) 31.

on the island, one of the school managers came to meet me at the airport. The next day, he gave me a tour of each area across campus and kindly explained everything to me. One of the places he led me through was a DTS session that was being done in English and Korean.

There, I heard the testimony of one middle-aged man. He said the following based on the parable of the unforgiving servant.

> "Before, I didn't know. But now I know that I am the sinner who was forgiven of the debt of ten thousand talents. I realized how great a sinner I really am. As I realized this, I was then able to forgive everyone. And I was able to not get angry or take offense at other people. It's because I have no right. Once in a great while, I will still get mad at people. I know that this is when I have been caught up in spiritual amnesia."

This is true. If we focus on the fact that we are the sinner who was forgiven of the debt of ten thousand talents, then we will be able to forgive automatically. Forgiveness will be easy. In Pastor Dong-won Lee's book, it says the following.

> "How can we possess the characteristic to be merciful? There is only one answer. Think of how the Lord has regard-

ed us. If you are truly someone who has been saved, then remember how God treated you and made you his believer. When we had no right, and still resented God, He had pity on us and forgave us unconditionally and called us blameless and righteous. ... Jesus forgave us when we could not be forgiven, and he brought us out of the hell that we deserved because of our wickedness and depravity and instead, saved us. So how can we not forgive the small mistakes and flaws of our brothers?

Sir Thomas More was a gentleman with many dreams and was among the respected Christians. Yet, he was falsely accused, caught, and killed. More famously, he left these words to the judge who was sentencing him to death.

'More have I not to say, my lords, but that like as the blessed apostle Saint Paul, as we read in the Acts of the Apostles, was present and consented to the death of Saint Stephen, and kept their clothes that stoned him to death, and yet be they now twain holy saints in heaven, and shall continue there friends forever: so I verily trust and shall therefore right heartily pray, that though your lordships have now in earth been judges to my condemnation, we may yet hereafter in heaven merrily all meet together to our everlasting salvation.'

Then the judge asked the following after listening to his words.

'I have sentenced you to death, yet what is the reason you are showing me goodness?'

That is when Thomas More answered succinctly. **'It is because the Lord first showed me mercy.'**[173]

Like so, think of all the times you have been shown mercy and all the sins you have been forgiven of. When you do so, there is no one you cannot forgive. No matter who it is, you will be able to forgive them.

Lastly, I want to say this to you. To be unforgiving does not only block the forgiveness of sins. For forgiveness is not the only result of being merciful. Healing and deliverance of spirits are also a result of being merciful.

"And Jesus in pity touched their eyes, and immediately they recovered their sight and followed him." (Matthew 20:34)

"As he was getting into the boat, the man who had been possessed with demons begged him that he might be with him. And he did not permit him but said to him, 'Go home to your friends and tell them how much the Lord has done for you, and how **he has had mercy on you.**'" (Mark 5:18-19)

---

[173] Lee, *Be Like This*, (1995) 68–69.

That is why when we forgive, many times illnesses are healed and evil spirits also depart. Jesus said the following.

> "And Jesus answered them, '**Have faith in God.** Truly, I say to you, whoever says to this mountain, "Be taken up and thrown into the sea," and does not doubt in his heart, but believes that what he says will come to pass, it will be done for him. Therefore I tell you, whatever you ask in prayer, believe that you have received it, and it will be yours. **And whenever you stand praying, forgive, if you have anything against anyone**, so that your Father also who is in heaven may forgive you your trespasses.'" (Mark 11:22-25)

At times we not only need faith for healing and rebuking of spirits but also need forgiveness. Without forgiveness, even if we believe, we can go to hell. In the same way, without forgiveness, faith for healing and rebuking spirits is useless. Therefore, forgive immediately. I pray that you will thus be free from illnesses and evil spirits.

6. AM I PURE IN HEART?

"Blessed are the pure in heart, for they shall see God."
(Matthew 5:8)

There is a book that was a world-wide sensation and a best-seller for a long time in South Korea. It is the book, *Heaven is So Real* by Choo Thomas, which was translated into Korean by Pastor David Yonggi Cho. In the book, it records the following topic five different times.

> "**WHERE ONLY THE PURE-HEARTED CAN GO**
> The Lord answered my questions clearly and emphatically. *'My daughter, we went to the kingdom.'* He quickly recognized the question that was forming in my heart: *How did we get there? 'The only ones who will go there are the obedient and pure-hearted children.'"* [174]

---

[174] Choo Thomas, *Heaven is So Real*, (Lake Mary, FL: Charisma House, 2006) 21.

"'**THE ONLY ONES** *who can come here are the ones whose hearts are as pure as the water,*' Jesus assured me after we arrived in heaven during the early hours of February 29."[175]

"Next, Jesus took me to a river. ... I noticed how clear and still the water was. It sparkled like the finest crystal I'd ever seen. The Lord reiterated the invitation He extends to all who want to follow Him and have an eternal home with Him in heaven, *'The only ones who can come here are the ones whose hearts have been made as pure as the wate*r.'"[176]

"This is what Jesus had been telling me—heaven is reserved for those who will obey. **Only the pure in heart will be able to enter and live there.**"[177]

"It was a place of purity and whiteness, and the roads and buildings were immaculately clean. ... A brilliance like sunlight was everywhere. Then the Lord showed me all the oceans of the world and the whole earth. Snow was covering the earth. The Lord explained: *'I must purify My people before I bring them to My kingdom. Unless they are pure-hearted, they cannot see*

---

[175] Ibid., 33.
[176] Ibid., 34.
[177] Ibid., 94.

My kingdom.' Then I remembered one of the Beatitudes: **'Blessed are the pure in heart, for they shall see God'** (Matt. 5:8)."[178]

What do you think? Do you believe this to be biblical? My question is not whether Choo Thomas' experience is biblical or not. I am simply asking whether the content of her writing is biblical. We need to put aside our own views and preferences and figure out if this verse actually holds such a meaning or not. For this verse is in direct correlation with the safety of our souls and our eternal future. That is why I laid down all my interpretations, and with a just and open heart, searched for the meaning of this verse. I wish to now share with you all the conclusions I have reached.

1) What Does Being Pure in Heart Mean?

On the basis of Matthew 4:17, the beatitudes are the characteristics of people who have repented and become disciples. On the basis of Mark 1:15, they are also the characteristics of people who repent and believe in the gospel.

Yet, people may wonder, "Does everyone who repent and believe in the gospel have a pure heart? Is everyone on the

---

[178] Ibid., 181.

same level?" Due to this, many scholars interpret this verse differently. For example, Douglas Hare said the following.

> "The Greek adjective **katharos** means both **clean**, as in 'a clean linen shroud' (Matt. 27:59), and **pure**, that is, unadulterated or unalloyed, as in 'pure gold' (Rev. 21:21)."[179]

Afterwards, he also claimed the following.

> "Since 'pure heart' is there in parallel with 'clean hands,' one is inclined to regard **the pure in heart as those who are innocent** not only of moral failures ('clean hands') **but also of evil intentions** (the heart being understood as the seat of the will). Here would be included both the 'adultery of the eyes' of Matt. 5:28 and other evil thoughts (15:19). **If such is the meaning, however, there are none who qualify for the blessing.**"[180]

Thus, he is saying that being pure in heart simply means the undivided nature of the whole heart rather than actually being pure in heart.

With an open heart, I viewed this interpretation to possibly be true and started researching the problem. First, I looked at

---

[179] Hare, *Matthew*, (1993) 41.
[180] Ibid., 41.

the original language. The Greek for "pure" is καθαρός *(katharos)* and it means "clean," or "pure". The word *katharos* is also explained as follows.

> "The Greek language has 2 adjectives signifying 'purity, cleanliness'; it is *hagnos* and *katharos*. *Hagnos* is a word originally connected with the root meaning to be 'holy', signifying a qualitative holiness or purity belonging to the deity and the associated things or persons (cultic objects and officials). The more common term used is ***katharos*** and its cognates. **These words mean a ritual, physical or moral purity of persons or objects."**[181]

I also looked at the grammar. To summarize, the grammar of the New Testament shows the following.

> "The adjective *katharos* appears 26 times in the New Testament and is used for the following meanings.
> (a) Katharos signifies physical purity. ...
> (b) Katharos signifies ritual purity and cleanliness. ...
> (c) **Katharos is used for moral purity.** ..."[182]

---

[181] Geoffrey W. Bromiley, *Theological Dictionary of the New Testament: Abridged in one volume*, (Grand Rapids, MI: William B. Eerdmans Publishing Company, 1985) 381.

[182] Ibid., 381.

Thus, I ascertained that it was more accurate to understand "pure" as purity of heart.

However, the reason Douglas Hare interpreted the word differently was not simply because of the original language. It was because he believed becoming pure in heart on this earth was impossible.

The Bible does say that what is deceitful above all things is the heart.

> **"The heart is deceitful above all things, and desperately sick"** (Jeremiah 17:9)

Moreover, it also says that all kinds of wicked things crawl out from the heart of man.

> **"For from within, out of the heart of man, come evil thoughts, sexual immorality, theft, murder, adultery, coveting, wickedness, deceit, sensuality, envy, slander, pride, foolishness.** All these evil things come from within, and they defile a person." (Mark 7:21-23)

Thus, Hare is saying, how can this heart of man become pure?

Many scholars actually believe that it is impossible to be

pure in heart. That is why they interpret pure in heart as follows: to not have a double heart and instead be purely devoted to God.

Then, is this really true and is it impossible to be pure in heart? No, it is possible to be pure in heart, even on this earth. The evidence for this is as follows.

① Jesus Believed It Was Possible to Be Pure in Heart.

"'Woe to you, scribes and Pharisees, hypocrites! For you **clean the outside of the cup and the plate, but inside they are full of greed and self-indulgence. You blind Pharisee! First clean the inside of the cup and the plate**, that the outside also may be clean. 'Woe to you, scribes and Pharisees, hypocrites! For you are like whitewashed tombs, **which outwardly appear beautiful, but within are full of dead people's bones and all uncleanness. So you also outwardly appear righteous to others, but within you are full of hypocrisy and lawlessness.'"** (Matthew 23:25-28)

What we need to particularly focus on is when Jesus says, "You blind Pharisee! First clean the inside of the cup" (Matt. 23:26). The word used here for "clean" is the same word katharos that was used to talk about the pure in heart. Yet, Jesus told the Pharisees that they need to clean their hearts (inside). Jesus would not have ordered them to do so if this was impossible. He also would not have condemned them so harshly. Therefore, it is without a doubt that Jesus believed having a pure heart was possible.

We also need to focus on the fact that Matthew 23 is a warning to the hypocrites that they will not be able to escape hell. No one can enter heaven in such a state of impurity of the heart. Thus, it is not strange that to be pure in heart is one of the beatitudes, which are the very characteristics of the saved. Therefore, I am positive that the meaning of this phrase is to actually be pure in heart.

② There Are People in the Bible Who Are Actually Pure in Heart.

> "Who shall ascend the hill of the LORD? And who shall stand in his holy place? He who has clean hands and **a pure heart**, who does not lift up his soul to what is false and does not swear deceitfully." (Psalm 24:3-4)

> "Truly God is good to Israel, to those who are **pure in heart**." (Psalm 73:1)

"**He who loves purity of heart**, and whose speech is gracious, will have the king as his friend."[183] (Proverbs 22:11)

"So flee youthful passions and pursue righteousness, faith, love, and peace, along with **those who call on the Lord from a pure heart.**" (2 Timothy 2:22)

Like the above, there were people who were actually pure in heart in the Bible. It is thus unbelief and wrong to still ignore the evidence and say it is impossible to be pure of heart.

③ The Bible Says the Hearts of All Christians Are Pure.

I previously explained that the beatitudes are the characteristics of those who repent and believe in the gospel. And I also said that the question of whether everyone who repents and believes in the gospel has a pure heart and is on the same level might arise. And that because of this, many scholars interpret this verse differently. Yet, surprisingly, in the Bible there are verses that say all Christian are pure of heart. There are two more verses apart from our main passage in this chapter that talk of this.

---

[183] Because those who hunger and thirst for righteousness will be satisfied, those who love purity of heart will also receive it.

First, is Acts 15:9.

"And he made no distinction between us and them, having **cleansed their hearts by faith.**"

If "having cleansed their hearts" is truly about being pure in heart, then it proves that one can be pure in heart on this earth. Additionally, just like in the beatitudes, this verse is also talking about the believer who is saved. It becomes proof that the pure in heart in the beatitudes is also about actually being pure in heart. So, I investigated this meaning while wrestling through reading commentaries. As a result, I discovered the following writings.

F.F. Bruce wrote the following about this verse.

"And if God accepted those Gentiles **and cleansed them in heart and conscience by the impartation of his Spirit as soon as they believed the gospel,** …"[184]

Howard Marshall also wrote the following on this verse.

"Peter referred to God as the *One who knows the heart* of all

---

[184] F. F. Bruce, *The Book of the Acts*, (Grand Rapids, MI: William B. Eerdmans Publishing Company, 1988) 290.

men, and he drew the conclusion that in thus pouring out the Spirit on the Gentiles **God was cleansing their hearts from sin in just the same way as he cleansed the hearts of Jews**. It followed, therefore, that what mattered in God's sight was the **cleansing of the heart**, and that outward legal observances, such as circumcision, were a matter of indifference."[185]

And John Stott said the following.

"God *did not discriminate between us and them, for he purified their hearts by faith* (9), demonstrating that it is the **inward purity of the heart** which makes fellowship possible, not the external purity of diet and ritual."[186]

Moreover, Darrell Bock said the following about this verse.

"God does the **work of washing their hearts clean**. This divine washing takes place in the context of faith."[187]

Lastly, Eckhard Schnabel said the following on this verse.

---

[185] I. Howard Marshall, *The Acts of the Apostles*, (Grand Rapids, MI: William B. Eerdmans Publishing Company, 1980) 249-50.
[186] John R. W. Stott, *The Message of Acts*, (Downers Grove, IL: InterVarsity Press, 2020) 226.
[187] Darrell L. Bock, *Acts*, (Grand Rapids, MI: Baker Academic, 2007) 500.

"God **'cleansed' the hearts** of the Gentiles by removing the impurity of the Gentile sinners, forgiving their sins, and granting them **purity.**"[188]

Above all else, we need to know that the verse is spoken by Peter while preaching the gospel to the house of Cornelius. That was when the Spirit came upon all who were present in the house. And the result of the Spirit falling upon them was their purity of heart. In other words, it is the work of the Spirit. Thus, we must see the cleansing of the heart as not a forgiveness of sins but rather as meaning to be pure in heart.

Next, we must look at Titus 1:15.

"**To the pure, all things are pure**, but to the defiled and unbelieving, nothing is pure; but both their **minds** and their **consciences** are defiled."

This verse is the same. If the "pure" and the "defiled" mentioned here are talking about actual purity and defilement of the heart, it becomes evidence that it is possible to be pure in heart. Moreover, the pure is again referencing all Christians, just like in the previous verse. This then can also become proof

---

[188] Eckhard J. Schnabel, *Acts*, (Grand Rapids, MI: Zondervan, 2012) 634.

that the purity mentioned in the beatitudes, which portrays all Christians, actually means being pure of heart. For these reasons, I further pursued finding the actual meaning of this verse.

First, I am sure that the pure in **"to the pure, all things are pure"** is about all Christians. It clearly means a moral and inner purity of the heart. However, some still believe this to be about pure or defiled food. Since the law is now abolished, they say that all food, namely all things, are now pure for Christians. They say this is the meaning of "to the pure, all things are pure." It technically is a plausible interpretation. However, even if this is the case, there is no question that "the pure" here is about the pure in heart. John Stott explained this well.

> "Second, they have a false understanding of purity. Like the Pharisees, they prize external and ritual purity above the true purity which is internal and moral. **It is not only that inward and spiritual purity is supreme ('Blessed are the pure in heart'); but once we have been made clean inwardly, Jesus said, 'everything will be clean for you.' Just so, Paul writes here: To the pure all things are pure** (15a), including of course the Creator's good gifts of marriage and food."[189]

---

[189] Stott, *1 Timothy and Titus*, (Downers Grove, IL: InterVarsity Press, 2021) 176.

Next, it is the same for "**but to the defiled and unbelieving, nothing is pure.**" William Mounce wrote the following about this section.

> "Paul's opponents were evidently teaching that one could attain ritual purity by following the ascetic laws. Paul asserts, rather, that **those who are morally defiled and do not believe cannot be made acceptable to God even by ritual purity because everything about them is unclean. To the (morally) impure, all things are (ritually) impure. Their real problem is not ceremonial but moral.**"[190]

This is the meaning of this verse. Therefore, it is also proof that "the pure" mentioned beforehand is about the pure in heart.

Lastly, it is the same for the phrase, "**both their minds and their consciences are defiled.**" John Stott however, understood this verse in the following manner.

> "*In fact, both their minds* [what they believe] *and consciences* [what they feel able to do] *are corrupted* (15b)."[191]

---

[190] William D. Mounce, *Pastoral Epistles*, (Nashville, TN: Thomas Nelson Inc., 2000) 401.
[191] Stott, *1 Timothy and Titus*, (2021) 176.

It is a very attractive interpretation! However, in the World Biblical Commentary, William Mounce understood them to each respectively be branded consciences and corrupted minds.[192] In particular, Duane Litfin wrote the following on this verse.

> "The 'commands' of verse 14 ['not devoting themselves to Jewish myths and the commands of people who turn away from the truth'], especially in light of the Jewish and possibly Gnostic influences, undoubtedly included ascetic rules about eating, drinking, and purification (cf. Col. 2:20-23; 1 Tim. 4:1-5). Paul set the matter straight by reminding his readers of the Lord's teaching that purification is largely a matter of the internal rather than the external (cf. Mark 7:15; Luke 11:39-41). **Nothing outside can corrupt one who is internally pure; but someone who is internally impure corrupts all he touches. The problem with the false teachers was that on the inside, in their minds and consciences, they were impure. ... Their impure interiors thus rendered them externally detestable (lit., 'abominable') to God, disobedient (cf. Titus 1:10), and unfit (adokimoi, 'disapproved'; cf. 1 Cor. 9:27) for doing anything good (cf. 2 Tim. 3:17)."**[193]

---

[192] Mounce, *Pastoral Epistles*, (2000) 402.
[193] A. Duane Litfin, *Titus*, (Wheaton, IL: SP Publications, Inc., 1983) 763.

Therefore, this verse also proves to us that all the hearts of believers are pure. Thus, it is entirely plausible to interpret the pure in heart in the beatitudes as actually being about those who have pure hearts.

④ If Your Heart Is Not Pure, You Cannot Enter the Kingdom of Heaven.

I cannot understand people like Douglas Hare who dilute the message of the pure in heart and interpret it in a different manner. As I have already explained, people do this because they believe that it is impossible to be pure in heart in this world. However, even if that is the case, nothing changes. For in the very same chapter, Jesus interpreted the seventh commandment as such.

> "You have heard that it was said, 'You shall not commit adultery.' But I say to you that everyone who looks at a woman with lustful intent has already committed adultery with her in his heart. If your right eye causes you to sin, tear it out and throw it away. For it is better that you lose one of your members than that your whole body be thrown into hell. And if your right hand causes you to sin, cut it off and throw it away. For it is better that you lose one of your members than that your whole body go

into hell." (Matthew 5:27-30)

Like so, not only those who commit adultery with their hands (actions), but also those who commit adultery with their eyes (heart) will be thrown into hell. In other words, if your heart is not pure, you cannot enter the kingdom of God. Therefore, even if you interpret it in such a manner, the results do not change. It is useless.

Moreover, in chapter 15, Jesus once again criticized the Pharisees for simply following the traditions of the elders by only washing their hands and not washing their hearts. He reprimanded them for worshiping God in vain. For when we look in parallel verses, we see that out of the heart come thoughts of sexual immorality, adultery, and sensuality.

> "For from within, out of the heart of man, come **evil thoughts, sexual immorality**, theft, murder, **adultery**, coveting, wickedness, deceit, **sensuality**, envy, slander, pride, foolishness." (Mark 7:21-22)

Additionally, Jesus once again criticized the state of the Pharisees who only cleaned the outside of their plates and not the inside. He sharply censured them saying, "How will you escape being condemned to Hell?" The heart of self-indulgence is mentioned in the following verse as well.

> "Woe to you, scribes and Pharisees, hypocrites! For you clean the outside of the cup and the plate, but **inside they are full of greed and self-indulgence.**" (Matthew 23:25)

This does not mean, however, that purity of heart is singularly related to immorality. It also has relations with all other evil thoughts. Yet, we cannot deny that immoral thoughts are the most typical representation of them.

Even apart from our main passage, Jesus mentioned three times in Matthew alone that only the pure in heart can enter heaven. Therefore, no matter what anyone says, if you are not pure in heart, you cannot enter the kingdom of heaven.

Thomas Watson said the following.

> "**Why purity must be chiefly in the heart.** (i) Because if the heart be not pure, we differ nothing from a Pharisaic purity. The Pharisees' holiness consisted chiefly in externals. Theirs was an outside purity. They never minded the inside of the heart.
>
> 'Woe unto you, scribes and Pharisees, hypocrites! ...'
>
> 'Ye are like unto whited sepulchres, which indeed appear beautiful outward, but are within full of dead men's bones' (Matthew 23:25, 27). ...

> We must go further. ... else ours is but a Pharisaic purity; and Christ says, 'Except your righteousness shall exceed the righteousness of the scribes and Pharisees, ye shall in no case enter into the kingdom of heaven' (Matthew 5:20)."[194]

This is true. If you do not have a pure heart, you will never enter the kingdom of God. Is it alright then to misinterpret the meaning of this vitally important truth and think it is impossible? To do so would be an act that gravely endangers souls. Yet, I have recently seen famous preachers on Christian TV channels commentating on The Sermon and preaching in such a manner. Thus, do not be fooled by these sermons.

As I have proven to you so far, purity of heart actually means to have a pure heart. John Stott gave a clear-cut explanation on this.

> "It is immediately obvious that the words in heart indicate the kind of purity which Jesus means, as the words 'in spirit' indicated the kind of poverty he meant. The 'poor in spirit' are the spiritually poor as distinct from those whose poverty is only material. From whom, then, are the pure in heart being

---

[194] Watson, *The Beatitudes*, (1971) 174.

distinguished?

> The popular interpretation is to regard purity of heart as an expression for inward purity, for the quality of those who have been cleansed from moral—as opposed to ceremonial—defilement. And there is good biblical precedent for this, especially in the Psalms. It was recognized that no-one could ascend the Lord's hill or stand in his holy place without having 'clean hands and a pure heart'. [Psalm 24:3, 4]"[195]

Stott is correct. Just as the word "in spirit" explains what kind of poverty Jesus was talking about, the word "heart" also shows us what kind of purity it is. It is a purity of the heart.

Additionally, our main passage in this chapter has a deep connection with Psalm 24. The following is recorded in that passage.

> "**Who shall ascend the hill of the LORD? And who shall stand in his holy place?** He who has clean hands and a pure heart, who does not lift up his soul to what is false and does not swear deceitfully. He will receive blessing from the LORD and righteousness from the God of his salvation. **Such is the generation of those who seek him, who seek the face of the**

---

[195] Stott, *The Message of the Sermon on the Mount*, (2020) 31.

God of Jacob. *(Selah)*" (Psalm 24:3-6)

This message goes well with the expression that one who has a pure heart sees God!

Yet, do you know where the "hill of the Lord" is? Do you know where the "holy place" is? The "hill of the Lord" is "Mt. Zion" and the "holy place" was the "temple" that was built on top of Mt. Zion. In other words, those who are not pure in heart do not have the right to go up to the temple and worship God nor meet him. We need to focus on this fact. If you do not have a pure heart, you do not deserve to go up to the temple. Then, can such a person even dare to enter heaven? They obviously cannot! That is why Jesus said that only those who are pure in heart can see God.

Therefore, do not listen to downgraded and wrongful interpretations that match the standards of the depraved state of man. No matter what anyone says, you must become one who is pure in heart and also believe that you can become one! I pray you will actually become such a person to then enter the kingdom of God.

2) What Does the Promise "to See God" Mean?

Jesus gave a very special promise to those who are pure

in heart.

"Blessed are the pure in heart, **for they shall see God.**" (Matthew 5:8)

Pastor Francis Frangipane also gave an example of this through his wife.

"My wife set herself apart to seek the Lord. Her cry during this time was, 'Lord, I want to see You.' As she sought the Lord, however, He began to show her certain areas of her heart where she had fallen short. She prayed,
'Lord, this is not what I asked for; I asked to see You, not me.'
Then the Holy Spirit comforted her, saying, 'Only the pure in heart can see God.'"[196]

This is true. Only those who are pure in heart can see God.

Then, what exactly is the meaning of the promise that Jesus made? Since long ago, I have been curious about this, but I've finally figured out that there are two meanings inside this promise.

---

[196] Francis Frangipane, *The House of the Lord* (Lake Mary, FL: Creation House, 1991) 21.

① Those Who Are Pure in Heart Can See God on This Earth.

It holds the very meaning that one becomes the king's friend.

> "He who loves purity of heart, and whose speech is gracious, will have the king as his friend." (Proverbs 22:11)

A person who is pure in heart befriends not an earthly king but the eternal King! It is truly a spectacular favor. Yet, as it is implied in the next verse, sin can interrupt one's fellowship with God.

> "Create in me a **clean heart**, O God, and renew a right spirit within me. **Cast me not away from your presence, and take not your Holy Spirit from me.**" (Psalm 51:10-11)

When our hearts become pure, such obstacles disappear. This is shown well in the following verses.

> "As I was in my prime, **when the friendship of God was upon my tent.**" (Job 29:4)

> "**The friendship of the L**ORD **is for those who fear him,**

and he makes known to them his covenant." (Psalm 25:14)

"You are my friends if you do what I command you." (John 15:14)

That the pure in heart will see God is like the above. It means that we can meet God deeply, have fellowship with him, and live a life walking with him. We can also re-confirm the actual meaning of this promise through Psalm 24.

"Who shall ascend the hill of the LORD**? And who shall stand in his holy place?** He who has clean hands and **a pure heart**, who does not lift up his soul to what is false and does not swear deceitfully. He will receive blessing from the LORD and righteousness from the God of his salvation. **Such is the generation of those who seek him, who seek the face of the God of Jacob.** (Selah)" (Psalm 24:3-6)

"The hill of the Lord" that comes out in this psalm is Mt. Zion, and the "holy place" is the temple. Therefore, what is promised to the pure of heart here is the ability to go up to the temple and through worship, spiritually meet God. It is not actually seeing God but spiritually meeting Him. Those who are pure in heart can spiritually meet God. Sinclair Ferguson explained this as follows.

> "The pure in heart—those who desire both to know and serve him—will see God (Matt. 5:8).
>
> **What can this mean?** Scripture tells us that no man has ever seen God because he is the invisible God (Jn. 1:18; Col. 1:15; 1Tim. 1:17; Heb. 11:27). How, then, can the pure in heart see him? Does Jesus mean that in some new way, in heaven, we will 'see God'? **The clue to understanding what it means to see God probably lies in those Old Testament passages that describe the experiences of those who are 'pure in heart.' Psalm 24:3-6 indicates that the pure in heart have the privilege of ascending the hill of the Lord and entering into the presence of God in his holy place**. ... Psalm 73:1 states that God is good to those who are pure in heart. In verses 24-28 of that psalm, Asaph (the author) tells us how he came to this conclusion: 'You guide me with your counsel, and afterward you will take me into glory... As for me, it is good to be near God.'
>
> **Both of these passages emphasise the privileges and joys of conscious fellowship with God and the knowledge that we are in his presence.**"[197]

---

[197] Ferguson, *Sermon on the Mount*, (1987) 52-3.

Therefore, to see God means to enjoy an intimate fellowship with God. On the topic of "seeing God," Arthur Pink wrote, "To 'see God' is to be brought nigh to Him (for we cannot see an object which is a vast distance from us), to be introduced into intimate intercourse with Him."[198]

Furthermore, John Wesley's writings on this are truly insightful. He expressed the meaning beautifully, basing it on his own experiences.

> "**The pure in heart see all things full of God**. They see him in the firmament of heaven, in the moon walking in brightness, in the sun when he rejoiceth as a giant to run his course. They see him 'making the clouds his chariots, and walking upon the wings of the wind.' They see him 'preparing rain for the earth', 'and blessing the increase of it'; 'giving grass for the cattle, and green herb for the use of man'. They see the Creator of all wisely governing all, and 'upholding all things by the word of his power'.
>
> 'O Lord, our Governor, how excellent is thy name in all the world!'
>
> **In all his providences relating to themselves, to their souls or bodies, the pure in heart do more particularly see God.** They

---

[198] Pink, *Exposition of the Sermon on the Mount*, (2011) 34.

see his hand ever over them for good; giving them all things in weight, and measure, numbering the hairs of their head, making a hedge round about them and all that they have, and disposing all the circumstances of their life according to the depth both of his wisdom and mercy.

But in a more especial manner they see God in his ordinances. Whether they appear in the great congregation to 'pay him the honour due unto his name, and worship him in the beauty of holiness'; or 'enter into their closets' and there pour out their souls before their 'Father which is in secret'; whether they search the oracles of God, or hear the ambassadors of Christ proclaiming glad tidings of salvation; or by eating of that bread and drinking of that cup 'show forth his death till he come' in the clouds of heaven. In all these his appointed ways they find such a near approach as cannot be expressed. They see him, as it were, face to face, and 'talk with him as a man talking with his friend' a fit preparation for those mansions above wherein they shall 'see him as he is'."[199]

In Psalm 24, the psalmist expressed those who went up to the temple to worship as "a generation that seeks God" and those who "seek the face of God." And he said their character-

---

[199] Wesley, *The Sermons of John Wesley*, (2013) 503.

istics are "not only clean hands, but a pure heart." It means that those who are pure in heart, by worshiping in spirit and truth, can spiritually meet God. This is also in sync with the following verses.

"Yet you are holy, **enthroned on the praises of Israel**." (Psalm 22:3)

"For where two or three are gathered in my name, there am I among them." (Matthew 18:20)

"And without faith it is impossible to please him, **for whoever would draw near to God must believe that he exists and that he rewards those who seek him.**" (Hebrews 11:6)

"The Spirit of God came upon Azariah the son of Oded, and he went out to meet Asa and said to him, 'Hear me, Asa, and all Judah and Benjamin: The LORD is with you while you are with him. **If you seek him, he will be found by you, but if you forsake him, he will forsake you.' As soon as Asa heard these words, the prophecy of Azariah the son of Oded, he took courage and put away the detestable idols from all the land of Judah and Benjamin and from the cities that he had taken in the hill country of Ephraim,** and he repaired the altar of the LORD that was in front of the vestibule of the house of the LORD.** And he gathered all Judah and Benjamin, and those from Ephraim, Manasseh, and Simeon who were residing with them, for great numbers had deserted to him from Israel when they saw that the LORD his God was with him. **They were gathered at Jerusalem in the third month of the fifteenth year of the reign of Asa. They sacrificed to the LORD on that day from the spoil that they had brought 700 oxen and 7,000 sheep. And they entered into a covenant to seek the LORD, the God of their fathers, with all their heart and with all their soul**, but that whoever would not seek the LORD, the God of Israel, should be put to death, whether young or old, man or woman. They swore an oath to the LORD with a loud voice and with shouting and with trumpets and with horns. And all Judah rejoiced over the oath, **for they had sworn with all their heart and had sought him with their whole desire, and he was found by them**, and the LORD gave them rest all around." (2 Chronicles 15:1-2, 8-15)

Those who are pure in heart can thus meet God through worship. They can also meet and experience God in the middle of praise, while praying alone, and even in their daily lives. They feel the presence of God and taste His goodness. They know that God is with them. This truly is something to desire after! Therefore, I hope all of you become pure in heart. And I pray that you will then experience God and enjoy Him in your life.

② Those Who Are Pure in Heart Will See God's Face in Heaven.

What I have just explained to you thus far is an exact interpretation. However, you might be feeling like it is not enough. You might wonder, "If that is all, why not say you will have intimate fellowship with God? Why use the strong expression to see God?" Such thoughts might make you think it is not enough of an explanation.

However, the fact that you feel this way does not mean that the aforementioned interpretation is inaccurate. For the promise of Jesus holds a salvation that has "already" come, and a salvation that has "not yet" come. It holds both meanings. As I have pointed out before, the promises in the second to seventh beatitudes are all in the future tense. Therefore, "for they shall see God," points not only to something we are enjoying now, but also to the ultimate salvation that the pure in heart will receive. Because of this, Dr. Yong-eui Yang wrote the following.

"The disciples, whose hearts are pure, are even happier for they will 'see God' in the kingdom of God that will be fulfilled in the future."[200]

When we see the following verses, it erases any doubt that this is the meaning of this promise.

"For now we see in a mirror dimly, **but then face to face**. Now I know in part; **then I shall know fully, even as I have been fully known**." (1 Corinthians 13:12)

"Strive for peace with everyone, and for the **holiness without which no one will see the Lord**." (Hebrews 12:14)

"Beloved, we are God's children now, and what we will be has not yet appeared; **but we know that when he appears we shall be like him, because we shall see him as he is**. And everyone who thus hopes in him purifies himself as he is pure." (1 John 3:2-3)

"Then the angel showed me the river of the water of life, bright as crystal, flowing from the throne of God and of the Lamb through the middle of the street of the city; also, on either side of the river, the tree of life with its twelve kinds of

---

[200] Yang, *How Will You Read the Book of Matthew?*, (2011), 96.

fruit, yielding its fruit each month. The leaves of the tree were for the healing of the nations. No longer will there be anything accursed, but the throne of God and of the Lamb will be in it, and **his servants will worship him. They will see his face**, and his name will be on their foreheads." (Revelation 22:1-4)

This is the perfect fulfillment of the promise "they shall see God." The Lord's promise, given to the pure in heart, includes both the intimate fellowship with God that is enjoyed on this earth, and heaven, the eternal enterprise. Therefore, "they shall see God" is a very accurate and perfect expression!

Is this then saying that only the pure in heart enter heaven? Certainly. Only such a person will be able to enjoy the heaven of their hearts on this earth (focus on the "righteousness" in Rom. 14:17!) They will also enter the new heaven and new earth where righteousness stands (2 Pet. 3:13) and will be able to see the face of God (Rev. 22:1-4). Therefore, you all must become pure in heart. I pray that this is how you will live, not only walking with the Lord in fellowship but also going to heaven and forever seeing God and enjoying eternal blessings and joy.

3) What Must We Do to Become Pure in Heart?

The Bible says that the heart is more deceitful than all things

(Jer. 17:9). Moreover, it says that all kinds of evil arise inside the heart of man.

> "And he said, 'What comes out of a person is what defiles him. **For from within, out of the heart of man, come evil thoughts, sexual immorality, theft, murder, adultery, coveting, wickedness, deceit, sensuality, envy, slander, pride, foolishness. All these evil things come from within, and they defile a person.**'" (Mark 7:20-23)

This is the heart of the descendants of the corrupted Adam, the natural man's heart.

Moreover, the hearts of the hypocrites, namely the scribes and the Pharisees, are also similar.

> "**Woe to you, scribes and Pharisees, hypocrites! For you clean the outside of the cup and the plate, but inside they are full of greed and self-indulgence. You blind Pharisee! First clean the inside of the cup and the plate, that the outside also may be clean. Woe to you, scribes and Pharisees, hypocrites! For you are like whitewashed tombs, which outwardly appear beautiful, but within are full of dead people's bones and all uncleanness. So you also outwardly appear righteous to others, but within you are full**

of hypocrisy and lawlessness." (Matthew 23:25-28)

But the heart of a Christian is different. Their heart is pure. That is why Jesus said the following in the beatitudes that portray the Christians.

"Blessed are the pure in heart, for they shall see God." (Matthew 5:8)

A person is either one of three: a natural man, a hypocrite, or a Christian. Of them, only the Christian will enter heaven. Therefore, we must become pure in heart.

Then, how can we become pure in heart?

Many have searched a long time for the special secret to becoming pure in heart. However, a special method does not exist. The answer is rather in the Bible that we read, for only the Bible is the real truth. Thus, I wish to introduce to you what I have found. It is not a special secret but what the scriptures are saying.

① We Must Repent!

John the Baptist, Jesus, the 12 apostles, and even Paul all cried out to repent before anything else. No one can be transformed without repentance. As I explained earlier, the beatitudes are the eight characteristics of those who have repented, having listened to the words of Jesus to, "Repent, for the kingdom of heaven is at hand" (Matt. 4:17). One of these characteristics is to be pure in heart. Therefore, we need to repent in order to be pure of heart.

In the Bible, after King David sinned due to Bathsheba, he repented and cried out to God in the following manner.

"Hide your face from my sins, and blot out all my iniquities. **Create in me a clean heart, O God, and renew a right spirit within me.**" (Psalm 51:9-10)

As a result, David was able to once again become pure in heart. Therefore, we must repent of our dirty hearts and thoughts and cry out to God to create in us a clean heart and renew a right spirit within us. That is how you can become a person who is pure of heart.

② We Must Believe!

In the book, Principles of Sanctification by Charles Finney, he wrote that one is sanctified by "faith alone."[201] In the same

---

[201] Charles G. Finney, *Principles of Sanctification*, (Minneapolis, MN: Bethany House Publishers, 1986) 142.

book, he also said the following.

> "Entire sanctification is to be attained by faith alone. … Both justification and sanctification are by faith alone."[202]

This is true, for the Bible records the following.

> "And he made no distinction between us and them, **having cleansed their hearts by faith.**" (Acts 15:9)

In this verse, Peter said that he cleansed the hearts of the gentiles by faith. When we also look at the context of Titus 1:15 that Paul wrote, we can see that faith is the key to having a pure heart.

> "**To the pure**, all things are pure, **but to the defiled and unbelieving**, nothing is pure; but both their minds and their consciences are defiled."

Defiled things and unbelief are partners. In the same way, faith and a pure heart are also partners. Therefore, in order to be pure of heart, we must believe. We must have faith to have a

---

[202] Ibid., 145.

pure heart.

The natural man, no matter who they are, cannot win against all sin. They cannot win against the sin of the mind and the heart.

> "For those who live according to the flesh **set their minds** on the things of the flesh, but those who live according to the Spirit set their minds on the things of the Spirit. **For to set the mind on the flesh is death, but to set the mind on the Spirit is life and peace. For the mind that is set on the flesh is hostile to God, for it does not submit to God's law; indeed, it cannot. Those who are in the flesh cannot please God.**" (Romans 8:5-8)

Yet, there is a reversal if the Holy Spirit comes inside of us.

> "**You, however, are not in the flesh but in the Spirit, if in fact the Spirit of God dwells in you.** Anyone who does not have the Spirit of Christ does not belong to him." (Romans 8:9)

And the prophecy of Ezekiel is thus fulfilled.

> "**And I will put my Spirit within you, and cause you to walk in my statutes** and be careful to obey my rules." (Ezekiel 36:27)

The Spirit comes upon us when we listen to the gospel and believe.

"Let me ask you only this: **Did you receive the Spirit by works of the law or by hearing with faith? … Does he who supplies the Spirit to you and works miracles among you do so by works of the law, or by hearing with faith?**" (Galatians 3:2, 5)

"So that in Christ Jesus the blessing of Abraham might come to the Gentiles, **so that we might receive the promised Spirit through faith.**" (Galatians 3:14)

Therefore, we must believe in the gospel. We must also rely on the Holy Spirit, who is given to us when we believe. That is how we can be pure in heart.

③ We Must Listen to the Word!

Do you know what makes our hearts pure? It is the Word.

"**Already you are clean because of the word that I have spoken to you.**" (John 15:3)

"**Sanctify them in the truth**; your word is truth. As you sent me into the world, so I have sent them into the world. And for their sake I consecrate myself, **that they also may be sanctified in truth.**" (John 17:17-19)

"**That he might sanctify her, having cleansed her by the washing of water with the word.**" (Ephesians 5:26)

"**The aim of our charge is** love that issues from **a pure heart** and a good conscience and a sincere faith." (1 Timothy 1:5)

Like so, it is the truth, namely the Word that makes our hearts pure. In other words, this book that you are reading helps make your hearts pure. Therefore, I hope you expect this to happen to you too as you continue to read.

Recently, one member of our church uploaded this testimony online.

> "'A Miraculous 16 Months Spent at Beloved Church'- ID: Jesus My Love
> The reason I had never truly transformed, even with my pastor in my previous church checking the rights and wrongs of even the smallest things and reprimanding me so, was because of the lack of truth. No one can change unless they eat

the word of truth and spend enough time before the Lord. Even though no one interferes and nitpicks me at Beloved Church, when I listen to our senior pastor's sermons, I naturally start to cry tears of repentance and make resolutions. The powerful sermons that are living and working here are clearly changing me and give me hope that, I too, can succeed."[203]

It is a very precious testimony! Yet, why was this individual transformed listening to our church's sermons but not when they were attending a different church? It is because our church preaches the truth and not orthodoxy. The commandments of men can only wash one's hands and cannot cleanse the heart.

> "Then Pharisees and scribes came to Jesus from Jerusalem and said, 'Why do your disciples break the tradition of the elders? **For they do not wash their hands** when they eat.' He answered them, 'And why do you break the commandment of God for the sake of your tradition?
> … You hypocrites! Well did Isaiah prophesy of you, when he said: **'This people honors me with their lips, but their heart is far from me; in vain do they worship me, teaching**

---

[203] http://cafe.daum.net/Bigchurch/7aS/7491

as doctrines the commandments of men.' And he called the people to him and said to them, 'Hear and understand: it is not what goes into the mouth that defiles a person, but what comes out of the mouth; this defiles a person.'" (Matthew 15:1-3, 7-11)

But the commandment of God cleanses the heart.

On the contrary, the sermons and teachings that have been distorted by doctrine and orthodoxy further defiles man. The following verses show this well.

"If anyone teaches **a different doctrine** and does not agree with the sound words of our Lord Jesus Christ and the teaching that accords with godliness, he is puffed up with conceit and understands nothing. He has an unhealthy craving for controversy and for quarrels about words, **which produce** envy, dissension, slander, evil suspicions, and constant friction among people who are **depraved in mind** and deprived of the truth, imagining that godliness is a means of gain." (1 Timothy 6:3-5)

"This testimony is true. Therefore rebuke them sharply, that they may be sound in the faith, not devoting themselves **to Jewish myths and the commands of people who turn away from the truth.** To the pure, all things are pure, but to the defiled and unbelieving, nothing is pure; **but both their minds and their consciences are defiled.**" (Titus 1:13-15)

While explaining these verses, Duane Litfin made this important remark.

"Once again Paul connected theological error with moral deficiency."[204]

This shows us why a biblical and upright truth is important.

Moreover, we are able to earn a very important touchstone here that will allow us to discern doctrines and sermons. Does the doctrine that you believe in and the sermons you listen to make you pure of heart? Or have you just been amassing Bible knowledge? If a congregation listens to a sermon and a portion does not become pure in heart, then it is the fault of the individual. However, if the majority of the church is this way, then it is the fault of the preacher. Thus, I hope this touchstone allows you to not only discern doctrine but also sermons.

While preparing for this book, I realized something that was very important and special. I thanked God profusely for this realization. While preparing for this book, the Holy Spirit

---

[204] Litfin, *Titus*, (1983) 763.

spoke to my spirit the following.

"The Word not only tells people what to do, but the Word itself does something.

The Word makes one born again.

'Since you have been born again, not of perishable seed but of imperishable, through the living and abiding word of God.' (1 Peter 1:23)

The Word makes one holy.

'Make them holy by your truth; teach them your word, which is truth.' (John 17:17, NLT)

The Word makes one clean.

'That he might sanctify her, having cleansed her by the washing of water with the word.' (Ephesians 5:26)

The Word works inside a believer.

'The word of God, which is at work in you believers.' (1 Thessalonians 2:13b)

Thus, it is important to listen attentively to sermons. If so, then the Word will transform those who listen to it."

In Hebrews 4:12-13, it shows the power of the Word.

> "For the word of God is living and active, sharper than any two-edged sword, piercing to the division of soul and of spirit, of joints and of marrow, and discerning the thoughts and intentions of the heart. And no creature is hidden from his sight, but all are naked and exposed to the eyes of him to whom we must give account."

To be honest, I only understood the above verses superficially. So, this time around, I decided to truly research its meaning. However, what I found was quite different from my first hypothesis.

In the World Biblical Commentary, William Lane said the following about this verse.

> "God's word, whose sanctions were imposed so effectively upon the Exodus generation, is performative today and confronts the Christian community with the same alternatives of rest and wrath. Those who remain insensitive to the voice of God in Scripture may discover that God's word is also a lethal weapon. When the past generation sought to contravene the oath of God and to enter Canaan, they were driven back and fell by the sword (mákhaira) of the Amalekites and the Canaanites

(Num 14:43-45). **The word of God poses a judgment that is more threatening and sharper than any double-edged sword** because it exposes the intentions of the heart and renders one defenseless before God's scrutinizing gaze."[205]

Thomas Schreiner also said the following about these verses.

"Verse 12-13 explain why the readers should strive to enter God's rest and why they should avoid unbelief and disobedience. **Disobedience is fatal, for the word of God is powerful and effective, so that those who disobey it will not escape punishment.**

God's word is compared to a double-edged sword. It seems here that the word's role in judgment is brought to the forefront. Perhaps the author thinks of the swords of Amalekites and Canaanites, which cut down Israel when they attempted to enter the land after the Lord told them they could not enter because of their disobedience (Num 14:39-45). **So too, the Lord's word hews down any and all those who disobey him.**"[206]

This verse was thus about judgment, which was different

---

205 William L. Lane, *Hebrews 1-8*, (Nashville, TN: Word Incorporated, 1991) 102.
206 Thomas R. Schreiner, *Commentary on Hebrews*, (Nashville, TN: B&H Publishing Group, 2015) 146-7.

from what I had first expected. This is the correct interpretation.

First, "the word of God" in this verse points to Psalm 95, or at the very least, has a deep connection to it.

> "For he is our God, and we are the people of his pasture, and the sheep of his hand. **Today, if you hear his voice, do not harden your hearts, as at Meribah, as on the day at Massah in the wilderness, when your fathers put me to the test and put me to the proof, though they had seen my work. For forty years I loathed that generation and said, 'They are a people who go astray in their heart, and they have not known my ways.' Therefore I swore in my wrath, 'They shall not enter my rest.'"** (Psalm 95:7-11)

Second, the passage starts with the word "for" (gar). The reason is then recorded in verse 11.

> "Let us therefore strive to enter that rest, so that no one may fall by the same sort of disobedience."

The above verse thus shows us the very reason. Therefore, we must see it as being related to judgment.

Third, Hughes excellently pointed out that the verse, "piercing to the division of soul and of spirit, of joints and of marrow," vividly depicts the Word of God as piercing and entering the deepest parts of an individual's entity.[207] Additionally, Donald Guthrie adequately explained that the "piercing to the division of soul and of spirit" does not mean that the soul and spirit are divided, but that the word pierces the whole man. In other words, it pierces both the soul and spirit to thus reveal one's nature.[208] The meaning of the final section, "discerning the thoughts and intentions of the heart," is also about how God's Word pierces our hearts and thoughts to reach the center. In other words, it is saying the Word of God pierces and reveals even the most secretive parts of our lives. God knows who we are and what kind of being we are. Accordingly, if we are disobedient like the Israelites and do not put in effort to enter that rest, then we will not be able to escape judgment. That is what these verses are showing us. Therefore, just as the double-edged sword in Revelations is connected to judgment, these verses are also about judgment.

As you can see, these verses were not how I had first understood them to be. I was flustered, and it led me to dive into more in-depth research. The following is the conclusion I reached.

Contextually, the interpretation above is correct. The Word

---

[207] Philip Edgcumbe Hughes, *A Commentary on the Epistle to the Hebrews*, (Grand Rapids, MI: William B. Eerdmans Publishing Company, 2015) 165.

[208] Donald Guthrie, *The Letter to the Hebrews*, (Grand Rapids, MI: William B. Eerdmans Publishing Company, 1983) 118.

of God acts to unclothe our sin and reality and reveals them to be judged. The Word that plays this role also transforms those who attentively listen to it. Like unclothing the heart, thought, and will of those who are listening, everything is exposed, awoken, and transformed. In this meaning, these verses are also still showing us the power of the Word that transforms people. Because of this, Thomas Schreiner wrote the following.

> "In context the focus is on the effectiveness of God's judgment, **but what is said here also applies more broadly to God's word in general.**"[209]

Besides Schreiner, many other scholars also spoke similarly. George Guthrie said the following.

> "**The same word** that at creation set the elements of the cosmos to their appointed tasks and still governs the universe toward God's desired intentions (1:2-3), **has the ability to effect change in people. It is not static and passive but dynamic, interactive and transforming as it interfaces with the people of God.**"[210]

---

[209] Schreiner, *Commentary on Hebrews*, (2015) 146.
[210] George H. Guthrie, *Hebrews*, (Grand Rapids, MI: Zondervan Publishing House, 1998) 156.

Thomas Long also spoke on this.

"A **hymnlike tribute** to the **power of God's word** (4:12-13). Sharper than any earthly two-edged sword... piercing into the depths of humanity, exposing to view the secret 'intentions of the heart.' ... the word of God unveils every human life, laid bare before the eyes of God. **The word of God takes an ordinary day and makes it 'today,' takes an ordinary moment and makes it the time of crisis and decision, takes a routine event and makes it the theater of the glory of God, takes an ordinary life and calls it to holiness. ... The living and active word of God refreshes hope and restores confidence. The word of God turns wandering human beings into principal actors in the magnificent story of divine redemption, transforms frightened people who hide in the garden and make excuses into holy partners of Jesus Christ who can, through him, stand up boldly and render an account.**"[211]

Moreover, Dr. Sang-geun Lee said the following.

"The Word of God is... **active**. [We know that] all living things are active. **This active action inspires hearts to repent and**

---

[211] Thomas G. Long, *Hebrews*, (Louisville, KY: Westminster John Knox Press, 1997) 61.

be saved."[212]

And I particularly like the words of Dr. Han-soo Lee.

"'For the Word of God is living and active.' This expression shows an active personality that the divine revelation has. It will do something."[213]

That is correct. Just like the Holy Spirit told me, the Word of God does not only tell us to do something. The Word itself does something. In other words, it makes us realize our sin. It awakens us. It makes us repent, decide, and cry out to transform us. This is represented well in the next verse.

"And we also thank God constantly for this, that when you received the word of God, which you heard from us, you accepted it not as the word of men but as what it really is, **the word of God, which is at work in you believers.**" (1 Thessalonians 2:13)

Certainly, for the Word to work in this manner, it must actu-

---

[212] Sang-geun Lee, *Galatians (In Korean)*, (Seoul, Korea: Christian Literature Press, 2008) 216.
[213] Han-soo Lee, *The Apostle's Love Letters: Hebrews & James (In Korean)*, (Seoul, Korea: Solomon, 2014) 63.

ally be the Word of God.

> "You accepted it not as the word of men but as what it really is, the word of God."

Then, if we just preach the real truth, will this work for all who listen? No. This will only work in those who listen to the Word, not as words of man, but of God and desire it with a humble heart. It is exactly as it is recorded that, "When you received the word of God, which you heard from us, you accepted it not as the word of men but as what it really is, the word of God, which is at work in you believers" (1 Thess. 2:13).

As a good example, there were people who gathered at the home of Cornelius. Cornelius, with a heart of desire, had gathered his relatives and close friends and was waiting when Peter arrived at the home. Then, Cornelius fell down in front of Peter's feet and worshiped him. Peter hastily lifted him up and said that he too was a man. Do you know how Cornelius responded?

> **"Now therefore we are all here in the presence of God to hear all that you have been commanded by the Lord."**
> (Acts 10:33)

Cornelius acknowledged Peter's words to be 100% the Word of God and listened with a humble and longing heart. That is when the Spirit came upon them.

"While Peter was still saying these things, the Holy Spirit fell on all who heard the word." (Acts 10:44)

Do you know how Peter referred to this event in Acts 15?

"'The apostles and the elders were gathered together to consider this matter. And after there had been much debate, Peter stood up and said to them, 'Brothers, you know that in the early days God made a choice among you, **that by my mouth the Gentiles should hear the word of the gospel and believe. And God, who knows the heart, bore witness to them, by giving them the Holy Spirit just as he did to us**, and he made no distinction between us and them, **having cleansed their hearts by faith.**'" (Acts 15:6-9)

Peter said to them that Cornelius and his relatives and friends, who listened to the sermon that day, cleansed their hearts.

Thus, what is the key to becoming pure in heart? It is to listen to the Word with this heart of desire. When we listen to sermons as the Word of God and humbly listen with a longing heart, it will cleanse our hearts. This is what happened in the home of Cornelius. And it is happening right now, here today. I do not doubt that this will happen to many of you who are reading this Sermon on the Mount series. I believe that this transformation has already happened for many and is happening to many as well. Richard Phillips said the following.

> "Consider the matter of our sanctification, that is, our own growth in holiness. What could be more effective than to shine the light of God's Word upon our lives, into our minds and hearts?"[214]

This is true. Therefore, I pray you will listen to the Word with faith and a heart of expectation. That is how it will make your hearts clean. Praise God!

④ We Must Strive to Live by the Word!

The Word and the Spirit give us strength to obey the truth. However, it does not force us to obey the truth. We are the ones who need to obey the truth. Therefore, we must make the

---

[214] Richard D. Philips, *Hebrews*, (Phillipsburg, NJ: P&R Publishing Company, 2006) 142.

decision to obey the truth and intentionally make an effort to do this at all times.

The following verses show us its importance.

"How can a young man keep his way pure? By guarding it according to your word." (Psalm 119:9)

"O Jerusalem, wash your heart from evil, that you may be saved. How long shall your wicked thoughts lodge within you?" (Jeremiah 4:14)

"You blind Pharisee! First clean the inside of the cup and the plate, that the outside also may be clean." (Matthew 23:26)

"So flee youthful passions and pursue righteousness, faith, love, and peace, along with those who call on the Lord from a pure heart." (2 Timothy 2:22)

Therefore, you must rely on the Spirit and make an effort. By doing so, I pray that you will cleanse your hearts.

Meanwhile, Jesus said the following while explaining the seventh commandment.

"You have heard that it was said, 'You shall not commit adultery.' But I say to you that everyone who looks at a woman with lustful intent has already committed adultery with her in his heart. **If your right eye causes you to sin, tear it out and throw it away.** For it is better that you lose one of your members than that your whole body be thrown into hell. And if your right hand causes you to sin, cut it off and throw it away. For it is better that you lose one of your members than that your whole body go into hell." (Matthew 5:27-30)

Jesus said that it is also adultery to look at a woman with lustful intent and firmly said, "If your right eye causes you to sin, tear it out and throw it away." John Stott wrote the following about this verse.

> **"We shall have to eliminate from our lives certain things which (though some may be innocent in themselves) either are, or could easily become, sources of temptation. …We may have had to become culturally 'maimed' in order to preserve our purity of mind. …it is better to accept some cultural amputation in this world than risk final destruction in the next."**[215]

This is correct. Joseph did not stand up and fight when Poti-

---

[215] Stott, *The Message of the Sermon on the Mount*, (2020) 70-71.

phar's wife tempted him. He ran away. Paul also told Timothy to "flee youthful passions" (2 Tim. 2:22). Thus, I want to make the following suggestion to you. Download R-rated blocking software on your computers. In other words, disable your computers. Nowadays, there are many lewd programs on TV and it makes staying up late at night dangerous. However, you can also configure the TV to block access to R-rated films and programs. By doing so, disable your TV as well. I hope that you will actually do this in your homes, not only for yourselves, but also for your children.

⑤ You Must Seek the Face of God!

"Who shall ascend the hill of the LORD? And who shall stand in his holy place? He who has clean hands and **a pure heart**, who does not lift up his soul to what is false and does not swear deceitfully. He will receive blessing from the LORD and righteousness from the God of his salvation. **Such is the generation of those who seek him, who seek the face of the God of Jacob.** (*selah*)" (Psalm 24:3-6)

Who has clean hands and a pure heart? It is the generation who seeks the Lord, and the one who seeks the face of the God of Jacob. Therefore, this is one of the methods for how you can become pure of heart.

If you look on our church blog, you will see a testimony from my old Sunday School teacher there. Because the testimony is so precious, I have kept it up all this time. My teacher served as a missionary for many years before becoming spiritually drained. That is when she read my book and came to our church. Here, she cried and prayed and met Jesus three times. She testified about the change in her life afterwards.

> "I simply changed at that point. Everything changed. As I realized that He was real, as I desired to see Jesus more, and as I longed to meet Him more, my interest in everything else disappeared. It became like this without any effort on my part. ...
>
> A while ago, after receiving the Holy Spirit at a revival conference at Ulsan Methodist Church, the world could not seem more beautiful in my eyes. But even after such an experience, I had been spiritually lost. I had supported my husband's ministry to the best of my abilities, but I was still sinning and I had many worldly values still mixed in me. **But all of that disappeared when I saw Jesus' face.**
>
> I shed so many tears. Countless tears. I had never cried that much in my life before. Until Jesus met with me at my home church, I had cried because of the difficulties of being a missionary. However, after meeting Him, tears streamed down like

a steaming waterfall, and my soul was continuously being restored. It was God's care for no one else but me. **My heart was washed clean.** Ever since I was in my thirties, I had suffered from dizziness, indigestion, back pains, and leg pains. Nothing was ever severe enough to be hospitalized, but my body had suffered much. However, I was miraculously healed of all of it, and even now, 7 years later, I feel perfectly fine. That was how healing had naturally happened for me.

I had thought, 'It is okay if my body is in pain. **All I want is to know God more and to see Jesus more.**' I had paid no attention to my body at that point, but it was suddenly healed just like that."[216]

Praise God! Is this not a touching testimony?

To be honest, if you commit to what I have previously introduced, you will be able to become pure in heart. Yet, seeking God and seeking His face is the key to completely purifying yourself. Therefore, we must become one who loves God and seeks His face. That is how all your hearts can become purer and purer.

---

[216] Seung-woo Byun, *Truth Like a Diamond*, (Seoul, Korea: HolyPearl Publications, 2016) 10-11.

I would like to now conclude this message on being pure of heart. And I would like to do so by saying two final things.

First, I started the explanation of this beatitude with the testimony of Elder-Deaconess Choo Thomas. As the book mentions, to say you must be pure of heart to enter heaven is not strange. For it is clearly shown in the teachings of Jesus on the seventh commandment that come after the beatitudes. Therefore, although we cannot believe all that is written in Heaven is So Real!, it is a valuable thing to emphasize that you must be pure of heart to enter heaven and to shock souls and shake them awake through this.

Therefore, we must seek after this purity of heart. However, being pure of heart is not talking about being perfect. If that were the case, then there would hardly be any who could enter heaven. The beatitudes are the eight characteristics of believers who listened to the kingdom gospel, repented and were saved. They are not the characteristics of those who are glorified or have achieved perfect glorification. Therefore, being pure in heart rather means to not have habitual sins as shown in 1 John. Even those who are pure in heart may at times sin with their eyes, heart, and mind. That will not automatically send them to hell. When that happens, they simply need to confess and immediately turn around to start again.

"If we confess our sins, he is faithful and just to forgive us our sins and to cleanse us from all unrighteousness." (1 John 1:9)

This verse in it of itself supports my explanation. Confessing shows that it is possible to commit sins, and it acknowledges it.

I believe that it is necessary to not only emphasize the need to be pure in heart like so, but also create balance by speaking out about how it is also not about being perfect either. That is how we can bring people to not only strive for a pure heart but also prevent people from falling into despair. Beloved, it is not impossible to have a pure heart. It is completely possible. Therefore, do not lose hope and I pray you will all seek after this and become pure in heart.

Next, what we should be focusing on, as the most profound teaching to gain from Matthew 5:8, is not on the purity of the heart but rather that God must be our ultimate goal. We must be pure in heart to enter heaven. Because of this, many people desire to become pure in heart and focus on it. However, if you start to only focus on becoming pure in heart, then even if you do gain a pure heart, you will feel empty and a lack of happiness. It is like how a virgin bride does not feel happiness due to her purity. Her husband is what brings about her happiness! We are the same. Therefore, we must take interest in God. We must be filled with God. That is how we can truly become happy.

Take a look at Psalm 24 carefully. The ultimate purpose is not to have a pure heart. The purpose was not simply to have a pure heart but to go up the mountain of God (Sinai) and to enter the holy place (temple) and meet God to worship and have fellowship with Him. That is why they were called, "The generation who seeks him" and those "Who seek the face of the God of Jacob." In other words, purity of the heart was just one of their characteristics, but seeking God's face was their entire identity. Therefore, we must not stop at just desiring a pure heart but must at all costs seek God and become one who seeks the face of God.

I say the following carefully and do not want to be misunderstood, but I would like to say that although it is most important for us to love God, we must not give our all to just loving God. We must love our God with all our heart, life, and will. But it is not just loving God that we need to give our all for. What is the greatest commandment of the law? It is to love God and love our neighbors (Matt. 22:37-40). Jesus also gave the new commandment that just as I have loved you, you also are to love one another (John 13:34-35). He even commanded us to love our enemies and persecutors (Matt. 5:43-44). Therefore, we should not only love God above all else, but also love one another, love our neighbors, and even love our enemies and persecutors. That is when true maturity will form. And you will not feel dull or empty but instead will overflow with life, joy, and peace. Thus, I pray that no matter the cost, you will all participate in this endeavor.

7. AM I A PEACEMAKER?

"Blessed are the peacemakers, for they shall be called sons of God." (Matthew 5:9)

If you look in church history, there is one great historical crime that Christians committed: The Crusades. At first, the uprising began with just motives, as they rose up with the fervor to reclaim the Holy Land. However, they utilized wrongful methods by using hatred and violence. As a result, countless families of believers in Europe were distressed. Tens of thousands of children became orphans, and countless women were left widows. Families were broken. It was an extremely dark age where Christianity was the furthest it had ever been from the Bible.[217]

At the time, while other Christians were all raising their overzealous voices in enthusiasm, there was one quiet voice that

---

[217] Lee, *Be Like This*, (1995) 91.

prayed a "Prayer for Peace." It was St. Francis. He prayed thus.

> "Lord, make me an instrument of your peace
> Where there is hatred, let me sow love
> Where there is injury, pardon
> Where there is doubt, faith
> Where there is despair, hope
> Where there is darkness, light
> And where there is sadness, joy
>
> O Divine Master, grant that I may
> Not so much seek to be consoled as to console
> To be understood, as to understand
> To be loved, as to love
> For it is in giving that we receive
> And it's in pardoning that we are pardoned
> And it's in dying that we are born to Eternal Life"

St. Francis was a peacemaker. Like him, we too must become peacemakers. Thus, let us discuss the blessing of the peacemaker.

1) The Duty of a Peacemaker!

In our main passage for the chapter, the word "peacemaker"

shows us that we have "a duty to be a peacemaker."[218] There are three such obligations that you and I have to make peace.

① The Duty to Be at Peace with One Another

First, we must be at peace with other people.

"If possible, so far as it depends on you, live peaceably with all." (Romans 12:18)

It is related to our ultimate salvation.

"But I say to you that **everyone who is angry with his brother will be liable to judgment; whoever insults his brother will be liable to the council; and whoever says, 'You fool!' will be liable to the hell of fire**. So if you are offering your gift at the altar and there remember that your brother has something against you, leave your gift there before the altar and go. **First be reconciled to your brother**, and then come and offer your gift. **Come to terms quickly with your accuser** while you are going with him to court, lest your accuser hand you over to the judge, and the judge to the guard, and you be put in prison." (Matthew 5:22-25)

---

218 Lee, *Be Like This*, (1995) 81.

> "**Strive for peace with everyone, and for the holiness without which no one will see the Lord.**" (Hebrews 12:14)

Therefore, we must at all costs, be at peace with others. Yet, Thomas A. Kempis said the following.

> "**GOODNESS AND PEACE IN MAN**
> **FIRST KEEP peace with yourself; then you will be able to bring peace to others.**"[219]

He also wrote the following on the next page.

> "Some people live at peace with themselves and with their fellow men [Rom. 12:18; 2 Cor. 13:11], but others are never at peace with themselves nor do they bring it to anyone else. These latter are a burden to everyone, but they are more of a burden to themselves. A few, finally, live at peace with themselves and try to restore it to others."[220]

It is the truth. I have personally seen that those who do not actually have peace in their own hearts are the ones who have discord with others and agonize them. On the other hand, I

---

[219] Kempis, *The Imitation of Christ*, (2003) 31.
[220] Ibid.

have seen that those who have peace in their hearts live peacefully with others. Therefore, if you desire to live in peace with others, you must first find peace in your own heart.

I believe this is one of the reasons why the peacemakers are placed after the pure in heart. For God repeatedly said that there is no peace for the wicked.

> **"'There is no peace,' says the LORD, 'for the wicked.'"** (Isaiah 48:22)

> **"'There is no peace,'** says my God, **'for the wicked.'"** (Isaiah 57:21)

Sin first breaks your heart of peace and then breaks the peace between you and others. That is why in James he said, "But the wisdom from above is first pure, then peaceable…" (James 3:17). Thus, we must first become pure of heart. Then, we must have peace overflowing in our hearts. After this, if you make the effort to live in peace with others, I believe that you will be able to do so.

There is another reason why the peacemakers fall after the pure in heart. It is because purity and peace must go hand in hand. We must love peace and live in harmony with others. However, this is not always possible because being a peacemaker is not a one-sided deal.

Some might ask, "Didn't the Bible say to 'live peaceably with all?'" Yet, this phrase has the conditional clauses "if possible" and "on you" which restricts it (Rom. 12:18). It means that no matter how much effort we make to be at peace with another, if the opponent rejects it, it becomes impossible, and we are not at fault. Because I have personally experienced this often, I know, very well, how true it is.

Additionally, we must be wary of unjust peace. John Stott said the following.

> "Although the followers of Jesus never have the right to refuse forgiveness, let alone to take revenge, **we are not permitted to cheapen forgiveness by offering it prematurely when there has been no repentance.** 'If your brother sins,' Jesus said, 'rebuke him', and only then 'if he repents, forgive him' (Lk. 17:3).
>
> **The incentive to peace-making is love, but it degenerates into appeasement whenever justice is ignored. To forgive and to ask for forgiveness are both costly exercises. All authentic Christian peace-making exhibits the love and justice—and so the pain—of the cross."**[221]

---

[221] John R. W. Stott, *The Cross of Christ*, (Downers Grove, IL: Intervarsity Press, 2006) 289.

Pastor Dong-won Lee also said the following.

"After discussing purity, Jesus gave a teaching on peace. It is because purity is the premise for peace. The scariest enemy that breaks peace is the sin of impurity. James 3:17 says that the 'wisdom from above is first pure, then peaceable...'

Peace without purity is nothing but compromised peace that lacks truth. That is why the Bible always emphasizes purity and then mentions peace. ... [222]

The peace of a Christian is not premised with compromise. Therefore, even though we try to make peace, because we do not compromise, the world responds with persecution. Christians desire peace, yet, this peace is a pure peace based on righteousness."[223]

However, currently, false peace runs rampant in South Korea. The masses are being played by this false peace. It is not true peace. Therefore, we must pray desperately for this country. While we strive for peace on a personal level, we must also always be careful to not sacrifice our purity nor our sense of justice.

---

[222] Lee, *Be Like This*, (1995) 81.
[223] Ibid., 93.

② The Duty to Make Peace Between Other People

We must not only be at peace with other people, but must also create peace between people who have discord and animosity towards one another. We must become a peacemaker and not someone who drives a wedge between people and further fans the flames. In order to do this, we need to be careful with our words.

> "A dishonest man spreads strife, and **a whisperer separates close friends.**" (Proverbs 16:28)

> **"Whoever covers an offense seeks love, but he who repeats a matter separates close friends."** (Proverbs 17:9)

Driving a wedge between two people is easy to do. However, making peace between two people in discord is not easy. This is how John Stott described the difficulty.

> "They will be called sons (or daughters) of God. He must have meant that peace-making is such a characteristically divine activity that those who engage in it thereby disclose their identity and demonstrate their authenticity as God's children.
> **If our peace-making is to be modeled on our heavenly Fa-**

ther's, however, we will conclude at once that it is quite different from appeasement. For the peace which God secures is never cheap peace, but always costly. He is indeed the world's pre-eminent peacemaker, but when he determined on reconciliation with us, his 'enemies', who had rebelled against him, he 'made peace' through the blood of Christ's cross (Col. 1:20). To reconcile himself to us, and us to himself, and Jews, Gentiles and other hostile groups to each other, cost him nothing less than the painful shame of the cross. We have no right to expect, therefore, that we will be able to engage in conciliation work at no cost to ourselves, whether our involvement in the dispute is as the offending or offended party, or as a third party anxious to help enemies to become friends again.

What form might the cost take? Often it will begin with sustained, painstaking listening to both sides, the distress of witnessing the mutual bitterness and recriminations, the struggle to sympathize with each position, and the effort to understand the misunderstandings which have caused the communication breakdown."[224]

As such, it is not easy to create peace between two people who are in discord. It only becomes possible if you pay numer-

---

[224] John Stott, *The Cross of Christ*, (2006) 289.

ous costs for it. Even so, we need to look towards God and Jesus, who paid the greatest cost for this and be more like them. That is when we will realize that the cost we must pay is so miniscule in comparison and will easily be able to pay it.

③ The Duty to Make Peace Between God and Other People

I believe that there is a more important and deeper meaning to the "peacemakers" than just the two explanations I have already given you. And I believe this last one to be the primary meaning of this message.

I read many books in order to research The Sermon, and I discovered that only the extreme minority have the same thoughts as myself on "the peacemakers." Even these sources only lightly mentioned it in passing.

First, Pastor Dong-won Lee wrote the following.

> **"When the gospel is spread, this peace expands soundlessly on earth.** Paul said, 'How beautiful are the feet of those who preach the good news' (Rom. 10:12). He quoted the message of prophet Isaiah, and Isaiah's words are as follows.
>
> 'How beautiful upon the mountains are the feet of him who brings good news, who publishes peace, who brings good news of happiness, who publishes salvation, who says to Zion, "Your

God reigns.'"

Peace expands where the gospel is spread." [225]

Sinclair Ferguson wrote on this more clearly and superbly.

"Like the other beatitudes, this one has been wrested out of its context many times. Jesus is not speaking about the mere cessation of hostilities among the nations. He is speaking about the cessation of hostilities between the man and God. This is the peace he came to establish.

The Old Testament word for peace is shalom. It is a rich word, and conveys the idea of wholeness, health, well-being. It could almost be translated 'salvation.' Those who make peace are those who earnestly seek the shalom, the salvation, of their fellows." [226]

These are the only two books that talk about this interpretation. Very few indeed!

Then, what is the reason that I still believe this verse means the above? It is because the order of the beatitudes has a systematic and logical association with one another. Sinclair Fer-

---

[225] Lee, *Be Like This*, (1995) 89.
[226] Ferguson, *The Sermon on the Mount*, (1987) 38.

guson explained this as follows.

> "**One beatitude flows into the next, as we have already seen:** the poor in spirit mourn for their sins, and as a result are marked by the meekness of those who know the truth about themselves in the presence of God. Such men and women hunger and thirst for righteousness, and receive it. Since they have been filled only because of the Lord's mercy to them, they become merciful to others.
>
> Three further words of blessing follow—to the pure in heart, the peacemakers, and the persecuted. ... As we become pure in heart (the meaning of which we will examine more carefully), we see God. But he is the God of peace (1 Thess. 5:23; Heb. 13:20), through the blood of the Cross (Col. 1:20). To see who he is, is to have a desire to bring others into his peace. The pure in heart are, therefore, also peacemakers. But what do they discover?
>
> Like Jesus they are persecuted. Yet they can rejoice, because this numbers them with the prophets of Christ who were persecuted before them."[227]

I want to explain this to you further. After one gains righteousness by becoming poor in spirit, mournful, meek, and

---

227 Ibid., 35-6.

one who hungers and thirsts for it, a true disciple does not act like the Pharisees and despise others. Rather, because of the mercy they received, they have mercy for other sinners. While doing so, they then further enthusiastically seek after a pure heart. They do not think only about their own souls but rather think of the souls of others. They pray desperately and spread the gospel for others to be reconciled with God. While doing so, they are persecuted due to the above. It is not simply that a disciple is dumbfoundingly persecuted even while portraying the seven beatitudes like the scholars say (although there is an element of this). The disciple is persecuted because they preach the gospel.

What do you think? Is this not a more natural interpretation? Thus, it is most natural and in harmony with the flow of the beatitudes to understand the peacemakers as those who pray and evangelize to others to be reconciled with God. It is why I believe it to be the main meaning of the peacemakers.

Yet, the following question might be asked after reading my explanation thus far.

"If the peacemakers mean what you say they mean, why didn't Jesus just say, 'Those who pray for salvation and evangelize'? Why did He use the ambiguous phrase 'peacemakers?'"

The above is a question that I also wondered and was curious about. Then, I came across this answer.

> **"I still have many things to say to you, but you cannot bear them now.** When the Spirit of truth comes, he will guide you into all the truth, for he will not speak on his own authority, but whatever he hears he will speak, and he will declare to you the things that are to come. He will glorify me, for he will take what is mine and declare it to you." (John 16:12-14)

The reason, as shown in this verse, is that the crowd and even the twelve disciples could not bear it if Jesus told them directly. If we read the four gospels attentively, we would know that what the disciples could not bear to understand was the death and resurrection of Jesus. The disciples could not bear this message.

Yet, our reconciliation with God happened through the death on the cross. It would have been impossible without the blood of Jesus. The disciples however, were in a state where they could not even accept the death of Jesus. That is why I believe He expressed it with such a euphemism. Moreover, I believe that because this was the case, when the apostles were thereafter able to bear this truth, the epistles they wrote showed an alignment and harmony with the expression, "peacemakers". The next verses then show us what the most important peacemaking is in our lives.

> "**Christ Jesus, whom God put forward as a propitiation by his blood.**" (Romans 3:24b-25)

> "**For if while we were enemies we were reconciled to God by the death of his Son.**" (Romans 5:10)

> "And through him to **reconcile to himself all things**, whether on earth or in heaven, **making peace by the blood of his cross.**" (Colossians 1:20)

> "**He is the propitiation for our sins, and not for ours only but also for the sins of the whole world.**" (1 John 2:2)

The following verses show us what kind of person the "peacemaker" really is.

> "All this is from God, **who through Christ reconciled us to himself and gave us the ministry of reconciliation; that is, in Christ God was reconciling the world to himself, not counting their trespasses against them, and entrusting to us the message of reconciliation.** Therefore, we are

ambassadors for Christ, God making his appeal through us. We implore you on behalf of Christ, **be reconciled to God.**" (2 Corinthians 5:18-20)

In this sense, a beatitude person, in other words, a Christian is a peacemaker.

My fellow Christians, if not you, then who will save souls? Only those who are saved can help save others. God is alive and heaven and hell truly exist. Therefore, pray with Jesus' heart for the unsaved souls. And I hope that you will use all the methods available to help people believe in Jesus and save them.

2) The Blessing That the Peacemakers Will Receive!

We have now learned what exactly it means to be peacemakers and who they are! To continue, we want to take a look at the blessing that the Lord promised them: "For they shall be called sons of God."

Receiving salvation means becoming a son of God.

> "And **because you are sons**, God has sent the Spirit of his Son into our hearts, crying, 'Abba! Father!' So **you are no longer a slave, but a son**, and if a son, **then an heir** through God." (Galatians 4:6-7)

The son receives an inheritance.

Moreover, the Bible mentions that not only those who seek holiness, but those who seek peace with all will receive the ultimate salvation.

> **"Strive for peace with everyone, and for the holiness without which no one will see the Lord."** (Hebrews 12:14)

Therefore, "for they shall be called sons of God" means that you have been saved and will receive the ultimate salvation. Many scholars agree with this. They explain it as a salvation that has already come and a salvation not yet come.

① Those Who Are Peacemakers Are True Sons of God, Namely the Truly Saved.

Thomas Watson wrote the following on the interpretation that the promise of the Lord means a salvation that is already here.

> "If God be our Father, we are of peaceable spirits. 'Blessed are the peacemakers: for they shall be called the children of God.' Matt 5:9. Grace infuses a sweet, amicable disposition; it files off the ruggedness of men's spirits; it turns the lion-like fierceness into a lamb-like gentleness. Isa 11:7. They who have God

to be their Father follow peace as well as holiness. ... [These furies] cannot call God Father. Nor can those who are makers of division. 'Mark them which cause divisions, and avoid them.' Rom 16: 17. **Such as are born of God, are makers of peace."**[228]

Arthur Pink said the following.

"To be called so is to be esteemed and regarded as such. The Lord Himself is 'the God of peace' (Heb. xiii, 20), and where this holy disposition is manifested by His people He owns them as His children."[229]

John Stott also said the following.

"He must have meant that peace-making is such a characteristically divine activity, that those who engage in it thereby disclose their identity and demonstrate their authenticity as God's children."[230]

Lastly, Sinclair Ferguson wrote the following.

---

[228] Watson, *The Lord's Prayer*, (1960) 9.
[229] Pink, *An Exposition of the Sermon on the Mount*, (2011) 39.
[230] Stott, *The Cross of Christ*, (2006) 288.

> "They will be called the sons of God. Jesus' logic is not difficult to follow. **God is described in Scripture as the God of peace.** As such, He has made peace for us through Christ; he has reconciled us to himself (2 Cor. 5:19-21). Making peace is part of God's gracious character. **Those who have become members of his family will share in his family likeness. His sons will be peacemakers.**"[231]

As it is expressed well in these writings, "For they shall be called sons of God" is a promise that means that they are truly saved and true children of God.

② Those Who Are Peacemakers Will Receive the Ultimate Salvation and Enter Heaven.

Sinclair Ferguson wrote the following on the interpretation that the promise of the Lord means a salvation that has not yet come.

> "...to be called a son of the living God. Does this seem to be an anticlimax after the promise that we shall see God? In fact, it is a wonderful climax, for there is no higher privilege we could ever experience than this—to see God as our father...

---

[231] Ferguson, *The Sermon on the Mount*, (1987) 38.

Best of all, since sons inherit their father's riches as well as their father's characteristics, this beatitude summarises all the beatitudes."[232]

Additionally, Dr. Yong-eui Yang wrote the following.

"The New Testament suggests that Jesus was the one who fulfilled the messianic peace and provided it (Luke 2:14, 19:38; Eph. 2:14-18, etc.). If this is true, then it is quite natural for Jesus to require his disciples, who are under this messianic rule, to be peacemakers.

The apodosis promises that the disciples who 'make peace' will be given the privilege of being called 'sons of God.' The New Testament often calls God the 'God of peace' (Rom. 15:33; Phil. 4:9, etc.). Disciples who 'make peace' can be called sons of God because they resemble the character of the 'God of peace'. **The declaration of their identity as sons of God at the fulfillment of God's kingdom guarantees that they will have the most intimate fellowship with God for eternity by being fully accepted by Him (Rev. 21:7)."**[233]

In particular, Rev. Dongwon Lee's following explanation

---

[232] Ibid., 54.
[233] Yang, *How Will You Read the Book of Matthew?*, (2011) 96.

brings forth excitement in our hearts.

> "As citizens of heaven, we need peace to enter heaven, the kingdom of peace. Romans 14:17 emphasizes that the kingdom of God is the kingdom of righteousness, peace and joy. Heaven is the kingdom of righteousness and it is the kingdom of peace.
>
> One day, the prophet Isaiah saw a vision of God's kingdom.
>
> 'The wolf shall dwell with the lamb, and the leopard shall lie down with the young goat, and the calf and the lion and the fattened calf together; and a little child shall lead them... The nursing child shall play over the hole of the cobra' (Isa. 11:6-8).
>
> Imagine this scene. A scene where a wolf plays with a lamb, where a leopard lies down with a young goat. An endlessly peaceful scene where a nursing child plays over the hole of the cobra. Imagine the beautiful scene of the kingdom of God which will come when the Lord makes this earth anew. This is the very reason why the Lord demands peace in the spirit and souls of the people of God."[234]

Is it not truly spectacular? The promise "to be called the sons of God" holds the meaning that they will enter heaven and be

---

[234] Lee, *Be Like This*, (1995) 82-3.

called the sons of God and live forever in peace.

Meanwhile, I told you all that the most important meaning of the peacemakers is their interest and effort for the salvation of souls. This is a very important touchstone! For it will differentiate who is a true Christian, from who is just a nominal Christian, or even a hypocrite when it looks like they are all living the same Christian life.

I deeply resonated with the following words of Thomas Watson.

"How far are they from being God's children who have no care to bring others into the family of God!"[235]

He is right. Even if you attend church, live a long life of faith, and partake in various volunteer work, you will not know the worth of salvation if you are not truly saved. It is the very reason why they have not been saved. They have not deeply realized their sin, the need for repentance, nor the need to be born again. They do not understand how desperately they need salvation.

Can such people really be interested in the salvation of others? Can they truly worry over other souls, pray for them, make an effort to evangelize to them, and pour out their time

---

[235] Watson, *The Beatitudes*, (1971) 233.

and money? There is no way this is possible!

On the other hand, true Christians are greatly interested in the salvation of others. This is the reason that the peacemakers are a characteristic of the beatitudes, a characteristic of a true believer.

As Jesus said, "Those who are well have no need of a physician, but those who are sick" (Matt. 9:12). Therefore, the first step to salvation is to deeply realize our sins. The next, is to deeply mourn for our sins, listen to the Word with a trembling heart, desire righteousness, be pure of heart, etc., and become a saved person who has the characteristics of the beatitudes. Such a person knows how great salvation is and that it is infinitely more important than gaining the world. They not only treat their own salvation as precious but also treat the salvation of others as precious. They pray and make an effort to save others. When they think of their parents, children, relatives, friends, coworkers, and neighbors, they are most interested in their salvation. And whether they do it well or not, they strive to evangelize. This is the person who will be called a true Christian, who will receive ultimate salvation, and who will be called sons of God forever in heaven.

Let us pause and think about this. The son of God and our elder brother Jesus died on the cross to save souls. Would you then think His younger siblings and fellow sons of God would be uninterested in the salvation of souls and simply live interested in money, success, and the pleasures of the world like non-believers? That cannot be the case.

It may not be to the extent of Paul's interest, but true Christians will all have a profound interest in the salvation of souls.

> "I am speaking the truth in Christ—I am not lying; my conscience bears me witness in the Holy Spirit—that I have great sorrow and unceasing anguish in my heart. For I could wish that I myself were accursed and cut off from Christ for the sake of my brothers, my kinsmen according to the flesh." (Romans 9:1-3)

> "Brothers, my heart's desire and prayer to God for them is that they may be saved." (Romans 10:1)

Although I am not at Paul's level, I too always have in mind the salvation of my family and relatives and never stop worrying about them. I am also gravely concerned and in endless agony over the nominal Christians in the church and for the salvation of the souls of non-believers. The greatest suffering while living has been the pain I've felt worrying and praying over my family and relatives who have not been saved. This is my deepest worry and pain. If you are truly saved and a child of God, you too will have this worry and pain inside of you. Therefore, I pray you use it as a touchstone to check if you are truly saved.

Lastly, I want to conclude this chapter with the following story. I am not sure exactly when it was, but near the end of preaching one Sunday at our first service, the Holy Spirit strongly poured out the following message to me. It was not in the original manuscript, nor something I was thinking of, but the Spirit suddenly said the following.

> "The beatitudes are the characteristics of those who are saved and show who will enter heaven. Thus, the beatitudes show the interests of Jesus. It shows what Jesus was focused on. Yet, what is your focus?
>
> The people of this world focus on money, on their own happiness, and success. However, this is not Jesus' focus. Jesus focuses on the soul and on salvation! Jesus's focus is on Heaven!
>
> Jesus came on this earth as our Savior and to save souls. That is what Jesus focused on in relation to people: to save souls, to allow us eternal life, and to allow us into heaven! This is Jesus' focus of interest. And the beatitudes clearly reveal Jesus' interests, focus, and His heart."

After saying this, I said the following during our third service that same day.

"I can say this in front of God with a good conscience of my faith. My interests while being a Christian, during ministry, and while preaching, have not been in anything else but souls. My concern has always been for the salvation of souls. It has centered around bringing them to heaven. I have not been concerned with the growth of the church or receiving a lot of offerings but solely on souls. And this is why my sermons are different.

Inherently, people realize and acknowledge things that they are interested in. I think about this frequently. It is why I have said the following many times to pastors from other denominations that I have relations with.

I ask them, 'How in the world are pastors looking at the Bible? How can they be so foolish? Why are they so obtuse and ignorant?'

What I am saying is, how can they be so ignorant of the soteriology that is biblical? I believe the answer is in the fact that their interests lie elsewhere. Their concern is for church growth, a successful ministry, and even for money and honor. If their interests lied with souls, they would see the Word that these souls need. If their focus was on salvation and heaven, when they look at the Bible, they would see correct soteriology that leads people to heaven.

Why can these pastors not see what I was able to see when reading the Bible in elementary school? Why do senior pastors still not see what I saw as a kid? It is because their concern is on other things. It happens because, although they might be sincere and good people, they are still only focused on their ministry without any real concern for souls, salvation, nor in bringing people to heaven.

However, my concerns are different. I have no desire to become a pastor of a megachurch, become president of committees, or the chairman of the Christian Council of Korea. I am not concerned with such things. Actually, in the past, there were forces that tried to make me the chairman of the Christian Council of Korea. If I had made up my mind to do so, even if it did not happen right away, it could have happened in the next couple of years. Yet, when these people tried to stir me up, I strongly declined. They asked me several times, and each time I declined them.

For I am not focused on such things. My interests lie in keeping my salvation and entering heaven, no matter what. This truly is my main concern, even when I look at others.

Let me ask you, what are you concerned with when thinking of your parents? I am concerned with my parents' salvation. When you look at your children, what are you concerned with? I am concerned with my children's salvation. And when looking at my siblings and relatives I am also concerned with their salvation. When I look at the Christian sphere, my concern is for the salvation of countless pastors and believers in the Korean Church. When I look at our nation, my concern is for the salvation of our people. For what is more precious than the world is a soul and because, most of all, hell truly exists.

I believe it is the grace of God that Jesus' main focus has become mine as well, and it is why I am thankful. Your focus, too, needs to be on the souls: on your own soul, the souls of your family members, your friends, your neighbors, and on the souls of this generation.

I am sure you are all frustrated because the COVID-19 pandemic is not quickly ending. You cannot go to restaurants or travel, and it is suffocating. I feel the same way. However, what is most regrettable and frustrates me the most is that we are unable to go on our Africa missions because of this. There are so many souls that could be saved through the missions, so many pastors and churches that could be awakened. It is most regrettable that this has been suspended and thus I pray daily.

'For COVID-19 to end..., for our Africa missions to start again..., to be able to save countless souls..., and for the great revival and great harvest to occur in Africa...'

Take heed of my words. If your interests do not lie in the salvation of souls, it will be hard to become a true Christian. Your interests must align with Jesus'. Your focus needs to align with Jesus'. What you value as most important must align with Jesus'. That is how your values will change, how you will change, and how your life goals will change.

Do you know why many pastors become corrupt when their church grows larger? It is because their focus is different from Jesus' focus. Their interests are different and what they value as most important is different. Believers are not an exception to this. Therefore, unless your interests and focus change, you will not be safe.

Thus, let us pray for such a change.

'Lord, we want Your interests to become our interests. We want Your focus to be our focus. We want to acknowledge the beatitudes as the true blessings like You have done and to desire them, to ask for them, and to seek after them. And we want to pray, not only for ourselves, but that others will also become beatitude people. We want to pray for this and rend our hearts to spread the real truth to them!'"

8. AM I ONE WHO IS PERSECUTED FOR RIGHTEOUSNESS?

"Blessed are those who are persecuted for righteousness' sake, for theirs is the kingdom of heaven. Blessed are you when others revile you and persecute you and utter all kinds of evil against you falsely on my account. Rejoice and be glad, for your reward is great in heaven, for so they persecuted the prophets who were before you." (Matthew 5:10-12)

If you look in the book *The Harvest*, it says the following prophecy about South Korea.

"There will be many changes in communism, and the world will have a brief respite from the unrelenting assault of the red tide. It will then make some further significant advances. South Korea, the Philippines, South and Central America (including Mexico, and most of Africa) will ultimately be swept up by it. This will be such a changed form of communism that communism will not really be an appropriate word for it, but it will be economic and political totalitarianism. ...

In some of the countries taken by the communists there will be an attempt to completely wipe out Christianity as well as other religions. At the same time, in some communist countries religious tolerance will increase but seldom to the degree that it could be considered true religious freedom. In the nations that remain 'free' or democratic, religious intolerance will increase until believers will be in some degree of danger in every nation on earth. ...

The most severe persecution against believers will come in countries which now enjoy religious freedom. A number of these governments will have aligned themselves with the false church. This false church will have allegiance and authority over most of the populations of what is left of the 'free world.' This church will incite governments and populations against all Christians who do not submit to its authority."[236]

This book was published in America in 1997. It was before Kim Dae-jung's administration came into power and if we had left North Korea as is, they would have self-destructed. The failure of communism was so clear, and it was the opportune

---

[236] Rick Joyner, *The Harvest*, (Charlotte, NC: Morningstar Publications, 1989) 153-4.

time for the North Koreans to be freed. Therefore, it seemed like the chances of this prophecy coming true were nonexistent and it was dumbfounding.

Yet, as time passed, it truly seemed like this prophecy would come true as our government started leaning to the left. Then, the leftist party actually took a hold of the government. Due to this, many were deeply worried over the possibility of the country becoming communized if things continued at this rate.

Yet, I would like to note that Pastor Bob Jones did not agree with the aforementioned prophecy when he was still alive. When I was invited to Pastor Bobby Conner's home, and I asked about this prophecy, he also adamantly replied that Pastor Rick Joyner was mistaken. And Pastor Ok-kyung Kim, who I trust in far more than the above pastors, continues to receive the word that our country will never be communized. Currently, I am holding on to this answer and praying for our country.

Even though this is the case, we cannot completely ignore the prophecy that I introduced.

> "In some communist countries religious tolerance will increase but seldom to the degree that it could be considered true religious freedom. In the nations that remain 'free' or democratic, **religious intolerance will increase until believers will be in**

some degree of danger in every nation on earth."[237]

The reason for this is due to the following prophecy of Jesus.

"Then they will deliver you up to tribulation and put you to death, and **you will be hated by all nations for my name's sake**." (Matthew 24:9)

Therefore, persecution is not completely irrelevant for us who are living in these end times. We must always be ready to respond to tribulations. Because of this, I believe that this eighth beatitude is a message we all truly need.

1) The Cowardly Cannot Enter the Kingdom of Heaven!

Some people might ask, "I have never heard of that before. Where in the Bible does it say this?" However, it is a clear biblical truth.

First, it is recorded in the beatitudes.

"Blessed are those who are persecuted for righteousness' sake, for theirs is the kingdom of heaven." (Matthew 5:10)

---

[237] Ibid.

In reverse, this verse means that those who avoid persecution, by cowardly submitting, cannot receive the inheritance of heaven. In other words, those who are cowardly cannot enter the kingdom of heaven.

Moreover, it is shown in the cost that the disciple must pay.

> "Now great crowds accompanied him, and he turned and said to them, **'If anyone comes to me and does not hate his own father and mother and wife and children and brothers and sisters, yes, and even his own life, he cannot be my disciple. Whoever does not bear his own cross and come after me cannot be my disciple.'"** (Luke 14:25-27)

We can clearly see in this passage as well that the cowardly cannot enter heaven. For, at times, unless we pay the cost through persecution, we cannot be a true disciple, i.e. a true Christian.

Additionally, it is also shown in Hebrews.

> "'For, yet a little while, and the coming one will come and will not delay; but my righteous one shall live by faith, **and if he shrinks back, my soul has no pleasure in him.' But we are not of those who shrink back and are destroyed**, but of those who have faith and preserve their souls." (Hebrews 10:37-39)

The author of Hebrews is warning us of the danger of apostasy that comes from persecution. In other words, if you shrink back because you are afraid of persecution, you will be destroyed. In order to not shrink back, we must be brave. It is just like the hymn that says, "Then it is the brave man [who] chooses while the coward stands aside." That is why the following is recorded in Hebrews 10:35.

> "Therefore do not throw away your **confidence**, which has a great reward."

The "great reward" here is talking about our ultimate salvation. Therefore, this verse also shows us that the cowardly cannot enter heaven.

Lastly, it is shown very clearly in Revelation.

> "**But the fearful**, and unbelieving, and the abominable, and murderers, and whoremongers, and sorcerers, and idolaters, and all liars, **shall have their part in the lake which burneth with fire and brimstone: which is the second death.**" (Revelation 21:8, KJV)

This is a spiritual hit list of all those who will be thrown into hell. They are the opposite of the overcomers. Yet, we see "the fearful" at the very front of this list. Who might they be?

The book of Revelation deals with the Great Tribulation, which is an unprecedentedly great persecution in all the history of mankind. "The fearful" are those who deny the Lord in fear of persecution. They are the complete opposite of the people in Revelation 12:11.

> **"And they have conquered him by the blood of the Lamb and by the word of their testimony, for they loved not their lives even unto death."**

As John recorded, "the fearful" cannot enter heaven. They will be thrown in the fires of hell, which is the second death.

However, do you know what other translations have translated "the fearful" as? The ESV, NASB, and NRSV all translated them as "the cowardly". So, is it true or false that the cowardly cannot enter heaven? It is thoroughly true!

With this in mind, let us take a look at the Christian sphere in Korea. You will be flabbergasted. Most of the pastors, media, and denominations are acting like cowardly mutes in order to avoid any persecution. Inside the church, they cower in front of the unjust heresy hunters and the tyranny of large denominations. Outside the church, almost all of them cower in front of our government that tries to rearrange anti-discriminatory laws, which are anti-Christian in nature. We have seen this happening for a very long time. And when you see one, you can see the rest as well. I question whether these cowardly people will be able to keep their faith when they face persecution that requires their own lives to be on the line. I believe they will not be able to keep their faith.

Meanwhile, while reading Thomas Watson's book, I saw the interesting phrase, "Our sufferings are light. This 'light affliction …' (2 Corinthians 4:17)." He made the paradoxical assertion that the persecution we receive is light for the following reason.

> "Our sufferings are light. This 'light affliction …' (2 Corinthians 4:17)!
>
> Affliction is light in comparison of hell. What is persecution to damnation? What is the fire of martyrdom to the fire of the damned? It is no more than the pricking of a pin to a death's wound. … Affliction is light in comparison of glory. The weight of glory makes persecution light. … And if persecution be light we should in a manner set light by it. Let us neither faint through unbelief, nor fret through impatience."[238]

---

[238] Watson, *The Beatitudes*, (1971) 292.

This is correct! Jesus said the following about the former point.

> "I tell you, my friends, do not fear those who kill the body, and after that have nothing more that they can do. But I will warn you whom to fear: fear him who, after he has killed, has authority to cast into hell. Yes, I tell you, fear him!" (Luke 12:4-5)

Paul wrote the following about the latter.

> "And if children, then heirs—heirs of God and fellow heirs with Christ, provided we suffer with him in order that we may also be glorified with him. **For I consider that the sufferings of this present time are not worth comparing with the glory that is to be revealed to us.**" (Romans 8:17-18)

Therefore, this interpretation is correct! We must all remember this and not become the cowardly. We must certainly not cowardly compromise, nor cowardly commit apostasy towards the Lord. We must also not, in fear of being misunderstood, cowardly go to a different church nor stop from registering. In all aspects, do not become the cowardly and instead become a brave person, befitting a believer.

2) Not All Who Are Persecuted Are Blessed!

For not all persecution is the persecution that Jesus spoke of.

"If I give away all I have, and if I deliver up my body to be burned, but have not love, I gain nothing." (1 Corinthians 13:3)

Pastor Dong-won Lee said the following.

"**What is not persecution?**

Christians can suffer difficulty or trouble as a consequence of handling something wrong. In this case, it is not persecution. It is punishment. One preacher interestingly contrasted the concept of persecution with the concept of punishment as follows.

'**Persecution is received from a bad person for doing something good. Punishment is received from a good person for doing something bad.**' We often try to regard the punishment we are receiving as persecution instead.

Firstly, any difficulty we are facing due to our mistakes is not persecution. In such an event as this, there will never be a reward from God. 'For what credit is it if, when you sin and are beaten for it, you endure?' (1 Pet. 2:20). Then, it says in 1 Peter 4:15, 'But let none of you suffer as a murderer or a thief or an evildoer or as a meddler.' In such a case like the above, where you are faced with difficulty by meddling in others' business or committing sins, it is not persecution.

Secondly, trouble due to a Christians' ignorant evangelism methods or fanatic acts is not persecution either. When Jesus sent the disciples out to evangelize, He taught, 'Behold, I am sending you out as sheep in the midst of wolves, so be wise as serpents and innocent as doves' (Matt. 10:16). Thus, we cannot think that the difficulty we experience from using wrong evangelism methods, due to lack of wisdom, is necessarily persecution."[239]

Therefore, not all persecution qualifies as the persecution that Jesus spoke of, and not all who receive persecution will be blessed. Only those who receive persecution for righteousness' sake will be blessed.

"Blessed are those who are persecuted for righteousness' sake, for theirs is the kingdom of heaven." (Matthew 5:10)

The Bible also says the following.

"An unjust man is an abomination to the righteous, but **one**

---

[239] Lee, *Be Like This*, (1995) 93–4.

whose way is straight is an abomination to the wicked." (Proverbs 29:27)

"We should not be like Cain, who was of the evil one and murdered his brother. And why did he murder him? Because his own deeds were evil and **his brother's righteous.**" (1 John 3:12)

"Indeed, all who desire to live a **godly** life in Christ Jesus will be **persecuted.**" (2 Timothy 3:12)

We must, like the people above, be persecuted for righteousness and not for our sins. Arthur Pink said the following significant words.

> **"This searching word 'for righteousness' sake' calls upon us to honestly examine ourselves before God when we are being opposed."**[240]

It is a critical comment. When we receive persecution, we need to stop immediately thinking that we are receiving it due to righteousness. We must, instead, humbly reflect upon ourselves.

---

[240] Pink, *An Exposition of the Sermon on the Mount*, (2011) 40.

Then, what should we examine ourselves with? It is with "righteousness!"

We must be aware of the fact that persecution is in the final beatitude. And what is important is not persecution, but righteousness. We must become one who is persecuted for righteousness' sake.

If so, then what is "righteousness?" Righteousness not only means the righteousness we hunger and thirst for and to be pure of heart, but it also holds an intimate relationship with all of the beatitudes. For we become righteous through all of the former seven beatitudes. Therefore, we must examine ourselves, with the seven beatitudes that come before the eighth, as touchstones.

There is a song by Young-nam Cho called, "The Third Daughter of Mr. Choi's Family."

"In a village nearby, Mr. Choi has three daughters.
Among them, the third one is the prettiest.
Rumor has it, their dad is fiercer than a tiger.
No guy has ever had a chance to see her face properly. …

But I opened the door wide and ran into the house.
And told him, 'Here I am, and I'm exceptional son-in-law material,'

Kneeling and bowing down to the man.

Mr. Choi was pleased and chuckled a hearty laugh. …

Hooray! How marvelous! Happy am I!

I became the fierce tiger Mr. Choi's son-in-law and got a beautiful bride.

Any man who sees me will make fun of me, saying, 'You got one out of seven blessings'.

They will make fun of me, they will make fun of me."

The important part is the final stanza.

"Any man who sees me will make fun of me, saying, 'You got one out of seven blessings.'"

Like the above, you might only get one out of the seven worldly blessings. However, the beatitudes are blessings you receive as a set. You either receive it all or nothing. A person will never enter heaven nor receive a great reward, even after being persecuted, if they are indifferent to the first seven beatitudes. Therefore, do not rest assured just because you are being persecuted. Instead, sincerely examine yourselves to see if you are being persecuted as the righteous one who has the first to seventh beatitudes. This is why I resonate with Peter's words.

"But let none of you suffer as a murderer or a thief or an evildoer or as a meddler. Yet **if anyone suffers as a Christian**, let him not be ashamed, but let him glorify God in that name." (1 Peter 4:15-16)

Peter says to not suffer as a murderer, thief, evildoer, or as a meddler, but to suffer as a Christian. A Christian is a beatitude person. Thus, I have understood this phrase, "to suffer as a Christian" to mean, "to suffer as a beatitude person." You all must first, become one who receives the first to seventh beatitudes. So, I pray that when you receive persecution, you will be blessed to receive it as a beatitude person.

3) Torture and Murder Are Not the Only Forms of Persecution!

When people think of the word "persecution," they think of torture or martyrdom, which are all physical actions. However, this is not the only means of persecution. There is also persecution through words.

"Blessed are you when others **revile you** and **persecute you and utter all kinds of evil against you falsely** on my account." (Matthew 5:11)

Dr. Yong-eui Yang said the following about this verse.

"This paragraph reveals the type of **persecution that the disciples received on earth to include, not just physical harm, but also verbal harm** (v.11)."[241]

Therefore, it is not just Emperor Nero, Japan during the Japanese colonial period, or Kim Il-Sung and his successors that are persecutors. The scope of a persecutor is far wider than that. What I am saying is that a pastor or a Christian might not actually be on the receiving end of persecution. They might be the very people who are persecuting others with their words.

Thomas Watson said the following on the topic of "several kinds of persecution."

"What are the several kinds of persecution? There is a two-fold persecution; **a persecution of the hand; a persecution of the tongue.**

1 **A persecution of the hand.**

'Which of the prophets have not your fathers persecuted?' (Acts 7:52). 'For thy sake we are killed all the day long' (Romans 8:36; Galatians 4:29). This I call a bloody persecution,

---

[241] Yang, *How Will You Read the Book of Matthew?*, (2011) 97–8.

when the people of God are persecuted with fire and sword. So we read of the ten persecutions in the time of Nero, Domitian, Trajan etc.; and of the Marian persecution. ... [many] have been scourged to death with the rod of the persecutor. ...

2 The persecution of the tongue...

(i) Reviling. This few think of or lay to heart, but it is called in the text, persecution. 'When men shall revile you and persecute you'. This is tongue persecution.

'His words were drawn swords' (Psalm 55:21). You may kill a man as well in his name as in his person. A good name is as 'precious ointment' (Ecclesiastes 7:1). ... Now to smite another by his name is by our Saviour called persecution. Thus the primitive Christians endured the persecution of the tongue. 'They had trial of cruel mockings' (Hebrews 11:36). David was 'the song of the drunkards' (Psalm 69:12). They would sit on their ale-bench and jeer at him. How frequently do the wicked cast out the squibs of reproach at God's children:

(ii) Slandering. So it is in the text: 'When they shall persecute you and say all manner of evil against you falsely'. Slandering is tongue persecution. Thus Saint Paul was slandered in his doctrine. Report had it that he preached, 'Men might do evil that good might come of it' (Romans 3:8). Thus Christ who cast out devils was charged to have a devil (John 8:48). The primitive Christians were falsely accused for killing their children and for incest. 'They laid to my charge things that I knew not' (Psalm 35:11)

Let us take heed of becoming persecutors. Some think there is no persecution but fire and sword. Yes, there is persecution of the tongue."[242]

Additionally, Frederick Price wrote the following on persecution of the tongue.

"We have this idea that persecution means you are going to be burned at the stake, put in a vat of oil like John, or have pitch put all over you and set on fire like they did the Christians during the days of the Roman emperor Nero.

That is not the only kind of persecution. Persecution can come from people talking and wagging their tongues about you. And it never stops.

I don't care how high up the ladder you get or how spiritual you become, people are going to talk about you. It is really not people; it is the devil. But the devil always has some person who is sitting around waiting to use his or her mouth to spew out a lot of garbage that is directed at the minister of God.

The person may not even know you, but he will criticize you.

---

[242] Watson, *The Beatitudes*, (1971) 260-1.

> You know that has to be a fool talking. ...
>
> People will talk about you, write books about you, use your name in print, and get on television and talk about you by name."[243]

You all may already know, but I have grown quite accustomed to receiving this type of persecution. Thus, I know a great deal about it. This type of persecution usually has a deep relationship with lies.

There is a Korean saying that says, "There's no smoke without fire." But according to the Bible, there is. There truly is smoke without any fire. Because of this, John Wesley wrote the following.

> "O you fools, did you suppose the devil was dead? Or that he would not fight for his kingdom? And what weapons will he fight with, if not with lies? Is he not a liar, and the father of lies?"[244]

Even today, Satan continues, without any rest, to create lies through his people. Therefore, we must not believe the rumors

---

[243] Frederick C. Price, *Practical Suggestions for Successful Ministry*, (Lake Mary, FL: Creation House, 2016) 27.

[244] John Wesley, *The Essential Works of John Wesley*, (Uhrichsville, Ohio: Barbour Publishing, 2011) 961.

we hear, news articles we read, decisions of denominations, or even TV broadcastings without checking the facts ourselves.

There was a time after reading the Bible that my heart grew heavy. It was when the High Priest and the scribes sent spies to Jesus and made them ask Him this question.

> "Is it lawful for us to give tribute to Caesar, or not?" (Luke 20:22)

Jesus saw through them and wisely said to them, "Then render to Caesar the things that are Caesar's, and to God the things that are God's" (Luke 20:25). Yet, do you know what they said when they brought Jesus in front of Pilate?

> "We found this man misleading our nation and **forbidding us to give tribute to Caesar**, and saying that he himself is Christ, a king." (Luke 23:2)

These are not your average believers but the religious leaders. How could they decide to say these clearly blatant lies? It's unbelievable! Yet, this is what is extensively happening inside churches today. I have received this type of slander countless times and continue to currently receive them. It's hard to list all the unjust decisions and wicked reports from the lies, perversions, and manipulations of the denominations, the false articles written by heresy hunters and greedy reporters, online posts and videos that slander us, and the books and false broadcasts that target me. I even spoke in front of the media at a press release, right before the Christian Council of Korea was about to announce their decision that I am not a heretic, but was wrongfully slandered. I said to them, "**This case against me and my church is not a problem of heresy but rather a problem of truth and lies.**"[245]

Meanwhile, those who receive persecution through the pen and through words actually experience severe pain.

"There is one whose **rash words are like sword thrusts**, but the tongue of the wise brings healing." (Proverbs 12:18)

Brother Yun also talked of this persecution and said, "This new kind of spiritual persecution was no easier than physical persecution in China, just different."[246]

Persecution with words also brings about severe pain. Many times, I truly felt torment and pain, like my heart was pierced by a sword, because of the blatant lies and slander against me. But what is more severe is that not only does this type of per-

---

[245] http://cafe.daum.net/Bigchurch/I1S/5806
[246] Brother Yun and Paul Hathaway, *The Heavenly Man*, (Grand Rapids, MI: Monarch Books, 2002) 309.

secution bring about great hurt for the victim, as Arthur Pink said, it works "to destroy the usefulness of God's ministers."[247] This fact pains me seven times more than the pain that I felt personally, and it terribly grieves me.

The Nestorians (they too were Christians) in 1305, violently attacked John of Montecorvino in Beijing. John had baptized more than 6000 people the previous year before this attack. But the Nestorians, out of jealousy, called him "a spy, magician, and a trickster." John later wrote, *"If not for all the slanders I should have baptized more than 30,000."*[248]

I, too, can confidently say the same. If our church was not falsely slandered by the denominations and pastors, then we would have saved ten times as much, if not a hundred times more souls. Not only this, but we would also have transformed churches in South Korea and all around the world.

Beloved, do you still think that God will not judge them for their sins on judgment day? The Bible clearly warns us of the following.

> "But as for the cowardly, the faithless, the detestable, as for murderers, the sexually immoral, sorcerers, idolaters, and **all**

---

[247] Pink, *An Exposition of the Sermon on the Mount*, (2011) 40.
[248] "Medieval Sourcebook: John of Monte Corvino: Report from China 1305." Internet History Sourcebooks Project: Ancient History, https://sourcebooks.fordham.edu/source/corvino1.asp.

liars, their portion will be in the lake that burns with fire and sulfur, which is the second death." (Revelation 21:8)

"**Outside** are the dogs and sorcerers and the sexually immoral and murderers and idolaters, and **everyone who loves and practices falsehood**." (Revelation 22:15)

Therefore, those who do not repent the sin of slandering through lies will not be able to escape hell.

Just because you do not torture or murder someone does not mean you are not a persecutor. There are few in the church who are persecuted for righteousness' sake. Yet, there are so many who persecute others through lies and falsehoods. If they do not repent, they will not be able to escape God's judgment. Therefore, I pray that they will quickly repent and right all the wrongs they have made.

4) The Tragedy of Spiritual Fratricide Is Still Happening Today!

One morning, I woke up and immediately thought of Matthew 5:10-12. I focused my interest on the section, "**For so they persecuted the prophets who were before you**." Then, I had the following thought.

"The prophets were persecuted in this manner? Who persecuted the prophets? It was not the heathens but rather the believers in the Old Testament. It was the Israelites! If this is true, then it also holds the meaning that the believers in this verse also persecuted fellow believers!"

Yes. The ones who persecuted the Old Testament prophets were not the heathens. It was the Israelites who believed in God. Stephen said the following.

"You stiff-necked people, uncircumcised in heart and ears, you **always** resist the Holy Spirit. As your fathers did, so do you. **Which of the prophets did your fathers not persecute?** And they killed those who announced beforehand the coming of the Righteous One, whom you have now betrayed and murdered." (Acts 7:51-52)

Additionally, Jesus said this.

"**If the world hates you, know that it has hated me before it hated you.** If you were of the world, the world would love you as its own; but because you are not of the world, but I chose you out of the world, therefore the world hates you. Remember the word that I said to you: 'A servant is not greater than his master.' **If they persecuted me, they will also persecute you.** If they kept my word, they will also keep yours." (John 15:18-20)

The "world" (v.18) persecutes the believers. Yet, the world first hated Jesus and persecuted Him. Because of this, Jesus in verse 20 said, "If they persecuted me." Who is the "world," and who are the "people" who persecuted Jesus? They are not unbelievers. They are the High Priest, elders, scribes, and Pharisees. In other words, they were those who believed in God. Surprisingly, these people are the "world." Today, there are so many pastors and believers inside the church who are like this. We cannot help but call them the "world." In the next chapter, Jesus also said the following.

> "I have said all these things to you to keep you from falling away. **They will put you out of the synagogues. Indeed, the hour is coming when whoever kills you will think he is offering service to God.**" (John 16:1-2)

Like so, the ones who persecuted Jesus and the apostles were not nonbelievers but those who believed in God. Even during the Old Testament era, the time of Jesus, and the time of the Apostles, Judaism continued to persecute the people of God that He used. And when we look through church history, we see that not only Judaism, but Christianity also participated in the same evil acts. And they are still continuing the same wicked acts today. The Korean Church is at the forefront of this. Truly, it is something to be appalled at.

John Stott, who is applauded as the one of the greatest evangelical theologians in the 21st century, wrote the following in *Authentic Christianity*.

> "**The persecution of the true church, of Christian believers who trace their spiritual descent from Abraham, is not always by the world, who are strangers unrelated to us, but by our half brothers, religious people, the nominal church. It has always been so.** The Lord Jesus was bitterly opposed, rejected, mocked, and condemned by his own nation. The fiercest opponents of the apostle Paul, who dogged his footsteps and stirred up strife against him, were the official church, the Jews. **The monolithic structure of the medieval papacy persecuted all Protestant minorities with ruthless, unremitting ferocity. And the greatest enemies of the evangelical faith today are not unbelievers, who when they hear the gospel often embrace it, but the church, the establishment, the hierarchy.**"[249]

---

[249] John Stott, *Authentic Christianity*, (Downers Grove, IL: InterVarsity Press 1996) 310.

It is almost difficult to believe that these are the words of John Stott! It is surprising that he said this at all.

If this is so, why did he say this? It's simple. This is the truth shown in the Bible and moreover, it is the undeniable reality. Long before Stott, Arthur Pink said a similar critique.

> "The words of Christ in John 15 have never been repealed: 'If ye were of the world, the world would love his own; but because ye are not of the world, but I have chosen you out of the world, therefore the world hateth you. Remember the word that I said unto you, The servant is not greater than his Lord. If they have persecuted Me, they will also persecute you; if they have kept My saying, they will keep yours also' (vv. 19 and 20). **Let it be carefully noted that it was the professing and not the profane "world" that Christ was alluding to**: it was from religious leaders, those making the greatest spiritual pretensions, that the Redeemer Himself received the worst treatment. **And so it is now: members and officers of the 'churches' stoop to methods and use means of opposition which those outside would scorn to employ.**"[250]

This is really true! And there is a shocking vision that clearly

---

250 Pink, *An Exposition of the Sermon on the Mount*, (2011) 41-2.

exposes this reality of the church.

"The demonic army was so large that it stretched as far as I could see. It was separated into divisions, with each carrying a different banner. The foremost divisions marched under the banners of **Pride**, Self righteousness, Respectability, Selfish Ambition, **Unrighteous Judgment**, and **Jealousy**.

There were many more of these evil divisions beyond my scope of vision, but those in the vanguard of this terrible horde from hell seemed to be the most powerful. The leader of this army was the Accuser of the Brethren himself. The weapons carried by this horde were also named.

The swords were named Intimidation; the spears were named Treachery; and the arrows were named Accusations, Gossip, Slander and Faultfinding. Scouts and smaller companies of demons with such names as **Rejection, Bitterness,** Impatience, **Unforgiveness** and Lust were sent in advance of this army to prepare for the main attack. ...

The most shocking part of this vision was that this horde was not riding on horses, but primarily on Christians! Most of them were well-dressed, respectable, and had the appearance of being refined and educated, but there also seemed to be representatives from almost every walk of life. ...

Many of these believers were host to more than one demon, but one of the demons would clearly be in charge. ... As I looked far to the rear of this army, I saw the entourage of the Accuser himself... **almost everyone in the forward divisions was a Christian, or at least a professing Christian. Every step these deceived believers took in obedience to the Accuser strengthened his power over them.**"[251]

I do not believe in Rick Joyner's vision as is, but I think it can be used as a reference. Still, this vision, at any rate, shows us an accurate depiction of our reality.

The church is a gathering of those who love one another. For the sign of the disciple, i.e. the Christian, is love.

> "A **new commandment** I give to you, that you love one another: just as I have loved you, you also are to love one another. **By this all people will know that you are my disciples, if you have love for one another.**" (John 13:34-35)

Therefore, it does not match the church at all to envy, distort, or lie to slander someone. Nevertheless, many modern-day churches, especially Korean churches, do this frequently.

I believe Brother Yun, who is a leader of the underground

---

[251] Rick Joyner, *The Final Quest*, (Fort Mill, SC: MorningStar Publications, 1996) 19-22.

churches in China, and I am clear evidence of this. Brother Yun, while evangelizing the gospel in communist China, was captured and tortured extensively. He was beaten near death, electrocuted by putting an electric baton in his mouth, used as a human toilet, and he even fainted after feeling the pain of having needles pushed underneath his fingernails. He also had metal pipes hit and break his two legs to the point where the bones were shattered completely.

It is famously known that he fasted for 74 days while in prison. But do you know why he fasted? In his book, *Living Water*, he confessed how the torture in prison was so painful that he believed it would be better to starve and die than live. Yet, he did not die and through a miracle, he was able to walk on his two legs out of the prison doors. Afterwards, he escaped to freedom.

Now free, Brother Yun and everyone else believed that the infernal persecution was finally over. However, it was not the end. It was no longer the Chinese government, but now the United States and the free churches that started to persecute him. In 2000 in California, one Christian reporter wrote a slanderous article against him. That article spread instantly around the world. Brother Yun greatly suffered due to this, and he wrote about that pain in his book.

"When I heard these words my heart was pierced with grief. ... Over the next few days our whole Canadian trip was thrown into jeopardy, as Christian leaders read the article and considered canceling our meetings.

Within twenty-four hours, various Chinese house church leaders, including all the elders of the Sinim Fellowship, were notified of the situation. Signed statements from well-known leaders such as Xu Yongze and Zhang Rongliang were faxed out of China, stating that these accusations were completely groundless, and confirming that I was an elder and authorized representative of the Sinim Fellowship.

In the days after this attack, which appears to have been carefully timed to coincide with the start of our Canadian preaching trip, **I struggled with this new form of persecution.**

In China I had been used to beatings, torture with electric batons, and all kinds of humiliation. I guess that deep in my heart I had presumed that now I was in the West my days of persecution had ended. I couldn't understand how someone who had never met me could write such a nasty article. I complained to my Christian friends,

'Why don't these people call us and read the documents? I don't understand! Why don't they find the truth out for themselves? It's right here for them to see!'

My translator told me,

'Brother Yun, these people don't want to know the truth. That's why they're not calling you or wanting to meet you. In China, Christians are persecuted with beatings and imprisonment. In the West, Christians are persecuted by the words of other Christians.'

This new kind of spiritual persecution was no easier than physical persecution in China, just different. I cried out in prayer, asking the Lord for his strength."[252]

Unfortunately, like the above, in the West and in South Korea as well, the church frequently persecutes the church.

Paul Hathaway, who is the co-author of Brother Yun's *The Heavenly Man*, compares this tragedy to "friendly fire."

"In recent years soldiers fighting in Iraq have used a new expression to describe the very worst kind of way to die or be injured in battle. They explain that if they were killed or wounded by an enemy bullet they would consider it a great honor, but the worst insult they could experience is to be wounded by **'friendly fire'**. It is a terrible feeling to be shot by fellow soldiers whom you thought were on the same side!

Unfortunately, and tragically, 'friendly fire' is alive and well

---

[252] Yun, *The Heavenly Man*, (2002) 307-9.

among God's people today. ... to come under fire from fellow Christians, who are meant to be fighting on your side, is a miserable and terrible thing to have to cope with. ...

How sad and grievous this is to the Holy Spirit! Although the term 'friendly fire' may be relatively new, sadly it has been practiced among believers since the Church was birthed in the Book of Acts. All throughout Christian history we can find God's revival fires being quenched by church leaders, many of whom did so out of ignorance and zeal to 'protect' the Gospel. More often than not, however, they were persecuting that which they didn't understand.

Many of the great Christian leaders throughout history have been the subject of brutal attacks from other Christians. ...

During the Welsh Revival of the early 1900s God used a young man named Evan Roberts as the main instrument of blessing to a dry and thirsty nation. Most Welsh clergy of the day, however, strongly opposed Roberts' ministry, fearing the influence he would have on 'their' congregations. Several full page advertisements were taken out by Welsh pastors in the newspapers of the day, denouncing Evan Roberts as a heretic and swindler. Dozens of pastors put their signature to the slanderous attacks. ... The same can be said of revivalists like Charles Finney and D.L. Moody, who were also strongly denounced by other Christian leaders.

Even Billy Graham has been strongly attacked throughout the years of his faithful ministry for his Lord. His autobiography records how a series of early meetings in England met with tremendous opposition from the churches, who opposed him and did all they could to send the evangelist back to America. A friend of mine who attended a Billy Graham crusade in the United States several years ago told me of his astonishment when he saw a group of Christians protesting outside the stadium, holding up signs saying things like, 'Don't listen to this man. His teaching will send you to hell!'" [253]

What is more dumbfounding is the fact that although this happens on accident in battle, it happens intentionally in the church. I believe that the occupational heresy hunters who purposefully do this and the professors and pastors who stand on the sidelines will be thrown into hell. For as Jesus said, heaven is somewhere those who are persecuted for righteousness' sake enter. It is not a place that persecutors can enter. Thus, I desperately wish that they would fear God and repent.

5) Blessed Are Those Who Are Persecuted, but Woe to Those Who Persecute Others!

---

[253] Paul Hathaway, "Open Letter Regarding 'The Heavenly Man.'" https://asiaharvest.org/open-letter-heavenly-man.

Jesus said that those who are persecuted for righteousness' sake are blessed. Then, what will happen to those who persecute others? Wrath (i.e. a curse) will fall upon them. This is shown through the context of the main passage and through the following verse.

> "Since indeed **God considers it just to repay with affliction those who afflict you**, and to grant relief to you who are afflicted as well as to us." (2 Thessalonians 1:6-7)

Therefore, it would be better to receive persecution over ever being the persecutor.

However, in order to not become a persecutor, we must first let go of jealousy. Behind every believer who persecutes another believer is jealousy. Why did the High Priest and Pharisees persecute Jesus? It was out of envy.

> "For he knew that it was out of **envy** that they had delivered him up." (Matthew 27:18)

> "For he perceived that it was out of **envy** that the chief priests had delivered him up." (Mark 15:10)

Additionally, why did they persecute the 12 apostles and

Paul? It was also out of jealousy.

> "But the high priest rose up, and all who were with him (that is, the party of the Sadducees), and **filled with jealousy**." (Acts 5:17)

> "But when the Jews saw the crowds, they were **filled with jealousy** and began to contradict what was spoken by Paul, reviling him." (Acts 13:45)

> "But the Jews were **jealous**, and taking some wicked men of the rabble, they formed a mob, set the city in an uproar, and attacked the house of Jason, seeking to bring them out to the crowd." (Acts 17:5)

In the same way, jealousy is the main cause of persecution today. That is why most heresy claims are against churches that are growing exponentially.

If we had been protected by our denomination when our church was part of the Presbyterian Church in Korea (Baek-Seok), everything would have been resolved then and there. However, when a choir member of the biggest church in that denomination moved to our church, Pastor Yang vengefully requested the committee to label our church as heretical. Even though the report of the professors who researched our church came back as there being nothing unbiblical in our doctrine, he took reigns at the General Assembly to illegally excommunicate me. And the Ulsan Polity that our church was a part of did nothing to protect me from this because of the jealousy of Pastor Kim (who was the senior pastor of the biggest church in this polity). Kim even went as far as to lie that he fainted to keep the chairman of the council from helping me, by calling him out of the general assembly meeting, so he could not defend me. Both of them did this out of jealousy. Therefore, if we do not want to become persecutors, we must let go of our jealousy. Apart from this, there are two more things we must be careful of in order to not become persecutors.

① Do Not Be Doctrine-Orientated If You Do Not Want to Be a Persecutor!

According to the Bible, there are commandments of men and commandments of God inside Judaism.

> "And he said to them, 'Well did Isaiah prophesy of you hypocrites, as it is written, "This people honors me with their lips, but their heart is far from me; in vain do they worship me, teaching as doctrines the **commandments of men**." You leave the **commandment of God** and hold to the tradition

of men.'" (Mark 7:6-8)

Those who believed in the commandments of men persecuted those who taught the commandment of God. It is the same today. Inside the church, there are commandments of men and the commandment of God. In each doctrine for each denomination, the things that are biblical are the commandment of God, and the things that are unbiblical are the commandments of men. Yet, on the contrary, because of a lack of discernment, those who are brainwashed by the commandments of men persecute those who biblically preach the commandment of God.

In the book *Jesus the Open Door*, Pastor Kenneth Hagin is first persecuted because of "divine healing" and later for "speaking in tongues."[254] This is not something to be persecuted for. Yet, he was persecuted because of cessationism, which is a commandment of men. However, according to 2 Timothy 3:15-17, what is most important amongst the truths of the Bible is not divine healing or speaking in tongues. It is soteriology. The greatest attacks and delusions that Satan gives is thus on soteriology. The area in the church that has become the most distorted and destroyed is thus soteriology. Therefore, what will happen when salvation is taught just as it is written

---

[254] Kenneth E. Hagin, *Jesus: The Open Door*, (Tulsa, OK: Kenneth Hagin Ministries, 1996) 111.

in the Bible? It is evident that even greater persecution will come their way.

Do you know why not only the Old Testament prophets, John the Baptist, and Jesus, but also the apostles, John Wesley, and Charles Finney were persecuted? They all share the common factor of having correctly preached on salvation. In the present day too, if you correctly understand soteriology, do not compromise and instead spread it. Then, you will be persecuted. Because of this, Arthur Pink said the following in *Authentic Christianity*.

> "Oh, how far, far below the New Testament standard is this modern way of begging sinners to receive Christ as their own personal 'Savior.'...
>
> Alas, alas, that modern evangelism is encouraging and producing just such hideous and Christ-dishonoring monstrosities. ... On almost every side today it is being taught, even by men styled orthodox and 'fundamentalists,' that getting saved is an exceedingly simple affair. So long as a person believes John 3:16, and 'rests on it,' or 'accepts Christ as his personal Savior,' that is all that is needed. It is often said that there is nothing left for the sinner to do but direct his faith toward the right object: just as man trusts his bank or a wife her husband, let him exercise the same faculty of faith and trust in Christ. **So widely has**

this idea been received that for anyone now to condemn it is to court being branded as a heretic." [255]

Pink also deeply worried over the false gospel rooted in the modern church.

"The terms of Christ's salvation are erroneously stated by the present-day evangelist. With very rare exceptions he tells his hearers that salvation is by grace and is received as a free gift; that Christ has done everything for the sinner, and that nothing remains but for him to 'believe'—to trust in the infinite merits of His blood. **And so widely does this conception now prevail in 'orthodox' circles, so frequently has it been dinned in their ears, so deeply has it taken root in their minds, that for one to now challenge it and denounce it as being so inadequate and one-sided as to be deceptive and erroneous, is for him to instantly court the stigma of being a heretic, and to be charged with dishonoring the finished work of Christ by inculcating salvation by works."** [256]

Is this not the truth? The reality is that those who preach

---

[255] Arthur W. Pink, *Practical Christianity*, (Grand Rapids, MI: Baker Book House, 1975) 20-1.

[256] Arthur W. Pink, *Present Day Evangelism*, (Pensacola, FL: Chapel Library, 2007) 9-10.

the gospel biblically today will be dumbfoundingly branded as "heretics who believe in salvation by works" by heresy hunters and unscrupulous denominations. Our church is the most representative case of this.

No matter who you are, if you are doctrinal, then you will persecute those who preach the biblical truth of salvation. Therefore, do not become doctrinal with soteriology or the assurance of salvation. I pray that you will, by all means, instead become biblical in this aspect.

② Do Not Be Religious If You Do Not Want to Be a Persecutor!

One of the reasons why the tragedy of spiritual fratricide occurs in the church is because many people are religious. In other words, they are influenced by the unbiblical doctrine of the cessation of the Spirit, and they treat revelation (illuminating revelation), gifts of the Spirit, and miracles as taboo.

Look at all the pastors in Korea who suffered immensely because of heresy claims, including Pastor Yonggi Cho and Pastor Seok-Jeon Yoon. Most of them had a healthy prayer life and had strong gifts of the Spirit.

Early on, Charles Finney wrote on the consequences that will follow when "filled with the Spirit."

"If you have much of the Spirit of God, you must make up your mind to have much opposition, both in the church and the world. Very likely the leading men in the church will oppose you. There has always been opposition in the church. So it was when Christ was on earth. ... Often the elders, and even the minister, will oppose you, if you are filled with the Spirit of God. You must expect very frequent and agonizing conflicts with Satan."[257]

Additionally, Pastor John Osteen, who was the founder of one of the largest churches in the U.S., boldly said the following.

"**As we have said, the Book of Acts is the pattern for the church in every age.** There has always been only one church, which is the body of Christ. All born again believers in all denominations are a part of that one church.

Acts chapter one emphasizes the fact that we need to have the Baptism in the Holy Spirit. Acts chapter two emphasizes how the Baptism in the Holy Spirit releases our spirits to communicate with the Father in true worship and praise. Acts chapter three emphasizes that the Baptism in the Holy Spirit is not an end, but a doorway into the supernatural flow of the miraculous.

---

[257] Charles G. Finney, *Lectures on Revivals of Religion*, (Great Britain: Oxford University Press, 1960) 117.

Now, we come to Acts chapter four in our pattern. Here we have the flow of PERSECUTION. Yes, that is in the pattern! We can expect to experience the same persecution as the disciples if we have the power of the Holy Spirit moving in our lives.

The Pharisees were the fundamentalists. The Sadducees were the modernists. ... These were just the denominations of their day. The persecution arose from them. The same is true today. ... Persecution is part of the pattern found in the Book of Acts. **As soon as the believers in the New Testament church got the Baptism in the Holy Ghost, the religious people of their day (not the sinners) were the ones that instigated the persecution in their lives...** Instead of being happy, these religious leaders said,

'What shall we do to these men?' (Acts 4:16)

This is what denominationalized, spiritually blinded, religious people in our day are saying:

'What shall we do with ... these people flowing in the power of God today?' ...

The leaders of the day said, 'But that it spread no further among the people, let us straitly threaten them that they speak henceforth to no man in that Name.' (Acts 4:17).

'And they called them, and commanded them not to speak at all nor teach in the Name of Jesus.' (Acts 4:18).

Listen! These religious people did not want this news to

spread any further! They were saying that they did not want any... incurables to be healed; no more merciful acts of God to be manifested!!! ... What a horrible attitude to take in the Name of Almighty God!

I love all of God's people in all denominations. But I am strongly opposed to that sectarian spirit that robs God's people and keeps them trapped in the cells of denominationalism that teaches them such foolishness...

God stirred me and called me to be a voice to them to let them know that there is more than a blind denominational creed and traditions of men... In our Baptist church, I was following the church pattern found in the Book of Acts. I was clothed with power... Then, of course, persecution arose...

When the flow of the supernatural begins, immediately persecution comes from organized religion...

Expect persecution when you begin to flow in the supernatural. Do not be so shocked. Do not be so startled. Do not give up when the persecution comes. ... **We need to love the people within every denomination. But we need to resist within every denomination. But we need to resist with a passion that sectarian, evil, devilish, denominational spirit that is not in line with the truth of the Bible."**[258]

---

[258] John Osteen, *How to Flow in the Super Supernatural*, (Houston, TX: John Osteen Publications, 1978) 56-63.

He also said the following grave confession.

"The Bible says, '**All that will live godly in Christ Jesus shall suffer persecution.**' (2 Timothy 3:12).

When I was the pastor of a Baptist church, I would question that scripture. I knew that I lived a godly life, but there was no persecution. That puzzled me.

One Sunday morning, I decided to preach a sermon that would name every sin that anybody could possibly commit. I thought I could stir up the congregation and generate some persecution. It did not work. My congregation loved me. They shook my hand after the service and went merrily on their way.

No persecution ever came in those days. **But soon enough I found out that all that a person has to do to experience opposition is to be filled with God's Holy Ghost power. When we begin to speak in tongues, cast out demons, pray for the sick and flow in that mighty river of God, persecution abounds on every side!!! There is a religious system that creates a sectarian spirit. It will not embrace the supernatural power of God. It will criticize every work of the Holy Ghost!**"[259]

Therefore, we cannot, by any means, avoid persecution. In

---

[259] Ibid., 15.

the past, I tried to avoid persecution for a long time. However, I no longer do this. I have accepted persecution. I realized that this is something that I cannot avoid, and that it is the cost I must pay as a servant of God. Therefore, you must all change your hearts like I did and be at peace with this.

Beloved, the enemy will always target a church and pastors who are filled with the Spirit. Yet, there are so many pastors today who are just religious. They do not desire the Spirit nor the gifts of the Spirit nor miracles. In other words, they are not filled with the Spirit. That is why they receive no persecution. Not only this, but because they are religious, they instead become persecutors. Anyone who becomes religious and fearlessly says, "The work of the Spirit is the work of evil spirits, mysticism, and heresy," has the possibility of committing blasphemy against the Holy Spirit. And when you commit blasphemy against the Spirit, that is the end. You are on the express train to Hell. Therefore, I urge you to be utterly careful to not become religious and then become a persecutor.

6) You Who Are Persecuted for Righteousness' Sake, Rejoice and Be Glad!

Surprisingly, Jesus told those who are being persecuted to rejoice and be glad.

"Blessed are you when others revile you and persecute you and utter all kinds of evil against you falsely on my account. **Rejoice and be glad**, for your reward is great in heaven." (Matthew 5:11-12)

The same advice is given in different places in the Bible.

"**Count it all joy**, my brothers, when you meet trials of various kinds." (James 1:2)

"But **rejoice** insofar as you share Christ's sufferings." (1 Peter 4:13)

Moreover, the Bible actually shows examples of this happening.

"And when they had called in the apostles, they beat them and charged them not to speak in the name of Jesus, and let them go. **Then they left the presence of the council, rejoicing that they were counted worthy to suffer dishonor for the name**." (Acts 5:40-41)

"The crowd joined in attacking them, and the magistrates tore the garments off them and gave orders to beat them with rods.

And when they had inflicted many blows upon them, they threw them into prison, ordering the jailer to keep them safely. Having received this order, he put them into the inner prison and fastened their feet in the stocks. **About midnight Paul and Silas were praying and singing hymns to God**, and the prisoners were listening to them." (Acts 16:22-25)

Why did Jesus tell the persecuted to rejoice and be glad? And how can we achieve this?

① The Reason We Can Rejoice While Being Persecuted Is Because Ours Is the Kingdom of Heaven.

"Blessed are those who are persecuted for righteousness' sake, for **theirs is the kingdom of heaven**." (Matthew 5:10)

This is natural! Only those who follow Jesus can enter heaven. However, one of the costs that we must pay when following Jesus is persecution.

"Now great crowds accompanied him, and he turned and said to them, **'If anyone comes to me and does not hate his own father and mother and wife and children and brothers and sisters, yes, and even his own life, he cannot be my disciple. Whoever does not bear his own cross and come after me cannot be my disciple.'" (Luke 14:25-27)

Persecution is evidence that they paid the cost and are true disciples who follow Jesus. Thus, persecution is the sign of the true believer or of true piety.

> "If the world hates you, know that it has hated me before it hated you. **If you were of the world, the world would love you as its own; but because you are not of the world, but I chose you out of the world, therefore the world hates you.**" (John 15:18-19)

A long time ago, I read something interesting in one of Charles Spurgeon's sermons. After saying, "When a man becomes a Christian, he straightway becomes different from the rest of his fellows," he told the following anecdote.

> "I was standing, one day, at the window, meditating what my sermon should be, and I could not find a text, when, all of a sudden, I saw a flight of birds. There was a canary which had escaped from its cage and was flying over the slates of the opposite houses—and it was being chased by some 20 sparrows and other rough birds. I thought of that text,

'My heritage is unto me as a speckled bird; the birds round about are against her.' Why, they seemed to say to one another, 'Here is a yellow fellow! We have not seen the likes of him in London. He has no business here—let us pull off his bright coat—let us kill him, or make him as dark and dull as ourselves.' **That is just what men of the world try to do with Christians!"**[260]

This is truly the case. That is why John Ryle said, "The very hatred of the world, therefore, is a satisfactory evidence that you are [Jesus'] disciples."[261] Blaise Pascal also said that persecution is "the best sign of piety."[262] Not only this, John Stott also said the following.

> **"Partly because persecution is a token of genuineness, a certificate of Christian authenticity,** *for in the same way they persecuted the prophets who were before you* (12b). **If we are persecuted today, we belong to a noble succession.** But the major reason why we should rejoice is because we are suffering, he said, because of me (11), on account of our loyalty to him and

---

[260] Charles Spurgeon, *Spurgeon's Sermons Volume 38*, (Grand Rapids, MI: Christian Classics Ethereal Library, 1892) 554-5.
[261] J.C. Ryle, *Expository Thoughts on the Gospel: St John Vol 3*, (New York, NY: Robert Carter and Brothers, 1874) 119.
[262] Blaise Pascal, *Pensees*, (New York: E. P. Dutton & Co., 1958) 257.

to his standards of truth and righteousness."[263]

This is the greatest reason why we must rejoice and be glad when we are persecuted.

We believe that when we become beatitude people, we will receive good remarks from our fellow peers of this world. That is not the case. We will receive persecution instead of praise. And this is not strange at all.

> **"And this is the judgment: the light has come into the world, and people loved the darkness rather than the light because their works were evil. For everyone who does wicked things hates the light and does not come to the light, lest his works should be exposed."** (John 3:19-20)

In actuality, the character and conduct of Christians bring out the sin in others and it makes them uncomfortable. That is why we cannot avoid being hated and receiving persecution. For example, Jesus excellently showed us the righteousness that must exist in a believer. Yet, even though this was the case, He still received such severe hate and persecution that He was nailed to the cross and killed. In addition, the Lord also said

---

[263] Stott, *The Message of the Sermon on the Mount*, (2020) 35-6.

that we would receive the same kind of treatment.

> "A disciple is not above his teacher, nor a servant above his master. It is enough for the disciple to be like his teacher, and the servant like his master. **If they have called the master of the house Beelzebul, how much more will they malign those of his household.**" (Matthew 10:24-25)

If you look in Sundar Singh's book, you will also see the following words of Jesus.

> "If in this world men persecute and slander you, do not let this surprise or distress you … **Neither be surprised if the world desert you, for it has deserted God Himself, so that in this you are seen to be a true son of your father.**"[264]

Beloved, they say that snakes do not eat prey that is already dead. In an actual nature documentary, when a toad was approached by a snake, the toad feigned death. Then, the snake did not eat the toad and slithered past. It is the same for the original snake Satan. Satan does not attack people like the believers from the church of Sardis, who have a reputation of

---

[264] Sadhu Sundar Singh, *At the Master's Feet* (Scotts Valley, CA: Createspace, 2009) 76-8.

being alive but are actually dead. He attacks the churches and believers who are alive. In other words, he only attacks real believers. Therefore, when you are persecuted, do not despair or become downtrodden. Instead, I pray you all will rejoice and be glad.

② The Reason We Can Rejoice While Being Persecuted Is Because Our Reward Is Great in Heaven.

> "Blessed are you when others revile you and persecute you and utter all kinds of evil against you falsely on my account. **Rejoice and be glad, for your reward is great in heaven.**"
> (Matthew 5:11-12)

When you are persecuted for righteousness' sake, your reward is great in heaven. To those who are persecuted, there will be a reward, a great reward. This is the reason why we must rejoice and be glad.

Missionary Phillip Yoon, who is diligently working in the Philippines, wrote the following in his book, *The Heart of Jesus Is Beating in Them*.

> "There are rewards in heaven and each will be given a different reward. ... This truth was more shocking to me than the fact that

heaven and hell exist. I was already a latecomer in this walk of faith, so there was so much I needed to catch up on. Thus, the fact that even the rewards in heaven also differ for each person made me speechless! Would this mean that when a completely new convert, who did nothing for God, dies and goes to heaven they would have to shrink back in a corner and sit there? The thought that I would be going to my eternal home, a place of no return, with empty hands truly woke me up. ... I came to God after failing to fulfill my dream in this world. I did not want to live at the bottom, even in heaven. Although I gave up on my dream here, I made the resolution to at least live gloriously like a king in heaven.

But **what must I do to get a big reward? I found the answer in the Bible.**

'Blessed are you when others revile you and persecute you and utter all kinds of evil against you falsely on my account. Rejoice and be glad, for your reward is great in heaven, for so they persecuted the prophets who were before you.' (Matt. 5:11-12)

I decided to put all my strength into 'receiving persecution for Jesus' and at the same time 'doing things to please God'. A Christian life of believing in Jesus itself is a series of persecutions from the world, but I came under the most intense persecution and mockery, particularly when I evangelized.

Evangelism thus satisfies both persecution and pleasing God simultaneously, so they are the greatest wings in regards to one's reward. Since 'quality' was important for me, I didn't stop the 'evangelism' that could bring me the most persecution and give the greatest delight to God. And in order to fulfill the 'quantity' aspect, I attended all the evening prayer meetings during the weekdays, in addition to Sunday services. I also joined the choir even though I was tone deaf and rhythmically challenged. Moreover, I never skipped cleaning the church on Saturdays."[265]

What a truly pure and precious idea. And it is a happy tragedy that when you become a member of our church, you automatically receive persecution. Thus, your reward in heaven stacks up to great heights. Is this not something to be thankful for?

If so, then how great must one's reward be for the persecution they receive for righteousness' sake? How great is the reward that even Jesus called it great? We cannot know the exact amount, but there is a scripture that can estimate how much it might be.

"By faith Moses, when he was grown up, refused to be called the son of Pharaoh's daughter, choosing rather to be mistreated

---

[265] Philip Yoon, *The Heart of Jesus Is Beating in Them (in Korean)*, (Seoul, Korea: Nachimvan Publishing, 2018) 75-6.

with the people of God than to enjoy the fleeting pleasures of sin. **He considered the reproach of Christ greater wealth than the treasures of Egypt, for he was looking to the reward.**" (Hebrews 11:24-26)

Many people envy the rich. In TV shows, they always have characters who are conglomerates or sons of billionaires. People want to be in their shoes and it attracts people to watch the shows. Yet, Moses considered "The reproach of Christ greater wealth than the treasures of Egypt." To put it in today's terms, it would be saying that he considered it greater wealth than the treasures of all of America. It truly is massive! This is how grand and massive the reward those who are persecuted for righteousness' sake will receive is. Therefore, I pray you will all rejoice and be glad.

Moreover, according to Philippians 2, Jesus became Lord by becoming obedient to the point of death. In the same way, we become "lords" through being persecuted for the Lord. What I am saying is that we become one who reigns together with Jesus Christ. This is foreshadowed in the following Bible verses.

"And James and John, the sons of Zebedee, came up to him and said to him, 'Teacher, we want you to do for us whatever we ask of you.' And he said to them, 'What do you want me to do for you?' And they said to him, **'Grant us to sit, one at your right hand and one at your left, in your glory.'** Jesus said to them, 'You do not know what you are asking. **Are you able to drink the cup that I drink, or to be baptized with the baptism with which I am baptized?'** And they said to him, 'We are able.'" (Mark 10:35-39)

It is also explicitly mentioned in Revelation.

"Then I saw thrones, and seated on them were those to whom the authority to judge was committed. **Also I saw the souls of those who had been beheaded for the testimony of Jesus and for the word of God, and those who had not worshiped the beast or its image and had not received its mark on their foreheads or their hands. They came to life and reigned with Christ for a thousand years.** The rest of the dead did not come to life until the thousand years were ended. This is the first resurrection." (Revelation 20:4-5)

Many years ago, Xu Yongze, who is written about in Brother Yun's book as being the leader of the largest faction of the Chinese underground church, came to Hanbat Methodist Church in Daejeon to lead a conference. I attended this conference with a heart of desire and was able to hear him preach in person. While listening, I heard that brother Xu Yongze, while in China, heard his fellow brothers had been captured. After hearing this news, he got on a train to rescue them. But in return, he too was captured and put in prison. One day, he was so sick of the abuse and torture in his prison life that he asked with resentment, "Lord, why did you allow us to be captured?" Jesus then answered him as follows.

"It is because you are all specially chosen. You are chosen as worthy of being rewarded and reigning as kings in heaven. Therefore, I allowed you to be arrested, so that you would participate in my suffering."

With these words, the Lord taught him that the persecution he received for the Lord was a "privilege." Like so, receiving persecution for righteousness' sake is a great privilege that is poured out to us. Therefore, I pray you will remember this and rejoice and be glad.

③ The Reason We Can Rejoice While Being Persecuted Is Because They Did So to the Prophets Before Us.

"Rejoice and be glad, for your reward is great in heaven, **for** so they persecuted the prophets who were before you."

(Matthew 5:12)

Recently, a President of a famous Christian newspaper company came to meet me. And he said the following.

"I've been watching for the past 15 years and I think you're the one who has been most severely, most awfully, and most unfairly oppressed. You've constantly suffered badly, making me wonder, 'How can someone be so badly oppressed like this? How can this be possible?' When the Tonghap denomination's amnesty committee reversed their decision, I couldn't help but be shocked and astounded - how can this happen in Christianity?"

To be honest, Beloved Church's sermons, healing ministry, alms-giving, missions, etc., are all unproblematic. Rather, we are a church that is a role model to other churches. Yet, why have we been slandered so and why are we continually mistreated? And why have we been slandered this viciously?

Beloved, do you want to know the reason? The answer is in the words that I will introduce to you right now. Reinhard Bonnke in Evangelism by Fire, said the following.

"Whenever the devil treats you as his foe, rejoice! He is paying you the greatest respect and best compliment possible. He is ranking you with those he hated in the past, the beloved servants of the Most High God."[266]

Additionally, Rick Joyner said the following in *Shadows of Things to Come*.

"When viewing the procession of Christians through history, it is apparent that persecution is the 'normal' state of people whose faith is genuine. True Christianity has always been an affront and a threat to those who live by the pattern of this present evil world and those professing Christians who have compromised with the world. This should never be a shock or a discouragement to us; in fact, we should be more concerned when we are not being persecuted. The absence of persecution can be a sign that we are not really living godly lives in Christ Jesus and are therefore not a threat to the powers of darkness."[267]

Brother Yun also wrote the following in *Living Waters*.

---

[266] Reinhard Bonnke, *Evangelism by Fire*, (Laguna Hills, CA: Reinhard Bonnke Ministries, 1993) 83.
[267] Rick Joyner, *Shadow of Things to Come*, (Nashville, TN: Thomas Nelson, Inc, 2001) 119.

"When God reveals His plans and strategies to us, we must move forward in obedience and be willing to withstand attacks and opposition. **We need to recognize that just because a heavenly calling has come to our lives, it doesn't mean everything will go smoothly. In fact, it could be argued that Satan only attacks those plans that he knows originate from God's throne. Other kinds of plans and programs that Christians are involved with are little threat to Satan's kingdom on this earth. But when our adversary senses something has God's anointing on it, he is afraid, for such strategies can blow his evil kingdom to pieces.** ...[268]

In this context, you should not be surprised when the vision you have received encounters such severe opposition, nor should you be surprised when hardship and persecution become your close companions as you walk on the road of obedience to God. ... [269]

Do you want to follow God and do something great for His kingdom? If so, then good. But you must first realize that the pathway to bearing fruit for the Lord is strewn with much opposition, slander, criticism, false accusation and pain. People will misunderstand you and doubt your motives, and Satan

---

[268] Brother Yun, *Living Water*, ed. Paul Hathaway (Grand Rapids, MI: Zondervan, 2008) 42.
[269] Ibid., 44.

will throw many roadblocks in your path in a bid to thwart your progress. This has been my experience over the years, and it has been the experience of every person I have known who has been used by God, from the apostles to the present day."[270]

In the same book, it mentions that during one of the meetings Brother Yun held in Europe, one mature Christian approached him and said the following.

"Brother Yun, I didn't know anything about you, but when I started to hear all the nasty accusations and rumors about how rotten you are, I was astounded. I realized that for Satan to go out of his way and deceive so many key Christian leaders to denounce and attack you, you must pose a threat to the kingdom of darkness. When I heard that even the Chinese government was trying to destroy your reputation, I understood that you must be a kingdom-minded person. Otherwise, it made no sense why these people would waste so much time and energy to attack you."[271]

Beloved, this is the reason why our church receives such severe slander in these impossible ways and is receiving persecu-

---

[270] Ibid., 46.
[271] Ibid., 278.

tion. Many pastors from other denominations said something similar and one older alumnus from seminary actually said the following to me.

"No matter how hard I think, the only reason Beloved Church, which is not heretical at all, is being so seriously slandered by other Korean churches is because the devil feels greatly threatened."

I know that this is true and believe you all know this too! Therefore, how glorious is this? So, rejoice and be glad.

Beloved, look carefully at the main passage! Jesus did not say, "For so they persecuted the Pharisees who were before you." Nor did He say, "For so they persecuted the Scribes or Rabbis who were before you." He said, "**For so they persecuted the prophets who were before you.**"

Of course, there are no High Priests or scribes today. However, as Apostle Paul recorded, there are apostles, prophets, evangelists, pastors and teachers (Eph. 4:11). Yet, people hardly persecute pastors or teachers. Evangelists receive a bit of persecution. The prophets are persecuted even more. And the apostles receive the most severe persecution. This is because, as I expressed during my sermon on the gifts of the Spirit, they correspond to the prophets of the Old Testament.

The reason our church has received so much persecution is

because although we are not foundational apostles (the apostles used for recording the Bible), we are following their footsteps. It is because as a non-foundational apostle, I am preaching the truth they preached as is and continuing their ministry with the Holy Spirit. This is a great joy for God but creates a great obstacle for Satan. How thankful and glorious a work is this? Therefore, do not be saddened over this level of persecution, and instead become one who rejoices and is glad like the Lord commanded. Praise God!

I would now like to give a final conclusion for the entirety of the beatitudes. The beatitudes are blessings. They are the blessing of blessings. Other blessings in life we might lose because they are just in the possession of the person. But the beatitudes are inside the person. Therefore, unless you give it up yourself, no one can take it from you. Moreover, the blessings of the beatitudes point towards heaven. Therefore, we must desire the beatitudes over all other blessings and we must receive them.

In the introduction of the beatitudes, I told you that the beatitudes are the portrait of a Christian. I have now extensively proven this. Through this, we have all been greatly challenged and have made the decision to become beatitude people. However, there must be a balance.

The beatitudes do portray the Christian, and every Christian is a beatitude person. It is also true that only this type of person will enter heaven. However, we must not think one is only a Christian if each beatitude is perfectly present in them. If that were the case, then there would not be a single person in this world who is a Christian.

The beatitudes are not talking about perfection. For example, "mourning" and "hungering for righteousness" show us that we are not perfect on this earth. David Turner, while explaining the Lord's Prayer said, "When disciples pray for pardon, they recognize that they are not yet perfect—their attitudes and activities often fall short of kingdom Standards."[272] Herman Ridderbos also wrote that, "And finally Jesus did not say that only those who are morally perfect will enter the kingdom. He merely asked for a righteousness that is better than that of the Pharisees and the teachers of the law."[273] Additionally, Lloyd-Jones wrote the following.

> "Neither is it a teaching of sinless perfection. Many people read these pictures at the end of the Sermon on the Mount, and say that they mean that the only man who is allowed or able to enter into the kingdom of heaven is the man who, having read the Sermon on the Mount, puts each detail into practice, always and everywhere. This again is obviously im-

---

[272] Turner, *Matthew*, (2008) 188.
[273] Ridderbos, *Matthew*, (1987) 102.

possible. If that were the teaching, then we could be quite certain that there never has been and there never will be a single Christian in the world."[274]

Therefore, we cannot weaken the absolute need for the beatitudes, but we must beware excessively raising the standards.

Beloved, a Christian is a beatitude person. Christians fundamentally, holistically, and practically are beatitude people. However, the standard is not to be a perfect person. A Christian is a beatitude person but at the same time someone who lives with the beatitudes as their goal. A Christian is someone who, through sanctification, becomes more and more a person of the beatitudes. Like how an infant is born and grows into an adult, a Christian is born fundamentally as a beatitude person and grows with the goal of becoming a perfect beatitude person. All people who are like this are true Christians!

---

[274] Lloyd-Jones, *Studies in the Sermon on the Mount Vol. 2*, (1961) 309.

2

Am I the Salt of the Earth and Light of the World?

"You are the salt of the earth, but if salt has lost its taste, how shall its saltiness be restored? It is no longer good for anything except to be thrown out and trampled under people's feet. You are the light of the world. A city set on a hill cannot be hidden. Nor do people light a lamp and put it under a basket, but on a stand, and it gives light to all in the house. In the same way, let your light shine before others, so that they may see your good works and give glory to your Father who is in heaven." (Matthew 5:13-16)

We believe that this message is spoken to all Christians. However, Arthur Pink's interpretation differs from such a way of thinking. He made the following unique assertion that is hard to dismiss.

> "'Ye are the salt of the earth.' These words (and those which follow to the end of verse 16) are frequently regarded as being

spoken of God's people at large, but this we think is a mistake.

First, because such an interpretation is out of harmony with the immediate context. In our last chapter we called attention to our Lord's changing of the pronoun in verse 11 from the 'they' in verses 1-10 to the 'ye.' In verse 10 Christ enumerated the general principle that 'blessed are they which are persecuted for righteousness' sake,' but in verse 11 He made particular application to His own ministers: persecution is the usual experience of God's people, but it is the special portion of His servants. Clear confirmation of this distinction is found in verse 12, where the maligned ministers of Christ are bidden to rejoice because 'so persecuted they the prophets which were before you'—not 'the saints,' but the official servants of God.

Thus, the 'Ye are the salt of the earth' obviously has reference to those who now occupy the same position as did the 'prophets' of old, namely those called of God to act as His mouthpiece and interpret His will.

Additional proof is found in what immediately follows, where after further designating them the 'light of the world' Christ added, 'A city that is set on a hill cannot be hid' a figure fitly pertinent to the officers of Christ, who are made a spectacle to the world.'

Finally, what is said in verse 15 plainly pertains to the ministers of God rather than to their hearers, for the candle on a candlestick again speaks of official dignity, and the giving 'light to all that are in the house' is plainly the one man ministering to the many."[275]

He also argued the following.

"Ere passing on it should be pointed out that the verse now before us also definitely confirms our explanation of the 'ye' in verses 13-16—a point which is disputed by many of our moderns. When treating of that passage we called attention to our Lord's change of the pronoun in His second division of the Sermon. In verses 3 to 10 the Saviour throughout used 'theirs' and 'they,' but in verses 11 to 16 He employed 'ye' and 'you.' We insisted that this second section has exclusive reference to Christ's official servants—the New Testament successors of the 'prophets' (verse 12), for they are, ministerially, the salt of the earth and the light of the world. That Christ continued to have in mind the same class, and was addressing Himself not to the rank and file of His people, but to His official servants, is clear from His 'Whosoever shall do and teach them.'"[276]

The point of Arthur Pink's argument is largely twofold.

---

[275] Pink, *An Exposition of the Sermon on the Mount*, (2011) 43.
[276] Ibid., 58-9.

First, Jesus used the word "they" till verse 10, but used the word "you" in verses 11-12. Therefore, He is talking about all believers till verse 10 and then talking about ministers in verses 11-12. And since verses 13-16 use "you" as well, Pink is saying that these verses must also only be for leaders, like the apostles. It seems highly plausible!

If you look at the aforementioned verses that Pink pointed out, it actually is so and his assertions seem correct. However, take a look at the verses that follow. Verses 18 and 20, along with verses 21-48, continue to use the word "you." If this is the case, then are the six antitheses only for the apostles? Certainly not. Not only this, but in chapters 6 and 7, it also continues to use the word "you." Yet, it is a message not just for the apostles but for all Christians. Therefore, although this interpretation looks plausible, it is not correct.

Next, is the argument that the "you" in verse 12 is about one who is in the ranks of the prophets. Furthermore, they argue the fact that verse 19 gives the lesson "to do and teach," and it shows that this is not about regular believers but about ministers. This too seems incredibly plausible!

However, if you read carefully, there is a shift in theme in verse 17. It is no longer about the salt and the light but about the law. Moreover, if you read verses 17-20, you would know that because Jesus came not to abolish the law but to fulfill it,

He said the following with the apostles and teachers in mind. "Therefore whoever relaxes one of the least of these commandments and teaches others to do the same will be called least in the kingdom of heaven, but whoever does them and teaches them will be called great in the kingdom of heaven" (19). Yet, this does not mean that Jesus was only talking to them. If you look in the following verse, He says the following to everyone.

> **"For I tell you, unless your righteousness exceeds that of the scribes and Pharisees, you will never enter the kingdom of heaven."** (Matthew 5:20)

Shall we read the main passage for this chapter to see if this is true?

> "Do not think that I have come to abolish the Law or the Prophets; I have not come to abolish them but to fulfill them. For truly, I say to you, until heaven and earth pass away, not an iota, not a dot, will pass from the Law until all is accomplished. Therefore whoever relaxes one of the least of these commandments and teaches others to do the same will be called least in the kingdom of heaven, but whoever does them and teaches them will be called great in the kingdom of heaven. For I tell you, unless your righteousness exceeds that of the

scribes and Pharisees, you will never enter the kingdom of heaven." (Matthew 5:17-20)

What do you think? It is exactly as I explained! Apart from this, take a look at the parallel verses where it talks about the salt and the light. First, let us look at the context of the parallel verses on salt. Mark 9:50 says, "Salt is good, but if the salt has lost its saltiness, how will you make it salty again? Have salt in yourselves, and be at peace with one another." Luke 14:34 says, "Salt is good, but if salt has lost its taste, how shall its saltiness be restored?" Both of these passages are not spoken to ministers. It was spoken to the crowd or to the believers who followed Him. Similar passages on light in Ephesians 5:8, "For at one time you were darkness, but now you are light in the Lord. Walk as children of light," and Philippians 2:15, "That you may be blameless and innocent, children of God without blemish in the midst of a crooked and twisted generation, among whom you shine as lights in the world," are the same. Both are not about pastors but about believers. Therefore, the message of the salt and the light was not a message just for ministers.

1. AM I THE SALT OF THE EARTH?

"You are the salt of the earth, but if salt has lost its taste, how shall its saltiness be restored? It is no longer good for anything except to be thrown out and trampled under people's feet." (Matthew 5:13)

Jesus said that Christians are the salt of the earth. Through this metaphor, He was speaking about the influence Christians have over the world. John Stott wrote the following.

"If the Beatitudes describe the essential character of the disciples of Jesus, the salt and light metaphors indicate their influence for good in the world."[277]

Dr. Yong-eui Yang also said the following.

"The 'salt' and 'light' show the influence of discipleship for

---

[277] Stott, *The Message of the Sermon on the Mount*, (2020) 40.

the world. ...

Verses 11-12 and verses 13-16 show two different points of view of **the result, in relation to the world, when the general principle of the beatitudes on discipleship is specifically applied to the lives of the disciples**. Verses 11-12 show the negative response from the world, which is the persecution the disciples will receive. **Verses 13-16 show the result of positive influence for the world, which results in worldly people giving glory to God."**[278]

The following two points are evidence that this interpretation and understanding is correct.

First, Sinclair Ferguson fairly pointed out that this verse was not written as a command but as an indicative. In other words, it is not commanding us to become something but a factual statement about the truth. Jesus did not command the disciples to become the salt of the earth. He proclaimed them as the salt of the earth. He is saying that He created them as the salt of the earth, so of course this is what they are.[279] Therefore, He is talking about their influence.

Next, we must pay attention to the order. In other words, it is important that the salt and light are mentioned after the be-

---

[278] Yang, *How Will You Read the Book of Matthew?*, (2011) 98-9.
[279] Ferguson, *The Sermon on the Mount*, (1987) 56.

atitudes. Scot McKnight said the following.

> "But we would also be wise to connect the sorts of influence we are to have to the themes of Jesus and, in particular, to the themes emerging from the Beatitudes (humble poor, pursuit of righteousness and justice, and creating peace and reconciliation). These would be the earliest 'applications' made by followers of Jesus when they heard Jesus say they were the salt in Israel."[280]

Focusing on this point is extremely important for properly understanding this passage.[281]

For it shows us that they are the salt of the earth and light of the world because they are beatitude people. Therefore, it is clear that the passage shows what kind of people Christians, who are beatitude people, are in this world and what kind of influence they must bring.

With this in mind, let us look at verse 13 in depth.

1) The Meaning of Being the Salt of the Earth!

There are a wide variety of roles and functions for salt. This

---

[280] McKnight, *Sermon on the Mount*, (2013) 57-8.
[281] Yang, *How Will You Read the Book of Matthew?*, (2011) 98.

in turn causes confusion. Michael Wilkins made a good point that, "The variety of uses for salt leads to different interpretations of what Jesus meant to communicate with the analogy."[282]

For example, I read many attractive writings about how the role of salt is to make one thirsty. Lorne Sanny wrote the following in *The Art of Personal Witnessing*.

> "The little girl in a Sunday school was asked: 'What is salt?' She said: 'Salt is to make people thirsty.' Now, perhaps you and I cannot make people drink, so to speak, but we can make them thirsty for spiritual things by the kind of a life that is filled with joy and victory in the Lord Jesus Christ. When they turn to Him they will be satisfied (John 4:10)."[283]

Louis A. Barbieri also wrote the following.

> "Jesus' followers would be like salt in that they would create a thirst for greater information. When one sees a unique person who possesses superior qualities in specific areas, he desires to discover why that person is different."[284]

---

[282] Wilkins, *Matthew*, (2004) 212.
[283] Lorne Sanny, *The Art of Personal Witnessing*, (Chicago, IL: Moody Press, 1957) 64-5.
[284] Louis A. Barbieri, *Matthew. The Bible Knowledge Commentary* (Wheaton, IL: SP

And the following is recorded in the Wisdom Collective Commentary.

"Salt makes us feel thirsty. Although it has the role of giving food its unique taste, if the saltiness is too strong, it can also make people feel thirsty. Thus, salt can simultaneously give taste to food and make one thirsty. In the same way, by acting out the inner characteristics of the beatitudes to the world, true disciples should make peace in a world filled with discord and conflict. They should prevent the corruption of a world filled with injustice and sin. Additionally, through living the model life that testifies of the internal characteristics they possess, the disciples need to make the people of this world thirst and long for such a life of possessing heaven through Christ. The disciples need to make it possible for them to turn to Christ."[285]

What an attractive interpretation! It is also a very valuable lesson.

However, is this really what Jesus was saying when He said, "You are the salt of the earth?" It is not. Yet, countless preachers go one step further and they list row after row the various

---

Publications, Inc., 1983) 29.
[285] Edited by Byung-do Kang, *Matthew 1: Wisdom Collective Commentary* (In Korean), (Seoul, Korea: CH-Wisdom Inc., 1993) 223.

functions of salt and preach that this is the meaning of "you are the salt of the earth." However, the chances of the message meaning the above are close to zero. They are simply concepts and lessons that pastors have conjectured. Therefore, it is not right to preach in such a manner.

Meanwhile, when we think about salt, the most representative functions that come to mind are as a "seasoning" and as a "preservative." Theologians are not an exception to this way of thinking either. That is why they interpret salt's role as making taste and preserving things from decay. Both are possible interpretations, for salt is used to make taste. The Bible also has verses on this.

> **"Can that which is tasteless be eaten without salt**, or is there any taste in the juice of the mallow?" (Job 6:6)

> "Let your speech always be gracious, **seasoned with salt**, so that you may know how you ought to answer each person." (Colossians 4:6)

However, our main verse, "You are the salt of the earth, but if salt has lost its taste, how shall its saltiness be restored?" is not about making food salty. I know very well that most who read this will think that "saltiness" is about making food salty and full of taste. Yet, most commentators agree that this is not the meaning of this verse. The real meaning of this verse is to "restore saltiness" and is the question of "how the saltiness that the salt itself has lost can be restored."[286] In other words, it is talking about the impossibility of it all. Thankfully, certain translators have kept this meaning alive in their translations.

> "You are the salt of the earth. **But if the salt loses its saltiness, how can it be made salty again?**" (Matthew 5:13, NIV)

> "You are the salt of the earth. **But what good is salt if it has lost its flavor? Can you make it salty again?**" (Matthew 5:13, NLT)

> "You are the salt of the earth; **but if salt has lost its taste, how can its saltiness be restored?**" (Matthew 5:13, NRSV)

However, this does not mean that it is impossible for the meaning of the salt to be about creating taste. The word "taste" is in the verse. Therefore, it is an adequate interpretation to think that Jesus was saying, "You are the salt. You were created as the salt. The world has already lost its taste, but you are

---

[286] Yon-gyong Kwon, *Do You Understand What You Are Reading? (In Korean)*, (Seoul: SFC, 2012) 74–5.

different from them. Therefore, you must keep your saltiness and must never lose your taste." Still, I believe the need to explain this verse as a preservative is also great. For just as how the darkness of the world is implied in "the light of the world," "the salt of the earth" implies the decay of the earth. Just as the light of the world is in contrast to the darkness, the salt of the earth is in contrast to the decay. Therefore, when explaining the salt of the earth, I believe it is important to emphasize its role as a preservative that dampens the decay of the earth. Thus, I desire to explain the salt of the earth by focusing on this point.

2) Why Must We Be the Salt of the Earth?

The reason we must become the salt of the earth is shown in the phrase "salt of the earth" itself. It is because it shows us the state of the world. Lloyd-Jones spoke clearly on this point.

> **"'Ye are the salt of the earth.' Now that is not only a description of the Christian; it is a description by implication of the world in which he finds himself.** … Now the Bible has always taught that, and it is put perfectly by our Lord when He says, Ye are the salt of the earth.'
>
> **What does that imply? It clearly implies rottenness in the**

earth; it implies **a tendency to pollution and to becoming foul and offensive**. That is what the Bible has to say about this world. **It is fallen, sinful and bad.** Its tendency is to evil and to wars. **It is like meat which has a tendency to putrefy and to become polluted.** It is like something which can only be kept wholesome by means of a preservative or antiseptic. **As the result of sin and the fall, life in the world in general tends to get into a putrid state.** That, according to the Bible, is the only sane and right view to take of humanity. Far from there being a tendency in life and the world to go upwards, it is the exact opposite. **The world, left to itself, is something that tends to fester.** ...

The Bible is full of endless illustrations of this. You see it manifesting itself in the very first book. Though God had made the world perfect, because sin entered, this evil, polluting element at once began to show itself. Read the sixth chapter of Genesis and you find God saying, 'My Spirit shall not always strive with man'. The pollution has become so terrible that God has to send the flood. After that there is a new start; but this evil principle still manifests itself and you come to Sodom and Gomorrah with their almost unthinkable sinfulness. That is the story which the Bible is constantly putting before us. This persistent tendency to putrefaction is ever showing itself."[287]

It's a really good point! Unfortunately, things will only get worse in the future. This world will only grow more evil and more corrupt till it becomes like the time of Noah and the time of Lot where God could not help but destroy it.

> "**Just as it was in the days of Noah, so will it be in the days of the Son of Man.** They were eating and drinking and marrying and being given in marriage, until the day when Noah entered the ark, and the flood came and destroyed them all. **Likewise, just as it was in the days of Lot**—they were eating and drinking, buying and selling, planting and building, but on the day when Lot went out from Sodom, fire and sulfur rained from heaven and destroyed them all—**so will it be on the day when the Son of Man is revealed.**" (Luke 17:26-30)

Then, before the Antichrist comes, the apostasy that Paul talked of will occur in the church. As the Antichrist the Bible prophesied about appears, the great tribulation will occur. Afterwards, Jesus will return and He will judge the corrupted world. Because of this, we must never follow the trends or cul-

---

[287] Lloyd-Jones, *Studies in the Sermon on the Mount*, (1959) 150-2.

tures of the world. We must solely listen to the Word of God that is the real truth and completely trust in it (Rom. 12:2).

However, it is not God's will for the world to continue to grow more evil and perverted. God desires to protect as much as He can against the decay and corruption of this world and to delay it. That is why He placed influences in this world that suppress it. The greatest of these are the state (the power to decide laws and enforce them) and family (including marriage and family life). Yet, this is not enough. That is why God desires Christians to more effectively take on this role of the salt. In other words, He desires Christians to become spiritual preservatives that can diminish the decay and rotting of the world. That is why Jesus said, "You are the salt of the earth."

Tasker said the following.

> "The disciples, accordingly, are called to be a moral disinfectant in a world where moral standards are low, constantly changing, or non-existent."[288]

This is correct. This is the call of Christians who have been tasked to be the salt of the earth. Therefore, we must never lose

---

[288] R.V.G. Tasker, *The Gospel According to St. Matthew: An Introduction and Commentary*, (Grand Rapids, MI: Wm. B. Eerdmans Publishing Company, 1961) 63.

our taste. We must never lose the characteristics of the beatitudes. That is how we will be able to take on the role of being the salt of the earth.

3) What Must We Do to Excel at Being the Salt of the Earth?

As the salt of the earth, we must skillfully cope with our role. In order to do so, we need the following two things: distinction and infiltration.

> "I have given them your word, and the world has hated them **because they are not of the world, just as I am not of the world. I do not ask that you take them out of the world, but that you keep them from the evil one. They are not of the world, just as I am not of the world.** Sanctify them in the truth; your word is truth. **As you sent me into the world, so I have sent them into the world.** And for their sake I consecrate myself, that they also may be sanctified in truth." (John 17:14-19)

Here, we clearly see the will of the Lord for us to be distinct from the world and to infiltrate it. These two things are also the key to helping us bear our role as the salt of the earth.

① We Must Live a Life Completely Distinct From the World.

Then what exactly is a life distinct from the world?

First, it is living the life of the beatitudes, which are present right before this verse. John Stott said the following.

> "The two metaphors of salt and light indicate the influence for good which Christians will exert in the community if (and only if) they maintain their distinctive character as set out in the Beatitudes."[289]

Additionally, Dr. Yong-eui Yang said the following.

> "In this scripture, Jesus points out that the characteristics of a disciple, as salt and light, comes from being distinguished from the world. And the characteristics of a disciple who is well distinguished from the world is revealed in the beatitude, which is the scripture that comes in the passage right before."[290]

Moreover, this is what is written in the Wisdom Collective Commentary.

---

[289] Stott, *The Message of the Sermon on the Mount*, (2020) 10.
[290] Yang, *How Will You Read the Book of Matthew?*, (2011) 99.

> "In the Sermon on the Mount, Jesus did not put the role of salt and light, which is what true disciples should be, before the beatitudes. By teaching the beatitudes first, He emphasized the internal characteristics the disciples, who possess the kingdom of heaven, should have. Then, He lectured on the actions and the ripple effect of those who possess the beatitudes. This fact shows that unless you possess the internal characteristics, it is impossible to live the life of the light and salt. Thus, the life of the light and salt can only be fulfilled when you possess the internal characteristics, which is the standard of heaven."[291]

Therefore, in order to bear the role of being the salt of the earth, we must be a beatitude person and continue to maintain the characteristics.

Next, a life that is distinct from the world is a life showing righteousness that exceeds that of scribes and Pharisees, which comes after our main verse. Scot McKnight said the following.

> "What is implicit in... the 'you are...,' is that Jesus assumes his disciples... [are] the blessed of 5:3-12, and the obedient ones of 5:17-48 and beyond. They are not salt or light automatically

---

[291] Kang, *Matthew 1*, (1993) 222.

but only to the degree that they 'are' followers of Jesus."[292]

Moreover, the Wisdom Collective Commentary wrote the following.

"**Jesus is, from 5:17-7, showing specific examples that match the life of the salt and light.**"[293]

Therefore, to bear the role of being the salt of the earth, we must not only become a beatitude person. We must also have the righteousness that exceeds that of the scribes and Pharisees through obeying the laws and commandments, as Jesus explained. That is the life that fulfills the role of being the salt of the earth. That is the life that Jesus expects from all Christians. Furthermore, that is the life of doing the will of the Father written about in Matthew 7:21. Therefore, I pray you all will live this life no matter what.

② We Must Live a Distinct Life from the World While Living Inside the World.

We are the salt of the earth. The Lord sent us to the world. Thus, where we need to be is not in a desert or in the moun-

---

[292] McKnight, *Sermon on the Mount*, (2013) 56.
[293] Kang, *Matthew 1*, (1993) 222.

tains. It is in the world. Therefore, although we can emulate the spirituality of the medieval monks, we must not emulate their lifestyle. In other words, we must be careful to not become pessimists like them. Professor Yong-eui Yang said the following on this.

> "The disciples were called the salt of the 'earth' and the light of the 'world.' This shows that the lives of the disciples are not only distinguished from the world but that it is deeply relevant with the world. The disciples do not live independently from the earth but live closely related to the world. However, in having this close relationship, they are not influenced by the world but rather ones who influence the world."[294]

In order to be the salt and light of the world, you must be inside the world. In other words, you must live with the people of this world. But while living with them, you must live as beatitude people and with righteousness that exceeds that of the scribes and Pharisees. That is how you can be the salt of the earth.

A long time ago, a man said the following to Pastor Kenneth Hagin.

---

[294] Yang, *How Will You Read the Book of Matthew?* (2011) 100.

"I am the only Christian in my department. Please pray that God will move me out of there."[295]

Do you know how Pastor Hagin responded?

He said, "Oh, no, why the whole department would putrefy if you were gone. You stay right there. You're the salt of the earth, so you stay right there and salt it."[296]

He's right. Many say they will never become a politician because the government is rotten to the core. However, that is exactly why the government needs salt. In order to fulfill the duty of the salt, true Christians need to go into Congress. It is the same for media, business, education, the entertainment industry, etc. To be the salt, you must enter these places. Therefore, hone and polish your skills and enter the various fields of the corrupt and unjust world. Be the salt there. I pray that you all will be the ones to push the brakes on the decay and corruption of that organization.

4) A Stern Warning - Do Not Lose Your Taste!

---

[295] Kenneth E. Hagin, *Bible Faith Study Course*, (Tusla, OK: Kenneth Hagin Ministries, 2000) 99.
[296] Ibid.

The main passage is in reality a warning. Jesus is warning us to never lose our saltiness.

"You are the salt of the earth, but if salt has lost its taste, how shall its saltiness be restored? It is no longer good for anything except to be thrown out and trampled under people's feet." (Matthew 5:13)

This is a hard message to understand for us because we make salt by drying sea water. Strictly speaking, sea salt cannot ever lose its taste because Sodium Chloride (NaCl) is a singular compound which cannot easily be divided. However, in Palestine, there are many rock salts. There are salt pillars where, when it rains, the salt gets washed away. Later, the pillar is left standing with all its salt gone. Moreover, during Jesus' time, the salt used in Palestine did not only have sodium chloride in it but a considerable amount of impurities as well. Thus, if not properly stored, the components of sodium chloride that dissolve easily in water would disappear and one would be left only with the impurities. The remaining white powder would still look like salt and be called salt but would be a useless thing that is no longer salty.[297] This is the kind of

---

[297] Yang, *How Will You Read the Book of Matthew?*, (2011) 99-100.

salt He was speaking about.

Salt that has lost its taste in the above manner is utterly useless. It cannot even be used as fertilizer. That is why it was thrown outside and trampled under people's feet. Sadly, this is the reality of the modern churches in Korea.

As previously introduced, salt losing its taste symbolizes losing the characteristics of the beatitudes and not living according to the Sermon on the Mount. We must protect this taste above protecting money, honor, or even our health. This is what is most important for Christians. Thus, I want to explain through the following three points why it is most important to protect one's taste as the salt.

① If You Lose Your Taste, You Are Useless!

If salt loses its taste, it becomes useless. While expressed in our main passage, it is shown better in Luke 14:34-35.

> "Salt is good, **but if salt has lost its taste, how shall its saltiness be restored? It is of no use either for the soil or for the manure pile. It is thrown away.** He who has ears to hear, let him hear."

God desires Christians to be the salt of the earth, as beatitude people with righteousness that exceeds that of the scribes and Pharisees. But if they lose their taste, then they cannot be the salt of the earth.

Certainly, people like the High Priest, elders, scribes, and Pharisees can still hold positions in society and the religious sphere. However, God cannot use them as the salt of the earth. There are so many pastors and believers like this today! Amongst them, there are those who not only cannot be used by God, but are instead used by Satan.

Many mistakenly believe that they are living for God, but God cannot use those who have lost their taste. George Campbell Morgan said the following.

> "According to the teaching of Jesus, the character of **the influence is the influence of character.** 'Ye are salt,' 'Ye are light;' not, Ye have salt, or, Ye have light. Much less does He say, Ye dispense the salt, or, Ye dispense the light. **There is all the difference between a living influence and a dead, official, attempt at influence.** If Christ had said, Ye dispense the salt, then we might have looked upon our position as official. There is no such thought. **The King began with the fundamental necessity of human nature, and He said, 'Ye are.'**
>
> As the father of a family, the influence you exert upon your boys and girls, is the influence of what you are, and not of

what you tell them they ought to be. It is the influence of your own personality in its deepest fibre that is going to make or mar your bairns. There is no escape from this.

We may tell our boys to be good; and, if we are bad, by the grace of God they may be good—some other hand may mold them, some other life may win them—but if we are going to win our boys for goodness, we must be good. Our influence comes out of what we are. …

What we are, determines the character of our influence in the world, whether we will or no."[298]

It is a little long, but I must also introduce to you Kathryn Kuhlman's writings.

"'Ye are the salt of the earth,' He said. Yes, the throngs of people sat before Him but it is evident that these words were not addressed to them. Jesus spoke these words to the inner circle made up of those who had met the qualifications of the first part of His sermon, and to those who would meet the qualifications in the future—today.

Jesus lists The Beatitudes first before continuing His sermon because only as we become poor in spirit, as we learn

---

[298] George Campbell Morgan, *The Gospel According to Matthew*, (Eugene, OR: Wipf and Stock Publishers, 1929) 46-7.

meekness, as we become pure in heart, are we enabled to reach out to others. These are the folk who are rightfully representing the invisible Church and whose influence counts for God. You cannot be the salt of the earth unless you are merciful, unless you are pure in heart, unless you are numbered among the peacemakers, unless you continue to hunger and thirst after righteousness.

Only as man has salt in his character can he be an influence for God to his generation. … It is impossible for one to give to someone else more than what he has himself. As a minister of the Gospel, I cannot give a greater spiritual depth to members of my congregation than I have experienced myself. If you are a pastor, remember something: it isn't how well you speak or the extent of your knowledge or the degrees you have earned that will make God real to members of your congregation. When you stand behind that pulpit, you cannot give any greater spiritual depth to the members of your church than you have yourself. …

So, in the same way that you can never give more to another than you have experienced yourself, neither can you exert a greater influence on another than you have experienced yourself. **The influence that you exert is always the influence of what you are**. No man exerts any influence upon another by the things he says…

I repeat—**no person exerts upon other people any great mea-**

sure of influence by what he says. Only as his words are the outcome of what he is in the deepest part of his own being, does he exercise real influence upon another. The influence that you as fathers and mothers exert upon your sons and your daughters is the influence of who you are. You can talk until doomsday telling them what they should be, but your words will mean nothing if they know you are not the man or woman you are urging them to be. Therefore, you have no influence. ...

I know we have all smiled at this commonly cited saying, but I quote it here because it is so very true:

'What you are speaks so loud that I cannot hear what you say.'

The most successful Christian living today is the man or the woman who is so consecrated to God that he does not have to sell his experience. **People are naturally sold on his Christianity by his life, and his influence leads them to Christ. That is exactly what Jesus meant when He said, 'Ye are the salt.'"**[299]

This is a truly challenging word. Thus, God does not look at our appearances or our qualifications. He looks, with eyes like a flame of fire, to see whether we are beatitude people or not and whether we are trying to live by The Sermon. With-

---

[299] Kuhlman, *In Search of Blessings*, (1989) 70-4.

out these two conditions, we are completely useless to God. Therefore, do not ever lose your taste and do not ever become useless to God. Instead, I pray you will become someone useful to God.

② If You Lose Your Taste, You Will Be Thrown Away!

If salt loses its taste, it becomes completely useless. Then, it is thrown away.

> "You are the salt of the earth, but if salt has lost its taste, how shall its saltiness be restored? It is no longer good for anything except to **be thrown out** and trampled under people's feet." (Matthew 5:13)

> "Salt is good, but if salt has lost its taste, how shall its saltiness be restored? It is of no use either for the soil or for the manure pile. **It is thrown away.** He who has ears to hear, let him hear." (Luke 14:34-35)

The message is obvious and clear! The Presbyterian doctrine, "once saved, always saved," is not the real truth. Yet, there are countless pastors and theologians who are still brainwashed by doctrine and distort this warning whenever the Bible warns us against this. It is obvious that these types of people will try to distort this message of the tasteless salt being thrown out to simply mean losing one's usefulness, namely being thrown out from being used. However, it is impossible for this verse to mean such. For the taste of salt symbolizes the characteristics of the beatitudes and righteousness that exceeds that of the scribes and Pharisees. And the beatitudes are the characteristics of the disciples. To lose that would mean returning to the state of a non-believer. Moreover, the Lord Himself warned that if you do not have better righteousness than the scribes and Pharisees, you cannot enter heaven (Matt. 5:20). Therefore, tasteless salt being thrown away cannot mean that you will not be used by God. In addition, if you look at the parallel verses to this verse and look at the context before and after, they are all related to not being saved or being forsaken and going to hell (Mark 9:50, Luke 14:34). Therefore, to say that tasteless salt will be thrown away does not simply mean that the Lord cannot use that person. It means that the soul will be forsaken. Therefore, the main passage is a very important verse that clearly shows once saved is not always saved.

Thankfully, these days, more scholars are acknowledging the passage to mean as it is written in the Bible. It is truly something to be thankful for.

First, Herman Ridderbos wrote the following.

"Salt that has lost its power is good for nothing and must be thrown away. Similarly Jesus' followers will have no future in the kingdom of heaven if no 'salty' influence emanates from them. The words 'thrown out' are highly significant in this context (cf. Luke 13:25; John 12:31; 15:6). In this sense good works can indeed be called conditions for entering the kingdom."[300]

Moreover, Dr. Yong-eui Yang said this.

"The saltiness of a Christian is the distinct Christian character described in the beatitudes. But if a Christian cannot reveal this character in his words and actions, he becomes useless before God and will be rejected by God in the end. This shows how fundamental it is for a disciple to have this distinguished character."[301]

Dr. Yon-gyong Kwon also wrote the following.

"If the disciples lose the natural taste the followers of Christ

---

[300] Ridderbos, *Matthew*, (1987) 94.
[301] Yang, *How Will You Read the Book of Matthew?*, (2011) 100.

should naturally show… they will be rejected. They will not be able to enjoy any future in heaven. … If we lose our saltiness, we don't become a second-class disciple. We completely lose the qualification to be a disciple (5:13-16)."[302]

Salt losing its taste means losing the characteristics of the beatitudes that come before this verse and not living by the standards of The Sermon that come after. However, in Matthew 7:13-14, Jesus compared being the salt to the narrow gate and narrow path that leads to life. This is the only path that leads us to life. All other roads are wide and lead us to destruction.

Additionally, Jesus said this warning in Matthew 7:21.

> "Not everyone who says to me, 'Lord, Lord,' will enter the kingdom of heaven, **but the one who does the will of my Father who is in heaven.**"

However, the "will of my Father" is to live according to The Sermon. Afterwards, Jesus said the following.

> "On that day many will say to me, 'Lord, Lord, did we not prophesy in your name, and cast out demons in your name, and

---

[302] Yon-gyong Kwon, *Salvation Without Works? (In Korean)*, (Seoul, Korea: SFC, 2012) 29-30.

do many mighty works in your name?' And then will I declare to them, 'I never knew you; **depart from me, you workers of lawlessness.**'" (Matthew 7:22-23)

"Lawlessness" here means not living according to the laws and commandments that Jesus further explained to us. In other words, they are those who do not have righteousness that exceeds that of the scribes and Pharisees. Lastly, Jesus said the following.

> "**Everyone then who hears these words of mine and does them** will be like a wise man who built his house on the rock. And the rain fell, and the floods came, and the winds blew and beat on that house, but it did not fall, because it had been founded on the rock. **And everyone who hears these words of mine and does not do them** will be like a foolish man who built his house on the sand. And the rain fell, and the floods came, and the winds blew and beat against that house, and it fell, and great was the fall of it." (Matthew 7:24-27)

What are "these words of mine?" It is certainly the Sermon on the Mount. For this parable is the final conclusion of The Sermon. Like so, in the conclusion, Jesus repeatedly said that those who do not live by The Sermon cannot enter the kingdom of heaven. Then, the salt that has lost its taste, namely those who have lost the characteristics of the beatitudes and do not live by The Sermon, are surely those whose spirits have been forsaken. To say otherwise would be a clear distortion and misinterpretation! Therefore, I pray that you will not listen to such distortions.

③ **If You Lose Your Taste, You Will Be Trampled On!**

If salt loses its taste, it becomes useless. So, it is thrown away and as a result, trampled on.

> "You are the salt of the earth, but if salt has lost its taste, how shall its saltiness be restored? It is no longer good for anything except to be thrown out and **trampled under people's feet**." (Matthew 5:13)

No one respects salt that has lost its taste. Not only does God not respect you, but you will be trampled under people's feet. Look at the Korean churches that are filled with tasteless salt. They are trampled on by the government, media, unions, and by the public. It is the same for churches in Europe and in America. These things are happening because the church has lost its taste.

Yet, the problem is not only that we are being trampled on. The greater issue lies with the fact that the glory of God is being hidden. When we excel in handling the role of being the salt and light of the world, it gives glory to God.

> "In the same way, let your light shine before others, **so that they may see your good works and give glory to your Father who is in heaven.**" (Matthew 5:16)

Oppositely, if we mishandle the role of being the salt and light of the world, God's name will be blasphemed by us, just like how God's name was blasphemed through the Jews.

> "You who boast in the law **dishonor God** by breaking the law. For, as it is written, **'The name of God is blasphemed among the Gentiles because of you.'**" (Romans 2:23-24)

God's name is not glorified because we pray, "hallowed be thy name," daily. We need to not lose our saltiness, be beatitude people, and be more righteous than the scribes and Pharisees. That is how we can glorify God's name in our families, schools, work places, and in the world. Therefore, I pray that you and I will never lose our taste.

5) The Heart-Breaking Reality of Modern Day Churches!

Do you know why seawater never rots? It is because of the salt in the seawater. They say the average salinity of the world's seawater is 3.5%. 3.5% saltiness maintains the rest of the 96.5%. With just 3.5% of salt, the remaining 96.5% of water can stay fresh. Is this not incredible? In the same way, if we just have 3.5% of real believers, this society will not grow ill.

On March 1st, 1899, the following article was written in the Korean Christian Advocate.

> "An influential man among the governors in the North has declared he will not go to a district where Christianity is rampant and asked to be moved to Youngnam District instead. Why could he not go to the Christian district? As our religion respects God and loves others, a true believer of this religion does not do the slightest wrong doing and does not disobey the leader but if the leader tries to steal the people's property, they would not allow it to be easily stolen. It is for this reason the man could not go to this district..."[303]

At the time, there were only around ten thousand Christians

---

[303] Moon-ho Kang, *To See the Peak from the Top (In Korean)*. (Seoul: Kukmin Ilbo, 1999) 221-2.

in Korea. With the population being 15 million, it would have been less than 0.1%. Still, in those areas with Christians, there was no possibility for injustices or corruption. Thus, as recorded, the corrupt official did not want to go to Pyongan Province or Hamgyong Province where there were many Christians, and instead, tried his hardest to go where there were no Christians. It is an unbelievably astonishing article.

Compared to back then, the percentage of Christians in Korea has risen dramatically and is now incomparable. Yet, why is our nation the way that it is? Why has it become so evil and so filled with deceit? It is because the church was not able to truly fulfill its role as the salt. To put it differently, that is how few true believers there are in the Church and how few people there are that are going to heaven. A long time ago, a famous Korean pastor said the following.

> "Jesus said in Matthew 5:13 'You are the salt of the earth'. What does this mean? **Even if we live as a minority on earth, we need to bear the role as the salt to preserve the whole.** The amount of salt that stops the sea from rotting is 3.5% of the sea water. The 3.5% of salt keeps the whole sea healthy. **They say that the number of Christians in our country is 25% of the entire population. What do you call this? A sham. If there were actually 25%, there would have been no place for evil to even take a

step in this country. And even if there are 25%, not all are true believers, which is why nothing is happening. Christianity does not take issue with how large or small the percentage. If we raise believers who are the true salt, even if it's just 3.5%, the world will change."

It is a message that we can deeply relate to. Therefore, this country's problem is Christianity's problem. The problem is not simply politicians, news outlets, nor the people. The problem is Christianity. The corruption of the church is the main culprit in creating this dumbfounding country. On account of this, I believe we all need to attentively listen to John Stott's words.

"And when society does go bad, we Christians tend to throw up our hands in pious horror and reproach the non-Christian world; but should we not rather reproach ourselves? No-one blames unsalted meat for going bad! It cannot do anything else. The real question to ask is: where is the salt? ...

What does it mean in practice to be the salt of the earth? To begin with, we who are Christians should be more courageous, more outspoken in condemning evil. Condemnation is negative, to be sure, but the action of salt is negative. Sometimes standards slip and slide in a community because there is no clear Christian protest."[304]

Sadly, Korean churches have currently become more corrupt than the world. Denominations and pastors have since long ago pretended to be mutes for their own safety. Pastors of the bigger churches are the quietest mutes. That is why our country has fallen to the state it is in now. Therefore, the church must change. That is the only way there will be hope and a future for this nation.

Lastly, I had always had regrets, thinking, "If our church had not been slandered so and we were able to grow into a megachurch, we would have been able to reform the Korean churches and transform this country!" But while thinking such thoughts, I read the words of Sinclair Ferguson, which comforted me and gave me hope.

> "It is all too easy for us to despair because of our frailty and insignificance, personally or numerically. However, we must never give in to Satan's lie that we can be effective only when we have large numbers and a show of strength. Jesus' illustration of salt is an encouraging reminder that the apparently cheap and insignificant can influence its environment out of

---

[304] Stott, *The Message of the Sermon on the Mount*, (2020) 47-8.

all proportion to our expectation."[305]

He is right. Perhaps what this country needs is not more Christians. Our church members and other believers, who are spiritually awake, might be enough. What is truly important is not a number but whether we are truly beatitude people. What is truly important is whether we have righteousness that exceeds that of the scribes and Pharisees. What is truly important is whether we are living by the Sermon on the Mount. Therefore, let us all truly become beatitude people and truly live by The Sermon. And by living in this manner, let us become the righteous ten who pray desperately for the Korean Church and this nation. Then, I believe that God will move to wake up the church and save this nation.

---

[305] Sinclair Ferguson, *Kingdom Life in a Fallen World*, (Colorado Springs, CO: NavPress, 1986) 85.

2. AM I THE LIGHT OF THE WORLD?

"You are the light of the world. A city set on a hill cannot be hidden. Nor do people light a lamp and put it under a basket, but on a stand, and it gives light to all in the house. In the same way, let your light shine before others, so that they may see your good works and give glory to your Father who is in heaven." (Matthew 5:14-16)

Jesus told his disciples, "You are the salt of the earth," followed by, "You are the light of the world." Jesus was talking about the role of Christians in the world and the two are, in actuality, the same thing. However, there is a minute difference. John Stott explained the difference as follows.

> "The function of salt is largely negative: it prevents decay. The function of light is positive: it illuminates the darkness.
> So Jesus calls his disciples to exert a double influence on the secular community, a negative influence by arresting its

decay and a positive influence by bringing light into its darkness. For it is one thing to stop the spread of evil; it is another to promote the spread of truth, beauty and goodness."[306]

Some scholars say that salt works through our lives and light works through evangelizing. Thus, they stretch the meaning of the light. This is not an accurate interpretation. For as shown in verse 16, what Jesus meant here was not evangelizing but rather about seeing our "good works." I will explain this later in detail when I deal with verse 16. But as of now, I will begin to explain our main passage chronologically.

1) Light of the World

"You are the light of the world." (Matthew 5:14a)

Just as in verse 13, verse 14 emphasizes the word "you." Not someone else, but "you," namely the disciples, are the light of the world. No other religious person of the world is the light of the world. They are the darkness. It is only the true disciples, Christians, who are the light of the world. Yet, the Jews believed themselves to be this light.

---

[306] Stott, *The Message of the Sermon on the Mount*, (2020) 47.

"But if **you call yourself a Jew** and rely on the law and boast in God and know his will and approve what is excellent, because you are instructed from the law; and if **you are sure that you yourself are** a guide to the blind, a **light to those who are in darkness**, an instructor of the foolish, a teacher of children, having in the law the embodiment of knowledge and truth." (Romans 2:17-20)

However, this is not true. We currently live in the New Testament era and not the Old Testament era. Therefore, the light of the world is now not the Jews, but Christians. Only Christians can be the true light of the world.

Originally, the word light was used to express the nature of God and Jesus Christ (Isa. 42:6, 49:6, John 8:12, 1 John 1:5). Jesus came as the light of the world. And those who believe in Jesus will become the sons of light. In other words, they become light (Eph. 5:8). Therefore, we are the light of the world. Charles Finney further organized this message and said the following.

> "The Lord Jesus Christ, first in His forerunner John, next in His own person, afterward in His apostles, and now in all His saints, is enlightening the world."[307]

---

[307] Charles Finney, *Principles of Christian Obedience*, (Minneapolis, MN: Bethany House Publishers, 1990) 97.

Without you all, the world is darkness. There is no hope. You are the only hope. For you are the only light in this world. The non-believers and believers of other religions in this world absolutely need the light that you shine. That is the only hope. Therefore, I pray that you will, no matter what, take responsibility to shine the light.

Meanwhile, just like the salt of the earth, many people misunderstand, "You are the light of the world!" as the command, "Become the light of the world!" However, Charles Finney said the following early on.

> "Observe[,] Christ does not say, 'ye ought to be the light of the world.' Christ says, 'Ye are the light of the world.'"[308]

Dietrich Bonhoeffer also said the following.

> "'Ye are the light.' Once again it is not: 'You are to be the light,' … Nor does Jesus say: 'You have the light.' The light is not an instrument which has been put into their hands, such as their preaching."

Moreover, Professor Yon-gyong Kwon said the following.

---

[308] Ibid., 101.

"Like the case of the salt, the words 'You are the light of the world' are not a command but a statement. Thus, this is not a command or suggestion to 'Be the light of the world', but a figure of speech that says, 'You are like the light of the world (so to speak)'. Like how the Lord explained the fundamentals of discipleship with the properties of salt, He is using the properties of light here to also explain the fundamentals of discipleship."[309]

Jesus's words are in the indicative mood and not the imperative mood. He is thus talking about their identity. Consequently, only a beatitude person can be the light of the world. This is shown well in Paul's writings.

> "That you may be blameless and innocent, **children of God without blemish** in the midst of a crooked and twisted generation, **among whom you shine as lights in the world.**" (Philippians 2:15)

Therefore, in order to become the light of the world, you must repent of your sins. Afterwards, you must believe in the gospel. In other words, you must become a beatitude person.

---

[309] Kwon, *Do You Understand What You Are Reading?*, (2012) 119.

Just as John Stott said, we must not forget that "our influence depends on our character."[310] We must also remember that God is light and there is no darkness within him. And in order to become a brighter light, we must never stop trying to resemble God.

2) A City on a Hill

"A city set on a hill cannot be hidden." (Matthew 5:14b)

It is easy to understand the message of "You are the light of the world!" However, the latter half of the verse suddenly talks about a hill and a city on top of it. This is not as easily comprehensible. "A city on a hill" is not a light. So, you might wonder, "What does a city on a hill have to do with shining the light?"

If you misunderstand the former half of verse 14 to mean, "Become the light," it is that much harder to understand. There is no way to know why "A city set on a hill cannot be hidden" is mentioned here. For there seems to be no connection between the meaning of the advice to be the light of the world and that a city on a hill cannot be hidden. That is why "a city on a hill" remains a puzzle. The fact that most sermons sneak past this

---

[310] Stott, *The Message of the Sermon on the Mount*, (2020) 50.

section and skip it clearly shows the very perplexity of this verse.[311]

Yet, Kathryn Kuhlman gave the following plausible interpretation of "a city on a hill."

"Note that Jesus uses the word 'city.' I am not a city and neither are you a city. A city is made up of many individuals; therefore, when Jesus speaks of a city, He is not talking about one person.

What exactly does He mean? Since we all know that a city is made up of many people; therefore, the city here refers to the church.

Jesus' church should be a shining light, shining in all of its majestic splendor in this world of darkness… In this world of darkness, the church should be a shining beacon there on that hill…" [312]

It is a very impressive interpretation. Kuhlman also said the following.

"My heart is burdened and I greatly fear that the light in some of God's cities is shining very dimly in this hour. The church has

---
[311] Kwon, *Do You Understand What You Are Reading?*, (2012) 120.
[312] Kuhlman, *In Search of Blessings*, (1989) 80.

lost much of its power, so much in fact that the hour has come when instead of beaming its light from the highest mountain peak and shining in majestic splendor, instead of challenging the world today, the world is challenging the church. God help us is my prayer!"[313]

This is not just a plausible interpretation but something we can deeply resonate with when we think of the circumstances of the modern church. However, although it gives us a good teaching, it is not a correct interpretation.

Then, what is the real meaning of this verse?

First, we must figure out the "city set on a hill" to truly know its meaning. Ancient cities were commonly constructed with white limestone. Because of this, it was not possible to hide the city from shining in the sun. At night, the white buildings became even more defined as the townspeople put up lamps. It could not be hidden. The Lord was focused on this very exposed nature of a city.

If you read, "A city set on a hill cannot be hidden," without much thought, it sounds like it is saying that the world cannot hinder or block the role of the church. Although this is not true, a similar meaning is held inside this message. John

---

[313] Ibid.

Wesley wrote as follows.

> "And, first, **it is impossible for any that have it to conceal the religion of Jesus Christ**. This our Lord makes plain beyond all contradiction by a two-fold comparison: 'Ye are the light of the world: A city set upon a hill cannot be hid.' **'Ye' Christians 'are the light of the world,' with regard both to your tempers and actions. Your holiness makes you as conspicuous as the sun in the midst of heaven. As ye cannot go out of the world, so neither can ye stay in it without appearing to all mankind. Ye may not flee from men, and while ye are among them it is impossible to hide your lowliness and meekness and those other dispositions whereby ye aspire to be perfect, as your Father which is in heaven is perfect**. Love cannot be hid any more than light; and least of all when it shines forth in action, when ye exercise yourselves in the labour of love, in beneficence of every kind. **As well may men think to hide a city as to hide a Christian: yea, as well may they conceal a city set upon a hill as a holy, zealous, active lover of God and man.**"[314]

Lloyd-Jones also expressed this point very well.

---

[314] Wesley, *The Sermons of John Wesley*, (2013) 519.

"We are to be like 'a city that is set on a hill', and 'a city that is set on a hill cannot be hid'. In other words, if we are truly Christian we cannot be hid. Put in a different way, **the contrast between us and others is something which is to be quite self-evident and perfectly obvious."**[315]

"The true Christian cannot be hid, he cannot escape notice. A man truly living and functioning as a Christian will stand out."[316]

Moreover, Douglas Hare said, "The context, however, strongly implies that the saying must be read as an imperative rather than as an indicative: 'You must be like a city on a hill, like a lamp in full view.'"[317] Yet, the person who best explained this is Professor Yon-gyong Kwon. He wrote the following in his book, *Do You Understand What You Are Reading?*

"A city set on a hill...

The picture of 'a city set on a hill' is not that of a random, un-welcome guest who interrupts this encouragement to become the light. This image is rather an excellent explanation of the Lord's intent to compare the disciples to the light. [This] is a city

---

[315] Lloyd-Jones, *Studies in the Sermon on the Mount*, (1959) 171.
[316] Ibid., 174.
[317] Hare, Matthew, (1993) 45.

built on a hill. It's not a small town that could be or could not be seen, but it is a 'Polis,' a city that includes many great buildings. ...

If a city like this was set on a hill, could you hide it? It would certainly be illogical to do so. Therefore, the point of this imposing image that Jesus brings is that it 'cannot be hidden.' That is to say, it is about exposure. A city built on a hill certainly 'cannot be hidden.' If you were trying to hide from other people, like at a secret military facility, you would from the start, dig underground and hide there. The fact that the city was set on a hill shows that from the beginning, there was a plan to fully reveal it to people. This is the intention of the Lord when He compared the disciples to the light. In other words, it is to be exposed.

First, it is clear that the 'city set on a hill' is an image drawn to emphasize exposure. Here, the meaning of the words on the light becomes clear. At a glance, a city set on a hill seems irrelevant to the light. But if you dwell on the theme of 'exposure,' the similarity of the two images of the light and a city set on a hill is quickly revealed. Just like a city set on a hill fulfills its natural duty by boasting its dignity to the people, the light exhibits its function when it is exposed to people. It is in this sense that the disciples are the light. Like how light fulfills its duty by being revealed, the disciples of the Lord are those who

fulfill their natural duty by being revealed."[318]

If this is so, then how is it possible to have this exposure that Jesus desired for us? It is possible through good works. That is how we can shine our light (v.16). That is the life of being the light of the world. And as the light of the world, we cannot hide as if we do not exist. We must be exposed and brought to attention through our good works.

> "For in Christ Jesus neither circumcision nor uncircumcision has any value. The only thing that counts is **faith expressing itself through love.**" (Galatians 5:6, ESV)

> "For when we place our faith in Christ Jesus, there is no benefit in being circumcised or being uncircumcised. What is important is **faith expressing itself in love**." (Galatians 5:6, NLT)

Like so, we must not just have faith in our hearts, but also have faith that is expressed as love. We must have this tangible faith that becomes clearly visible through the good works done by love. That is the call for all Christians.

---

[318] Kwon, *Do You Understand What You Are Reading?*, (2012) 120-1.

3) A Lamp on a Stand

"Nor do people light a lamp and put it under a basket, but on a stand, and it gives light to all in the house." (Matthew 5:15)

Because I was ignorant in the past, I thought the following after reading this verse. "After telling people to be the light of the world, why did Jesus tell them to give light to all in the house? Is He saying we need to start, in our families, to live correctly and shine the light?" Yet, this is not what it means. It is a repetition of the latter half of verse 14. In other words, Jesus is once again emphasizing the importance of exposure, as He did by saying that a city on a hill cannot be hidden. This time, He is re-emphasizing it with this new example of a lamp.

As evidence, the "basket" that comes out in this verse was a wooden bowl that was used to measure amounts of grain. It has the capacity to hold around 8.25L. Moreover, the word "stand" is in the Gospels four times and eight times elsewhere. In most of these mentions, the stand does not mean a holder for candlestick, but a "lampstand." In Israel, the structure of the house required a stand to be installed in each room. While the stand helps a lamp to shine far across the room, the basket stops the lamp from shining. To put a lamp under a basket would, in particular, completely block out the light. Therefore, this verse is emphasizing the fact that we must shine the light so all can see and not hide it. Professor Yon-gyong Kwon explains this point well.

> "A lamp on a stand
>
> The second image used to explain the meaning of the light is a lamp. The lamp is an object that shines, which is closer to the word 'you are the light of the world.' ... But it is not different from the meaning of 'the city set on a hill.' People turn on a lamp when it gets dark. Certainly, you don't put a shining lamp under a basket. ... Under normal circumstances, you don't light a lamp because it's dark and then hide it under a basket. For a lamp fulfills its duty by being revealed, not by being hidden. ...
>
> If you light a lamp, you put it on a stand. Only then can it 'give light to all in the house.' You can tell by the comparison of 'under a basket' and 'on a stand,' that the point Jesus wants to give is a simple comparison of being hidden or being exposed. If you zoom-in on a still image of a light on a stand, you would easily observe the truth that it holds the same meaning as the 'city set on a hill.' It is common sense to put a lamp on a stand to expose it to all in the house, like going on top of a high mountain would. Here, the words of the Lord come together to mean 'exposure.'

Like this, the image of a city set on a hill and the image of a lamp on a stand all deliver the same meaning of exposure. Of course, the secondary explanation of 'exposure' is the explanation of the figurative statement 'you are the light of the world.' **Then, it is clear why the disciples are compared to the light. They are to be exposed. Like how a light that is not exposed does not fulfill its duty, a disciple cannot fulfill the role of a disciple if they are not revealed to the people.**

Verse 16 connects this importance of 'exposure' to a specific command. In this context, 'in the same way' would mean that the point of the city set on a hill or a light on a lamp is all in the 'exposure.' **The Lord's command would be 'shine your light before the people.'** At a glance, it might be easy to read it as 'shine light on the darkness of the world.' But the first emphasis in this scripture is 'before others.' Our light should not be hidden under a basket but it should shine before people, thus be 'exposed' to people. … **Therefore verse 16 also emphasizes that the disciples are the light that needs to be exposed before others like a city set on a hill or a lamp on a stand. Only then will the people 'see' the light and give glory to the Father in heaven."**[319]

---

[319] Kwon, *Do You Understand What You Are Reading?*, (2012) 122-4.

Moreover, Dr. Yon-gyong Kwon said the following on "Discipleship and being exposed."

"Being the light of the world means that the core essence of a discipleship that follows Jesus is in being revealed or seen. This proceeds the command to be the light that shines on the world. The community of disciples cannot be hidden. A church exists to show something by being exposed to the people in this world. Like turning on a lamp and setting it on a stand for all to see, Jesus made the community of His disciples to be set on the stand of this world to shine on all people. Again, this is not advice to be the light of the world. Rather, it is a proclamation that the foundations of a disciple are in the role of 'showing.' Therefore, **a church that does not function as the light is not a bad quality church. It is a community that has given up being a church**. A church that cannot be shown is useless like the light hidden under a basket. …

Whether inside or outside of the church, the reality of today's church is a tragedy showcasing the strangeness of how the gospel we proclaim is not verified in our lives or the autonomy of our lives contradicting our words. …

We have to clearly realize, through this message, the importance of being exposed or shown. We occasionally hear people say, 'You believe because of God, not because of people.' Al-

though it is an understandable statement, it is not biblical. The Lord told us to 'shine.' So, to instead say, 'Look only at God, not us,' would be a dereliction of duty as a disciple. To give a more modern example, the community of disciples are like a showcase at a department store selling the gospel. Depending on the quality of the objects displayed in the showcase, the messianic business might succeed, or it might flounder. If we do not properly display ourselves in the showcase, the Lord's gospel business cannot help but flounder."[320]

I am sure you now sufficiently understand how necessary and important it is to shine the light for the world through good works. We have become beatitude people through repentance and faith. We ourselves are this light. We have this light inside of us. However, non-believers cannot see this light. Thus, just like how we put a lamp not under a basket but on a stand, we must also through our good works, reveal our light to all and not hide it. We must help non-believers to see this too, for that is how they will be able to give glory to God. Therefore, I pray that by actively doing good, you will be able to shine light on the world that is growing darker each day.

---

[320] Kwon, *Do You Understand What You Are Reading?*, (2012) 124-6.

4) Good Works

"In the same way, let your light shine before others, so that they may see your good works and give glory to your Father who is in heaven." (Matthew 5:16)

You are the light of the world. Herman Ridderbos said the following about this.

> "One does not place a lamp under a bowl but on an elevated stand where it can be seen. Similarly it would be absurd to think that a person from whom no light shines could belong to the light of the world."[321]

Therefore, just as how a city on a hill cannot be hidden and just as how a person does not put a lamp under a basket but on a stand to give light to all in the house, we must shine the light.

Then, what is the light we must shine? I believe that Jesus is saying in our main passage the same thing that Peter and Paul said in the following verses.

"for at one time you were darkness, but now **you are light in**

---

[321] Ridderbos, *Matthew*, (1987) 95.

the Lord. **Walk as children of light** (for the fruit of light is found in **all that is good and right and true**)." (Ephesians 5:8-9)

"Beloved, I urge you as sojourners and exiles to abstain from the passions of the flesh, which wage war against your soul. **Keep your conduct among the Gentiles honorable**, so that when they speak against you as evildoers, they may **see your good deeds and glorify God on the day of visitation**." (1 Peter 2:11-12)

As evidence, after saying, "You are the light of the world," (v.14) Jesus said in verse 16, "**In the same way, let your light shine before others, so that they may see your good works and give glory to your Father who is in heaven.**" Therefore, the light is good works.

However, some scholars believe that the light means proclaiming the gospel. For example, Scot McKnight made the following argument.

"But the image of 'light' impacting darkness was connected to Israel telling of their God to the 'nations' (Gentiles, world) in Isaiah. Here are two primary texts:

'Listen to me, my people; hear me, my nation: Instruction will go out from me; my justice will become a light to the nations'

(Isa 51:4).

'Nations will come to your light, and kings to the brightness of your dawn' (60:3).

Here is where reading the Sermon on the Mount in light of the Bible's Story reshapes both what we look for and what we see in the text. **These texts suggest that 'light of the world' is not a generic metaphor for moral influence in our local context, but actually anticipates the Gentile mission. ...**

Here are the words from Isaiah 9:1–2 Matthew cites at 4:14-16:

'Nevertheless, there will be no more gloom for those who were in distress. In the past he humbled the land of Zebulun and the land of Naphtali, but in the future he will honor Galilee of the nations [Gentiles], by the Way of the Sea, beyond the Jordan—The people walking in darkness have seen a great light; on those living in the land of deep darkness a light has dawned.'

We suggest, then, that with 'light of the world' in Matthew 5:14 Jesus is pointing to the Gentile mission when the gospel is taken beyond the land of Israel to the whole world." [322]

It makes a lot of sense! Lloyd-Jones also saw the light as

---

[322] McKnight, *Sermon on the Mount*, (2013) 58-9.

having a relationship to the truth of the gospel. He said the following.

> "For the real force of the statement is this: 'Ye, and ye alone, are the light of the world'; the 'ye' is emphatic and it carries that suggestion. Now at once you see there are certain things implied. The first is that the world is in a state of darkness. This, indeed, is always one of the first statements that the Christian gospel has to make.[323] ...
>
> We must go even further than that, however. Our Lord not only pronounces that the world is in a state of darkness, He goes so far as to say that nobody but a Christian can give any helpful advice, knowledge or instruction with respect to it. That is our proud claim and boast as Christian people."[324]

Moreover, he said the following.

> "There is obviously no light at all in this world apart from the light that is provided by Christian people and the Christian faith. That is no exaggeration. ...
>
> Let us never forget that Plato, Socrates, Aristotle, and the rest, had given their full teaching several centuries before

---

[323] Lloyd-Jones, *Studies in the Sermon on the Mount*, (1959) 159.
[324] Ibid., 161-2.

these words were uttered. It was after that amazing flowering of the mind and the intellect that our Lord made this statement. **He looked at this band of ordinary, insignificant people and said, 'You and you alone are the light of the world.' Now this is a tremendous and most thrilling statement. ... It says 'ye'. In other words its claim is that the ordinary Christian, though he may never have read any philosophy at all, knows and understands more about life than the greatest expert who is not a Christian."**[325]

Amen! This is a very attractive argument and is true in and of itself. However, this is not what Jesus was saying here. For the Lord was not talking about the truth but about good works (v.16).

Charles Finney properly detected this. That is why he repeatedly said the following about shining one's light.

> "**How Christians can enlighten the world.**
>
> What constitutes the Christian's light and renders him a light to others?
>
> ... his **light** consists in his temper, in his spirit, and **in his good works** in strict regard to the universal law of love."[326]

---

[325] Ibid., 162-3.
[326] Finney, *Principles of Christian Obedience*, (1990) 97.

"How? By consistently exhibiting your good works in contrast with their evil works."[327]

"... Christ has said to them, 'Ye are the light of the world.' And now 'let your light so shine before men that they, seeing your good works, (**not merely hearing your good doctrines, but seeing your *good works***), may glorify your Father who is in heaven.' **Nothing can prevent your enlightening the world but a refusal on your part to perform good works. If you perform good works people will see them. If they see them they will be constrained to glorify your Father which is in heaven. If then people are not enlightened, it is because you do not perform good works. In other words, it is because you are not Christians.** ...

It is only by strong and constant contrast that the conviction of the necessity of a radical change in themselves is to be forced home upon them. The more striking and constant this contrast, the better. The more universal and perfect this contrast is, the more sudden and irresistible will be their conviction of the necessity of a great and radical change in themselves."[328]

Herman Ridderbos also said the following.

---

[327] Ibid., 99.
[328] Ibid., 101-2.

> "Jesus thus emphasizes the unbreakable connection between having light and shedding light, between spiritual membership in the kingdom and good works."[329]

Of course, there are more verses in the Bible than just the verse that Scott McKnight cited that mention the light as truth. For example, Romans 2:17-19 is one of them.

> "**But if you** call yourself a Jew and **rely on the law and boast in God and know his will** and approve what is excellent, because you are instructed from the law; and if you are sure that you yourself are a guide to the blind, **a light to those who are in darkness.**"

Yet, what is important is the context of our main passage. In the context of the passage, the light is not the truth. It is good works.

> "In the same way, let **your light** shine before others, so that they may see **your good works** and give glory to your Father who is in heaven." (Matthew 5:16)

---

[329] Ridderbos, *Matthew*, (1987) 95.

In this way, Jesus clearly equated the light to "good works." Additionally, in this verse, Jesus said it was done not to get people to believe but to "give glory." Therefore, the light here is not talking about proclaiming the gospel but clearly rather about good works.

Now, I would like to conclude this book. Many people live diligently evangelizing. Yet, compared to all their hard work, their fruit is meager. Why? It is because they evangelize only with their words and without showing any good works. That is why their words have no influence. Kathryn Kuhlman said, "The only Bible that the unsaved man or woman may read is the life of the person who professes to be born again."[330] She also said the following.

> "The greatest compliment that can be paid a Christian is for an unbeliever to say, 'I don't understand it, I am not spiritual myself, but I have confidence in what you believe because you live it.'"[331]

In *The Gospel of Sadhu Sundar Singh*, an agnostic English professor found Sundar Singh and confessed to him the following.

---

[330] Kathryn Kuhlman, *Gifts of the Holy Spirit*, (North Haven, CT: Lulu, 2022) 68.
[331] Ibid., 68.

"It is not your preaching which has converted me, it is yourself; you, an Indian, are so like Christ in spirit and in bearing; you are a living witness to the Gospel and to the Person of Jesus Christ."[332]

Is this not the greatest praise one can receive that challenges all of us?

Even if we cannot exactly be like Sundar Singh, we must do two things if we want to achieve similar results. First, we must repent and become beatitude people. Next, we must diligently do good works. The reason I say this is because you stop at the 8th beatitude of receiving persecution if you only become beatitude people. Yet, if you become a beatitude person and you shine the light through good works, you will be the cause of people giving glory to God, just like Jesus said. Moreover, a portion of them will also be saved. Because of this, I believe churches need to start the "goodness revolution" that Patricia King talked about in *Light Belongs in the Darkness*.

> "Starting a Goodness Revolution
>
> Graham Cooke once said, '**The problem with the world isn't that there is too much corruption, violence, immorality, or per-**

---

[332] Friedrich Heiler, *The Gospel of Sadhu Sundar Singh*, (Delhi, India: Samuel Frese ISPCK, 2020) 82.

version. The problem is that there is not enough good-ness.' He explained how his church in England took on a neighborhood as a project and, each day, engaged in acts of goodness. They mowed lawns, washed windows, took dogs for walks, and drove folks to doctor's appointments or grocery shopping. They simply found out what people's needs were and then met them. As a result, the neighborhood's spiritual climate drastically changed; everyone was happier, friendlier, and some came to Christ. The 'goodness team' caused a positive reaction. ...

Graham's suggestion triggered the vision in me that starting a goodness revolution would be quite easy. **If the Body of Christ used the anointing to simply do acts of goodness, we could change the spiritual climate of our cities.**

Fear dissipates in the presence of goodness, and cruelty loses its power and influence. Jesus taught us to fight evil with good. Goodness is a powerful force. ...

After Graham's word, **I suggested that our team should launch a goodness revolution.** The whole event ended up being so much fun! That particular summer, 12 members of our team lived together in the same house for over three months. Now, such a set-up definitely has some potential for fallout! We committed to focusing on living in an environment of goodness, which turned out to be infectious. When one person starts, then others respond in like manner. We would say things like, 'I'm going to help you with the dishes, even though it's not my assignment, because I am working on a goodness revolution.' Then someone would respond, 'No, it's okay. I want to bless you! You go rest and let me do the dishes.' Another person would come in and say, 'Hey why don't we all do it together because I want to help, too.'

We had daily contests for who would go get coffee treats for everyone, because so many wanted to 'treat.' **As was often the case, a number of them ended up going out together to get treats. We cut the neighbors' lawns, made grocery hampers for those in need, and helped people at the supermarkets take groceries to the car. Everyone had fun as we worked on it together. I firmly believe that spiritual and relational environments in homes and families can change dramatically if everyone gets committed to launching a goodness revolution. After that, take it to the neighbors, the workplace, church, and school.** Once the 'movement' begins, then everyone will jump on board.

Let's look at definitions and synonyms of the words goodness and revolution. Then apply these concepts to your imagination as you ponder what a goodness revolution might look like in your home and community. Goodness is 'the state or quality of being good, upright, honorable, charitable, moral, righteous, considerate, tolerant, generous, kind, agreeable, pleasant, and genuine.' Revolution is 'a complete or radical change of any kind.'

You don't need too much spiritual discernment to discover the need for such a revolution in today's world. People are often uncaring and thoughtless of others. Imagine a radical change in your sphere of influence. Instead of current words, kind words would be spoken. Instead of immorality, purity would prevail. Instead of violence, gentleness would be shown. Instead of greed and selfishness, generosity would be lavished on others. Goodness is a powerful force that can change the world!"[333]

In the biography of St. Francis that I read long ago, I remember reading about how St. Francis and his disciples went out to evangelize. Yet, they did not evangelize and instead helped people on their farms and fields, helped with cleaning, and carried burdens all day. He spent the entire day working, but on his way back, he said that he evangelized well today! Good works open people's hearts. It makes difficult evangelizing easy. Even those who are hard to reach through words can be reached through actions of evangelism. That is why for those who think evangelism is difficult and have a hard time start-

---

[333] Patricia King, *Light Belongs in the Darkness*, (Shippensburg, PA: Destiny Image Publishers, 2005) 102-4.

ing, I believe the greatest evangelism they can do is evangelism through good works. A great advantage to evangelizing by works is that you don't have to go up to a stranger and talk to them. You don't even have to ring the doorbell or force your way into someone's home. You don't have to be thick skinned. Therefore, I think it would be a great idea to make an evangelizing team centered on good works for our evangelism ministry in Seoul and at all our satellite churches for whoever wants to apply. They would meet up periodically for the sole purpose of doing good works around our churches and for our neighbors. Whether you apply to join this team or not, you must all individually be the light of the world through good works. You must thus shine light on the darkness of this world, make non-believers give glory to God, and have more souls respond to the gospel. For the Lord has created you as the light of the world.